Victims or Villains

Victims or Villains:
Jewish Images in Classic English Detective Fiction

Malcolm J. Turnbull

Bowling Green State University Popular Press
Bowling Green, OH 43403

Copyright 1998 © Bowling Green State University Popular Press

Library of Congress Cataloging-in-Publication Data
Turnbull, Malcolm J.
    Victims or villains : Jewish images in classic English detective
fiction / Malcolm J. Turnbull.
        p.   cm.
    Includes bibliographical references.
    ISBN 0-87972-783-7 (cloth) -- ISBN 0-87972-784-5 (pbk.)
    1. Detective and mystery stories, English--History and criti-
cism. 2. English fiction--20th century--History and criticism.
3. Jews--Great Britain--Public opinion. 4. Jews in literature.
I. Title.
PR888.J4T87   1998
823'.08720935203924--dc21   98-27702
                                                                  CIP

Cover design by Dumm Art

Contents

Acknowledgements

In the course of researching and writing *Victims or Villains* (the former over several years), I have had input and assistance from a number of people, who either provided copies of relevant articles and other material, responded to queries, tendered advice, or alerted me to specific sources. I am grateful to individual staff members at the University of Cambridge and British Libraries,who cheerfully eased access through red tape when time was especially limited, as well as to Christopher Dean and Susan O'Brien of the Dorothy L. Sayers Society, Beverley Davis, OAM of the Australian Jewish Historical Society (Vic), Professor Jon L. Breen, Dilys Wynn, Jacquie Binns and Colin Thornton-Smith. John Willis tirelessly (as always) located material, organised photocopying and helped make the rounds of bookstores in Australia and overseas. Professor W.D. (Bill) Rubinstein of the University of Wales, Aberystwyth, a fellow Golden Age enthusiast, provided several sources and very kindly read and commented on an early draft. (His recent and controversial history of Anglo-Jewry was, of course, a key reference and point-of-departure when I looked at the position of the Jew in Britain). Finally, I owe a particular debt of gratitude to Marcia Harriman who acted as a virtual (and voluntary) research assistant by providing numerous references to Jews culled from her own extensive reading within the genre.

Introduction

The phrase "classic English detective story" conjures up immediate and comforting images of an insulated, complacent, even cosy Britain, a neverland in which genteel slayings are perpetrated, promptly investigated and solved, often by gifted, if eccentric, amateurs, against the reassuring backdrop of pre-Blitz London, peaceful rural villages or fully staffed Wodehousian country estates. These images are, of course, only part of a much more diverse and substantial whole; crime fiction in the first half of the century was more wide-ranging in conception and execution than is generally recognised. Fundamental to its existence and perpetuation, however, was the primary goal of entertainment. Escapist fare, conservative in outlook and execution, conforming to standardised patterns, forms and principles, unconcerned, as a rule, about subtleties of characterisation, or the unpleasant realities of sudden and violent death, and dedicated above all to the greater glorification of the literary puzzle and its solution, detective stories and novels enjoyed an enormous readership in the interwar years.[1] As Colin Watson has noted:

Novels of detection flowed from the presses month after month, year after year, in an ever-increasing tide. The appetite for them seemed to be insatiable. Here was no passing fashion; the weekly ration of whodunits came to be one of the staples of life for thousands of middle-class families. Housewives brought it home in the shopping basket as conscientiously as they remembered to renew the family supplies of bread and sugar.[2]

Having survived "the vicissitudes of literary taste and the sometimes suffocating paraphernalia of scholarship," the more durable specimens, and their descendants, continue to sell in large quantities today.[3] What analysts have come to regard as the Golden Age of English crime and detective fiction—usually cited as the 1920s and 1930s,[4] although a case could be made for including at least part of the 1940s in the time-frame—is distinguished by a massive catalogue documenting the exploits of such fictional immortals as Hercule Poirot, Lord Peter Wimsey, Miss Marple, Superintendent Alleyn, Drs Fell and Thorndyke, Inspectors French and Mallett, Albert Campion, Roger Sheringham, Mrs Bradley, Nigel Strangeways, Sir John Appleby, and dozens of lesser luminaries.

I came to the detective story along what I have since learned is a pretty standard route—i.e. through the chance discovery of Agatha Christie. As a college student and neophyte teacher in the 1970s, I read steadily, and delightedly, through the complete Christie over successive term vacations spent in country Tasmania. I retain a nostalgic fondness and admiration for the "Queen of Crime" to this day, although I remember my bemusement, even then, at some of the outdated attitudes and elitist and racist lapses in her work. From Christie, I moved on, predictably enough, to Sayers (again, disconcerting in some of her statements) and hence through a sturdy diet of Ngaio Marsh, Cyril Hare, Margery Allingham, A.B. Cox (in my view, one of the greatest of them all) and other major representatives of that wonderful and prolific era. Crime fiction has evolved significantly since World War II, yet with all due respect to the leading British and American crime writers of the current (and previous) generation I remain a slavish devotee of the whodunit and howdunit as entertainment personified, and an unabashed advocate of the Golden Age at its best.[5]

This preference does not blind me to generalised defects which impinge even on some of the finest achievements of the Golden Age—a sometimes outrageous class-consciousness, entrenched social snobbery, marked chauvinism and, most glaringly, an extensive and untenable racism. "[O]ld-style thrillers had long been packed with despicable and evil-intentioned foreigners," writes Watson, "and the writers of the more sedate detective stories saw no reason why they should not devote part of their talent to splenetic portraiture of characters with dark complexions or funny accents."[6] With Britain perceived and depicted as the effective hub of the civilised world, Britishness, by definition, entails a degree of intellectual, ethical, physical and racial superiority, and inevitably, anything or anyone non-

British (or "foreign") is suspect. The ultimate propagandists for this world view are the enormously popular, and thus influential, thrill-mongers John Buchan, Sydney Horler and H.C. McNeile, but it is expounded, to varying degrees, by crime writers in general.

Temperamental, exotic, and dubious continentals of all descriptions, unscrupulous Levantines, "hunnish" Germans, radical Russians, Mafia-connected Italians, licentious Frenchmen, as well as brutish blacks and malevolent Asiatics, are frequent targets of writers of interwar detective fiction; the derisive term "dago," originally aimed specifically at Spaniards or Portuguese, encompasses, at times, anyone not lucky enough to have been born in England's "green and pleasant land." Furtive Hindus perpetuate a retributive tradition dating back to Wilkie Collins and *The Moonstone*. (See J.S. Fletcher's *The Perilous Crossways* or Ronald Knox's short story "Solved by Inspection," for example.) Sinister orientals, i.e. the "yellow peril" staple of nineteenth-century penny-dreadfuls and "boys-own" pulp fiction, reinvigorated by Sax Rohmer's enormously popular Fu Manchu series, continue to surface throughout—and beyond—the Golden Age, often in connection with the drug trade, and notwithstanding recognition that their presence had become an all-too-predictable or mundane fictional device. (Manifestations include Edgar Wallace's *The Yellow Snake,* J.S. Fletcher's *The Mysterious Chinaman*, Agatha Christie's *The Big Four*, Margery Allingham's *Mystery Mile*, or John G. Brandon's *Death of a Socialite.*)[7] Negroes and natives of diverse origin, Kaffirs, East Indians, Africans, Black Americans, etc., are characterised as "niggers," "black devils," even as akin to "savages" and "cannibals"; not infrequently they appear as "heavies," thugs (Gladys Mitchell's *The Saltmarsh Murders*) or oversized professional fighters (the late Sherlock Holmes story "The Adventure of the Three Gables" or the Father Brown tale "The God of the Gongs").[8]

The most frequent butts of negative remarks, description or analysis, however, are Jews. Dilys Wynn has written:

For all the reasons a reader may be drawn to English mysteries of the Twenties and Thirties—nostalgia, a certain elegance of phrasing and tone, that classic plotting—there is an equally good reason for slamming the books shut and tossing them from one's home: a strain of antisemitism that runs deep, constant and pervasive.[9]

Historians of Anglo-Jewry and literary analysts differ somewhat in their assessment of the strength and significance, even incidence, of unflattering references to Jews in the detective story. Colin Holmes, for instance, notes cautiously that "negative Jewish stereotypes were sometimes in evidence" in the work of Dorothy L. Sayers and thriller-writer John Buchan, but warns that "we have to be careful in ascribing views to the author" on the basis of his/her novels.[10] Watson cites "several popular authors of the period who put antisemitic sentiments into print," adding that "there is nothing to suggest that their assumption of the aproval of their readers was misplaced."[11] W.D. Rubinstein notes an increase in the depiction of Jews as sinister foreign characters in thrillers, detective stories and other popular fiction following the Russian Revolution, and concedes that "noted detective writers" like Christie, Freeman, Berkeley (Cox), *et al*, "routinely employed unpleasant or sinister Jewish characters" in their work in the 1920s and early 1930s. He goes on to argue, however:

While disconcerting to us, and certainly indicative of a strand of popular fiction, more should not be made of this than meets the eye: the overwhelming proportion of popular British fiction of this type contained no Jewish characters, while virtually all identifiable groups— ethnic, national, occupational and class-based—are stereotyped in this way. Until the rise of Nazism . . . such negative group stereotyping was a commonplace device of lazy writers, even those of some distinction.[12]

Wynn is much more sweeping. "Something more powerful is operating here than a casual disdain of the outsider," she insists. In her estimation, derogatory references to Jews far outstrip unflattering comments made about other groups. "Christie, Sayers and the bulk of the Golden Agers [are guilty] . . . It [the antisemitic slur] is as much a part of their books as the corpse. And just as unlikeable. And, in most cases, even more offensive."[13] In examining anti-Jewish sentiment in England during

World War II, Tony Kushner makes the important point that fictional stereotyping of Jews persisted longer than generally supposed.[14]

The current study originated as a personal response to the disconcerting remarks and references to Jews I encountered in the course of reading through Agatha Christie, Dorothy L. Sayers and other practitioners of the Golden Age. Added impetus came from first reading Wynn's article and, subsequently, the viewpoints of the other analysts cited above. *Victims or Villains* proceeds from the premise that Jews, negatively depicted according to a range of demeaning stereotypes, and often introduced quite gratuitously, are a recurring and frequently encountered feature of English crime writing in its heyday. Multiple, and wide-ranging, examples will confirm the commonness in the literature of derogatory descriptions and depictions. My exploration of the topic seeks to ask why this is/was so, to determine the real significance of such fictional stereotyping, with reference to recent debate over the profundity of antisemitism in Britain, and to trace the evolution of fictional Jewish images in the context of socio-historical trends and events. Although the main focus is on the period between the two world wars, a time when anti-Jewish sentiment was escalating internationally, my study also looks at relevant aspects of the treatment of Jews in crime and detective fiction before and after the Golden Age.

Central to my thesis is the contention that Jewish images in popular fiction of the period(s) under review were a reflection of mainstream attitudes to Jews as a group within British society. Holmes notes that detective stories and thrillers, written to appeal to a mass readership, necessarily employed readily identifiable stereotypes in order to insure an immediate response. Hostile representations of Jews were there because readers could relate to them.[15] Implicit here is the belief that Golden Age stories are valuable sources for the social historian supplying, in this case, important evidence of normative perceptions of the Jew in early twentieth century England. Watson writes: "The habits of people, their ways of thought, their ambitions and prejudices, all may be divined more clearly from a reading of their favourite books than from the theses of the historian or sociologist."[16] "You cannot deny," argues Claude Cockburn:

that if Book X was what a huge majority of book-buyers and book-bor-rowers wanted to buy or borrow in a given year, or over a period of years, then Book X satisfied a need . . . of all indices to moods, atti-tudes and above all, aspirations, the bestseller list is one of the most reliable.[17]

It is true that all reading and writing is, to some degree, selective, and that popular literature can never be "a total reflec-tion of the popular ethos," yet fictional renderings of the Jew during this period undoubtedly echo real-life prejudices or per-ceptions.[18] "The Jew was the favourite object of British middle-class scorn," deduces Watson from his reading of interwar fic-tion. "His mere existence was felt to be an affront."[19] With that in mind, the current study is intended as a contribution to the debate on British antisemitism.

I am well aware of the diversity of sub-genres which come together as crime, mystery and detective fiction (see Julian Symons' discussion of the parameters in *Bloody Murder*).[20] Accordingly, I have opted for inclusiveness, taking for my guide the encompassing coverage of such authorities as Steinbrunner & Penzler, John M. Reilly, Barzun & Taylor and the *Dictionary of Literary Biography*.[21] I have not hesitated to refer where I thought relevant to John Buchan, William Le Queux, E. Phillips Oppenheim, H.C. McNeile ("Sapper"), Dornford Yates and Sydney Horler, or other writers (as diverse as Graham Greene, W. Somerset Maugham, Arnold Bennett or Robert Hichens) whose varied output conformed on occasion to either the pure detective or adventure/thriller traditions. Primarily, however, my sources are what have come to be known as classic who-dunits. Any such survey must take into account an enormous panorama of material. I have attempted to look in detail at the work of the genre's "big names" (Christie being an obvious example), but a study of this nature, inevitably, must be highly selective, dictated by availability, accessibility and serendipity. Although I have aimed at a comprehensive overview of the sources, I acknowledge realistically that some important evi-dence is bound to have been overlooked. American detective fic-tion clearly does not fall within the scope of my study; I suggest, however, that it might well provide a fertile field for future researchers. Sexism, homophobia and racism are part-and-parcel of the so-called "hardboiled" school, and Raymond Chandler's writing springs to mind as an obvious example.[22]

In addition to the important secondary sources already cited (Wynn, Watson, Kushner, Rubinstein, *et al*), prior research into antisemitism in popular fiction includes Gina Mitchell's studies of Buchan and McNeile, and Bryan Cheyette's analyses of Buchan and G.K. Chesterton.[23] David Stafford pays some attention to the treatment of Jews in the spy sub-genre, and the collection *Synod of Sleuths* includes a short survey of Jewish investigators by James Yaffe.[24] The attitudes towards Jews of Christie and Dorothy L. Sayers are discussed, in varying degrees, by the writers' biographers/critics. (See Chapter 3). Some peripheral but useful information is also available in a number of general surveys of the Jews in English literature (including Modder, Fisch and Rosenberg).[25] This study, however, claims to be the first detailed overview of a particular phenomenon.

Negative fictional renderings of Jews peaked in the 1920s and 1930s parallel with renewed fears of international conspiracies and Jewish manipulation of finance in the traumatic aftermath of the Great War, concurrent concerns at alleged Jewish connections to Bolshevism and the Russian Revolution, the rise of Fascism at home and abroad, economic turbulence and social discontent caused by the Great Depression, and influxes of refugee immigrants—all against the backdrop of a rapidly deteriorating Europe. The phenomenon built also on a lengthy literary tradition: centuries of disreputable dealers, underworld operatives, sinister aliens, Shylocks, and other fictitious manifestations of villainy. As well, Golden Age writers drew on more direct antecedents. Given that the "birth" of Sherlock Holmes in 1887 is cited customarily as the full-fledged beginning of the homegrown English detective story, it is possible to trace a Jewish presence in the genre from its outset. Pioneer contemporaries of Conan Doyle, such as C.L. Pirkis and E.M. Hornung, acknowledged the upward mobility of Anglo-Jewry in the second half of the nineteenth century by cheerfully associating Jewish parvenus with the more suspect and seedy circles of fashionable London society. (Jews were, if not the only, certainly the most prominent non-Anglo-Saxon minority to penetrate British high society before the Great War).[26] During the same period, E. Phillips Oppenheim speculated on the involvement of Jews in international intrigue while George Griffith populated the illegal gemstone trade with Jewish opportunists in his stories of the South African diamond fields.

Popular perceptions that Jewish individuals or conclaves dominated and dictated world financial markets clearly had a basis in the ascendancy and influence of the Rothschild and Warburg dynasties, although Charlotte Lea Klein notes wryly that the more the Rothschilds decreased in international importance, the more frequent were literary manifestations of Jews as "cosmopolitan financiers with global interests."[27] Such perceptions were reinforced by claims that the Boer War had been fought primarily to the advantage of Jewish capital or, subsequently, by claims of Jewish involvement in the Marconi and Indian Silver scandals. It is scarcely surprising, therefore, that Jews appeared regularly as stock financiers or moneylenders, at a range of social levels, in pre-1920 thrillers and detective tales. Notable instances occurred in the writing of Arnold Bennett, Baroness Orczy, E.C. Bentley and G.K. Chesterton. Common variants on the image extended financial dexterity to the manipulation by Jews of "the fate of nations," via international politics, terrorist networks, or multinational criminal enterprise. (Oppenheim's Marquis Lefant in *Mr Laxworthy's Adventures*, Chesterton's Dr Hirsch, or the alleged conspiratorial forces in John Buchan's *Greenmantle* and *The Thirty-nine Steps,* are prime examples). Implicit here was the view that, in their enthusiasm for murky milieux of subterfuge and espionage, Jews were, in the last analysis, "un-English," irredeemably "foreign," "clannish," and "alien." At its extreme, this view encompassed tacit speculation about racial inferiority, as in the Buchan story "The Grove of Ashtaroth."

Allied perceptions of Jewish unscrupulousness, venality, and predisposition to criminality—even outright evil—were reflected in the more prosaic activities of fictional underworld figures, again at all social levels: from petty pickpockets and fences like Billy Marks in *The Four Just Men,* through somewhat more up-market embezzlers, like Harry Jacobs in *The Adventures of Romney Pringle* or Judith Lyon in *The Exploits of*

Danby Croker, to big league crime "czars" (Sir Leopold Messinger in *Skin'o'My Tooth* or Isidore Barcovitch in *The Perilous Crossways*). Similarly, presumptions of Jewish hunger for money, and resentment at economic success, clearly underpinned depictions of such nouveaux-riche vulgarians as the Jacobis in *The Count's Chauffeur* and Madame Wachner in *The Chink in the Armour.*

Any questioning of such negative images, or attempts to "redress the balance," were rare in pre-Golden Age writing, the most notable early exception probably being A.E.W. Mason's enlightened comment on Dreyfus-inspired *Judeophobia* in *At the Villa Rose.* The normative images themselves had become established literary conventions within the genre, and allied subgenres, by 1920. Reinforced by the immense popularity of xenophobic thrill-purveyors like McNeile and Horler, manifestations recurred in thrillers and the closely-related detective story form throughout the interwar period and beyond. Topical variations also emerged. The stereotype of the sinister plutocrat, or Jewish mastermind bent on attaining or maintaining control over international affairs, gained new impetus from the proliferation of the *Protocols of the Elders of Zion.* (Sir Marcus in Graham Greene's *A Gun for Sale* or Sir Herman in Agatha Christie's *The Secret of Chimneys* are two examples.) Literary renderings of the Jew as revolutionary, involved in dastardly Communist plots, and intent on overthrowing law, order, stability, and all things British, reflected real public concerns at the outcome of the Russian Revolution and the spread of the "Bolshie bogey." Fictional Bolshevism was a particularly common theme in the 1920s, as conceived by the diehard Buchan and more recent arrivals like John Rhode, Richard Keverne, H.C. McNeile, Agatha Christie and Francis Beeding. Sometimes the images converged, with Chesterton, for instance, fantasising diabolical alliances between bankers and revolutionaries (the desire to serve shadowy "Jewish interests" thus apparently over-riding the fundamental differences between Communist and capital!).

Meanwhile, time-honoured financial stereotypes, from lofty banker to humble old-clothes-man, continued to outnumber other fictional depictions of Jews. In general, they ran true to form (Goldstein in *The Groote Park Murder,* Isaac Levinsky in *The*

Missing Moneylender, or Feldman in *Death on the Borough Council*), although treatment was uncharacteristically sympathetic on a couple of occasions (Sir Reuben Levy in *Whose Body* or the deliberately non-conformist financier in *The Silk Stocking Murders*). Jews continued to inhabit the multicultural underworld, sometimes as crime bosses (Wallace's Mo Liski), more often as gang members or individual "operatives" (Fletcher's Percy Neamore, Horler's "Jewey" Jacobson, Grierson's Barney Morris). Unflattering pictures abounded of the Jew as self-serving opportunist, devotee of sharp practice, financial—sometimes sexual—predator or ostentatious vulgarian, together with images of physical repulsiveness and, by implication, physical inferiority.

Unflattering stereotypes were not the total picture in the Golden Age, however. Although they remained a presence, albeit a declining one, during World War II and, to a diminished degree afterwards, more positive characterisations and references provided some balance. For instance: unnecessary references to Jews, some of them blatantly derogatory, appeared in most of Agatha Christie's books prior to the mid 1930s, yet, on occasion, she offset her one-dimensional insensitivities with surprisingly incisive deviations from the norm. Manders in *Three Act Tragedy* and Papopoulos in *The Mystery of the Blue Train* are examples. Notwithstanding a scepticism about Jews which was partly nurtured by her political conservatism and her fervour for High Church theology, Dorothy L. Sayers also balanced her stock Jewish grotesques with more thoughtful delineations. W. Somerset Maugham, allegedly antisemitic in private life, nevertheless described a minor Jewish character in positive terms in *Ashenden*; Anthony Berkeley Cox deliberately made fun of the Jew-financier stereotype in *The Silk Stocking Murders* and *Cicely Disappears*, while Margery Allingham discarded it in *Look to the Lady*.

In part, change was a natural by-product of the detective story's evolution, as a newer breed of writer reacted against overused cliches and conventions within the genre. Much more influential, though, was the impact of current events as Hitler's policies precipitated Europe towards World War II. While, on the one hand, Manning Coles, Horler, Keverne and John G. Brandon explored such variations on tradition as the Jew as black-marketeer, draft-evader, fifth columnist and even Nazi-collaborator (!), on the other, Marsh, Cox, Nicholas Blake, Christianna Brand and Raymond Postgate mused perceptively on the plight of the Jewish refugee or on the spectre of Fascism making inroads in Britain. In some cases, "old offenders" like Buchan, R. Austin Freeman, Christie and Oppenheim rethought their earlier hostility or flippancy in light of the persecution of European Jewry. One powerful thriller, John Bentley's *Pattern for Perfidy,* written and published just after 1945, took as its central theme the possibility of organised antisemitism taking lethal hold in tough-guy America, just as it had done in Germany.

The end of the war and revelation of the "final solution" marked, as Gina Mitchell has observed, a watershed in the clichéd depiction of Jewish villainy in popular literature.[28] As a general rule, negative Jewish stereotypes have disappeared from that time. There have been occasional regressions. For instance, pawnbrokers, patterned after generations of their kind, continued to surface as late as John Cassells' *Meet the Picaroon* in 1958. By and large, however, Jews of any description have become a relative rarity since the mid 1940s, major exceptions being occasional sympathetic treatments of Holocaust survivors (by Cyril Hare, Anthony Gilbert, Leo Bruce, P.D. James) or commentary on issues of Jewish identity and functioning in the late twentieth century (Laurence Meynell's *Die by the Book* or Barbara Vine's *A Fatal Inversion*, for instance).

In tracing the evolution and progress of Jewish images summarised above, I look initially, and by way of background, at the broader literary tradition to which crime writers fell heir in their engagement with the Jews. My exploration of the treatment of Jews in crime fiction prior to 1920 starts with Conan Doyle and confirms that stereotypes usually associated with the "classic" period were in evidence much earlier. Chapter 2 focuses specifically on the Golden Age (1919-1939), providing an overview of the particular conceptions and representations which prevailed during that critical era. By way of case studies, I look in detail at the work of three of the greatest Golden Age practitioners, Agatha Christie, Dorothy L. Sayers and Anthony Berkeley Cox. Chapter 4 traces changes in attitude and approach during the period, notably the transcendence of stereotype in light of world events. (Accordingly, I extend the Golden Age time-line to 1945 in that chapter, so as to take into account variations on cliche which emerged during World War II.) Chapter 5 looks at Jewish images in post-war crime fiction and, by way of conclusion, my final chapter draws together the various strands and summarises key themes and issues.

Finally: I have made reference a couple of times to the recent debate over British antisemitism. Before moving on—and given that one aim of *Victims or Villains* is to weigh up the extent and degree to which images in crime fiction accurately reflected Jew-consciousness in real life—I feel a short summary of the debate would be of value.

Not unexpectedly, strong disagreement exists amongst historians of Anglo-Jewry as to the significance of antisemitism in British society, in particular over the two generations or so, before World War II. One group has tended to follow the lead of "elder statesman" Cecil Roth who concludes that, from the time of their resettlement under Oliver Cromwell in 1656, Jews have enjoyed an enviable tradition of toleration and extraordinary levels of acceptance in Britain. "In this happy land," writes Roth, "they have attained a measure of freedom (and thereby of collaboration) which has been the case in scarcely any other."[29] The leading representative of this school of thought, W.D. Rubinstein, affirms that "British Liberalism . . . successfully engendered the integration of the Jewish community with the mainstream," and that, compared with the situation on the continent, antisemitism in Britain was, by and large, "minor and marginal, generally associated with the most atavistic and reactionary elements in British society."[30] Minor hiccoughs aside, the history of Anglo-Jewry may be seen as an ongoing "success story." Prior to World War I, concedes Todd Endelman in *Radical Assimilation in English Jewish History,* hostility towards Jews in Britain, although always present to some extent, was more muted than elsewhere in Europe. In her study of political antisemitism between the wars, Gisela Lebzelter concludes that Fascism ultimately failed to gain a foothold in Britain during the critical interwar years because of the absence there of a "historical tradition" of Jew-hatred.[31] According to Rubinstein, most leading British politicians over the past century, including many on the far right, have been demonstrably philosemitic.[32]

A less positive point of view has characterised the writing, over the past twenty years or so, of representatives of the "younger school" of Anglo-Jewish historiography (so called by Professor Rubinstein). Frank Felsenstein, for instance, suggests that Cecil Roth's assessment of English toleration contained an element of "wishful thinking":

However well meant, his analysis smoothed over (and at times consciously chose to ignore) the extensive undergrowth of antisemitic allusion that permeates the rhetoric of eighteenth-century English popular culture [i.e. Felsenstein's area of research] . . . [I]n the so-called age of Enlightenment, the nation that half a millenium before had been the first in mediaeval Europe to expel its Jews, a nation that (as far as records reveal) was also the first to promote the myth of the Wandering Jew and the obscenity of the blood libel, showed a purblind refusal to let go of its primitive superstitions with anything like the genial quiescence that many later scholars would have us suppose.[33]

Modern antisemitism, at one and the same time a logical and discernible outgrowth of traditional religion-based Jew-hatred, and a response to perceptions of Jewish "otherness" in context of the rise of the nation state, the growth of capitalism and the flowering of nationalism, was an established social phenomenon by the middle of the nineteenth century. (Geoffrey Field echoes Poliakov in finding that the Aryan-Semite cleavage was "already part of the intellectual baggage of all cultivated Europeans" by that time.)[34] In his incisive *Modern British Jewry,* Geoffrey Alderman identifies it as "the primary mode of shaping Anglo-Jewry's response and image during the past century," and he notes elsewhere that "most of the ingredients one finds in the antisemitism of the European continent have shown themselves at one time or another in Britain, at both the street and state levels."[35] Tony Kushner maintains that British antisemitism, both organised and otherwise, had strong and enduring ideological roots and impacted greatly on the Jewish community up until, and during, World War II. Indeed, he argues that the war years "witnessed a climax" in expressions of popular dislike of the

Jew.[36] Colin Holmes traces a clear tradition of anti-Jewish prejudice in Britain from the 1870s until World War II, manifestations
of which cut across class and political party boundaries. Even so,
Holmes acknowledges, at no time during that period were there
any official, government-sanctioned measures against Jews in
Britain, a point taken further by Rubinstein who notes that no
legislation or policy, between 1890 and 1945, excluded Jews
from fee-paying schools, universities, exclusive clubs, expensive
residential districts or Government. Nor was there any quantifi-
able evidence of discrimination in private employment. This was
in marked contrast to the Jewish experience in most of the rest of
the world; Endelman agrees that "Jewishness [in England] was
not the impediment to social success or occupational mobility
that it was in Germany or elsewhere in Europe."[37] Elaine R.
Smith, on the other hand, suggests that political antisemitism
often posed as "anti-alienism," and that the Aliens legislation of
1919, for example, actively discriminated against non-naturalised
immigrant Jews and their British-born offspring in the 1920s.[38]

Field observes that in Britain, unlike Weimar Germany, the
Jew never became "an integral part of a widely-shared nationalist world view . . . The ideological and psychological terrain of
anti-Jewish feeling in the two countries was widely dissimilar
even before the Nazi era." He goes on to argue, however, that
British antisemitism was never inconsequential: "Not at all. It
surfaced in private life in slights, rebuffs and various forms of
discrimination . . . It also, in an indirect fashion, played a role in
public policy."[39] Lebzelter, by contrast, maintains that any antisemitic agitation was usually greeted with indifference by the
British public, while W.F. Mandle credits (at least in part) that
nebulous entity "national character" with the ultimate political
failure of Sir Oswald Mosley and the British Union of Fascists.
Rubinstein cites a wealth of evidence to support his contention
that antisemitism, in real terms, was so minor as to be almost
non-existent in twentieth-century Britain. In his view, historians
of the "younger school" have tended systematically to exaggerate and overstate antisemitic aberrations—generally from a post-
Holocaust standpoint.[40]

Clearly, historians are unable to come to a consensus as to
the depth and breadth of anti-Jewish feeling in the interwar

years. Was it ever, on one hand, much more than a relatively minor, albeit distressing, irritant within an otherwise generally benign scheme of things? Was it, on the other, the contemporary manifestation of an age-old, profound and pathological prejudice which, by sheer good fortune, and the vagaries of history, did not achieve widespread transmission? It is indisputable that the Jews of Britain found themselves infinitely better off than their co-religionists elsewhere in Europe at the outbreak of World War II, or that historical circumstance continued to favour them as Britain withstood the German military machine. These facts can tend, however, to colour assessments of the pervasiveness or profundity of prejudice against them, both as individuals and as a group within British society, up to and during the period under review. I contend that analysis of Jewish images in popular fiction, specifically crime fiction, before, during and after the interwar years, can add considerably to our understanding of the true extent and nature of British antisemitism.

1

Prelude:
From Sherlock Holmes
to the Treaty of Versailles

Golden Age representations of Jews obviously did not exist in a vacuum but expanded rather on established public perceptions, prejudices and images, and well-entrenched literary conventions. Literary depictions of the Jew-as-villain can be traced back at least as far as mediaeval times. Indeed, it might be argued that the concept has Biblical antecedents, notably the child-slaying King Herod, Judas "the original businessman with a contract in his pocket," or the "anonymous *farceur*" who offered the dying Christ vinegar rather than water. Thus, argues Edgar Rosenberg, "the Jewish criminal—as Christ-killer, traitor, financial hog . . . had Scriptural sanction from the first."[1] The Jew subsequently appeared frequently in mediaeval literature, functioning as "a well-established and necessary myth, ubiquitous, coloured . . . , unmistakable . . . , declaring himself in grotesque gestures, stimulating in the reader or audience what, in literary criticism, is known as a 'stock response.' "[2]

Reverberations of the image were strong enough, long after the expulsion of the Jews from England, for Chaucer, Shakespeare and Marlowe to render their own definitive variations on the stereotype. In the century and a half following their readmittance to England under Oliver Cromwell (the time-frame which Frank Felsenstein refers to as the "longer 18th century"), Jews surfaced habitually as "tenacious minor figures," depicted unflatteringly in folklore, chapbooks, tracts and more orthodox published sources. Felsenstein has uncovered a sturdy antisemitic undergrowth in the popular culture of that period and he cites such examples as the blackguard Jew dealer whose face contorts into that of the Devil at the sight of jewellery in Daniel Defoe's novel *Roxana* (1724), or the heroine's recoil at the mere mention of the word "Jew" in Fanny Burney's *Cecilia* (1782).[3]

Although negative interpretations have always been evident, Harold Fisch notes that a duality has existed in literary renderings of the Jew since mediaeval times. Usurious merchants, moneylenders, and the like —with crooked noses and wobbly ethics—have been often depicted in company of (and "in ominous contrast to") their beautiful and virtuous daughters, for instance.[4] One thinks immediately of *The Jew of Malta* or *The Merchant of Venice* and, in the nineteenth century, of Sir Walter Scott's *Ivanhoe* (1819) which Rosenberg claims made "the Jews' fortune in the novel" in the same sense in which Shakespeare "gave them a permanent place in the theatre."[5] Scott's Isaac of York combines many of the traditional characteristics of the stock literary usurer although, significantly, he cannot be described as a villain; daughter Rebecca is goodness, wisdom and beauty personified. Charles Dickens, of course, made his own contribution to this "dual image" with his renderings of the criminous Fagin, in many ways the evil Jew of legend, in *Oliver Twist* (1838) and the golden-hearted, unworldly Riah in *Our Mutual Friend* (1865).[6]

Modder argues that a number of Jewish types stand out in nineteenth-century literature and that they exemplify the "close interrelation between literary and social trends." He notes that the fictional old-clothes man, pedlar or "ghetto Jew" resulted directly from influxes of impoverished immigrants from Russia and the Rhine districts; Jewish pedlars featured in some of the adventure stories of Captain Marryat, such as *Peter Simple* (1834), *Snarley You* (1836), and *Japhet in Search of a Father* (1836), and ultimately became a staple of music hall comedy. With political emancipation at mid-century and the movement of Jews into the middle classes, there evolved both the Jewish hero, notably the scholarly Sidonia in Disraeli's *Coningsby* (1844) or Daniel and Mordecai in George Eliot's *Daniel Deronda* (1876), and the assimilated non-Jewish Jew, such as Miriam in Charles Kingsley's *Hypatia* (1853) or Pash in *Daniel Deronda*. The hitherto pervasive image of the wandering Jew became something of an anomaly once Jews gained emancipation; even so, George du

Maurier's Svengali perpetuated the notion of the eternal alien in the immensely popular *Trilby* (1894), as did that pathological antisemite Hilaire Belloc in his clichéd *Emanuel Burden* (1904). Without doubt the most persistent and frequent type, though, played variations on the traditional Shylock image. As well as usury, the image often encompassed mastery of mysticism and the healing arts, and an extraordinary—even suspect—level of learning.[7]

Rosenberg agrees with Modder that changes in depicting Jews in the nineteenth century reflected evolving attitudes and circumstances within British society:

The historical argument can tell us a good deal why Jews could not be presented sympathetically before the 18th century; why the typically bad Jew of the 1830s wore dirtier linen than the typically bad Jew of the 1870s; why the sentimentally good Jew of the 1780s differed from his near-relations a hundred years later in being older, more of a monkey, and less of a public figure.[8]

Yet Rosenberg notes an essential conflict between the rational and populist misconceptions and prejudices in post-Georgian literature. He points, for example, to the persistence of the "evil Jew"/"black priest" myth centuries after Jews ceased to be suspected of poisoning wells or of cutting up babies for Passover.[9] Mayhew's mid-century survey of the London poor concluded that Jews were commonly regarded as "an entire people of misers, usurers, extortioners, receivers of stolen goods, cheats, brothel keepers" by the working classes; influxes of impoverished Eastern European Jews after 1880 compounded the situation, eliciting cries that "hordes of Russians" were swamping the East End, and culminating in anti-alien quotas in 1905. The Jewish population of London alone grew from 47,000 to 150,000 through immigration between 1883 and 1902. At another social level, historian Geoffrey Field points to emergent middle-class resentment and envy at the rise of upwardly mobile Jews (including disdain of the parvenu), as well as ongoing evangelical opposition.[10] Unsurprisingly then, Charlotte Lea Klein identifies increasing hostility in the fictional depiction of the Jew after 1870, heralded by Anthony Trollope's characterisation of the wicked Melmotte in *The Way We Live Now* (1875).

Klein suggests that persistent association of Jews with moneylending and business manipulation "stems from secretly felt envy that he (the Jew) should be so rapidly at home in the turmoil and rootless, unsettled conditions of modern life." More and more, she argues, Jews came to be seen as a threat to traditional values, and this perception was reflected in the literature of the time.[11] For example, Guy Thorne's *When It Was Dark* (1903), one of the best-selling novels of the Edwardian era, features Constantine Schaube, M.P., multi-millionaire, and press-baron. Schaube is "a figure straight out of the *Protocols of the Elders of Zion*" (according to Claude Cockburn)—the Jew, effectively, as anti-Christ or within the old "Jew-devil" mould. (Duplicates of Schaube would resurface—as Cockburn observes—"with fascinating frequency in British literature right through the first third of the century.")[12] Elsewhere, Marie Corelli identifies Jews with "spiritual wickedness in high places" in *Temporal Power* (1902); H.G. Wells uses a family of Jewish plutocrats as a symbol of unwanted change and modernity overtaking an ailing England, in *Tono-Bungay* (1909); the enormously popular H. Rider Haggard posits basic Semitic inferiority by portraying debased Abyssinian Jews "in the last stage of decadence from interbreeding" in his "ripping yarn" *Queen Sheba's Ring* (1910).[13]

Just as precedents for interwar depictions of Jews can be found in mainstream English literature of the late nineteenth and early twentieth centuries, a short survey of the Crime and Detective story in its infancy and formative years (i.e. from *A Study in Scarlet* until the end of World War I) is sufficient to show that Jews were already being employed as stereotyped underworld figures, grasping moneylenders and merchants, international conspirators, etc, by the genre's founding "fathers" and "mothers." Before looking in detail at key images in Golden Age fiction, we should examine their forerunners—starting logically with Sir Arthur Conan Doyle and his immortal Sherlock Holmes, the first of the superman sleuths or, in H.R.F. Keating's words, "the Great Detective as memorable human being."[14]

There are a couple of very minor references to Jews in the Holmes canon but it would be stretching the point unduly to describe them as offensive. In the very first Holmes case, *A Study in Scarlet* (1887), Dr Watson muses on the odd characters visiting Baker Street to seek help from the eminent sleuth:

One morning a young girl called, fashionably dressed, and stayed for half an hour or more. The same afternoon brought a grey-headed, seedy visitor, looking like a Jew pedlar, who appeared to me to be much excited, and who was closely followed by a slipshod elderly woman. (p.14)

A case might be put that the great female inspiration of Holmes' life, singer Irene Adler, could be Jewish ("A Scandal in Bohemia," *The Adventures of Sherlock Holmes,* 1892). Although at no point is Ms Adler's ethnicity stated (we are told that she was born in cosmopolitan New Jersey), the name does have a clear Jewish resonance. In "The Adventure of the Cardboard Box" (*The Memoirs of Sherlock Holmes,* 1894), Watson learns that Holmes purchased his immensely valuable Stradivarius violin, for 55 shillings, from "a Jew broker's in Tottenham Court Road." At the very end of Holmes' career, a jeweller known as Ikey Sanders refuses to cut a diamond and "peaches" on the thief in "The Adventure of the Mazarin Stone" (*The Casebook of Sherlock Holmes,* 1927).

In addition to the Sherlockiana, Conan Doyle's bibliography encompasses a number of miscellaneous early crime and horror stories, collected under the title *Round the Fire Stories* (1908). In one tale, "The Story of the Jew's Breastplate," a priceless museum artefact is tampered with; the narrator speculates that, as the item in question is "a Jewish object of great antiquity and sanctity," the mischief might be the work of "the antisemitic movement"!

Conan Doyle appears to have been actively philosemitic in private life. He was vocally pro-Dreyfus and he co-headed the campaign to free Oscar Slater in 1927. (The German-born Slater was convicted—wrongly, it is now generally believed—of the murder of a wealthy Scotswoman in 1909. Debate then and now has focused on the extent to which Slater's Jewishness might have impacted on the verdict. More than one analyst has dubbed the case "the Scottish Dreyfus affair.")[15] Doyle's crime-writing contemporaries and successors were generally less sanguine in their attitudes/comments on Jews.

Canadian critic Derrick Murdoch cites William Le Queux, Edgar Wallace, E. Phillips Oppenheim, Robert Barr, A.E.W. Mason, E.C. Bentley and G.K. Chesterton as, after Sherlock Holmes' illustrious creator, the most significant or influential English forerunners of the Golden Age. H.R.F. Keating holds a torch for Chesterton and John Buchan, while Julian Symons strongly endorses the contributions of Mason, Chesterton and Bentley, as well as E.M. Hornung, Baroness Orczy, Ernest Bramah, R. Austin Freeman, J.S. Fletcher, Mrs Belloc Lowndes and Arthur Machen.[16] Less significant, but important in their day, were Arnold Bennett and C.L. Pirkis. My survey of these pioneering writers has been limited yet it has pinpointed Jewish images (usually negative—albeit generally fleeting) in the work of all but Bramah and Machen.

Hornung (who was Conan Doyle's brother-in-law) recorded the adventures of A.J. Raffles, gentleman cracksman, cricketer, modern-day Robin Hood, sometime prober of mysteries (in the words of Charles Shibuk, "unquestionably the greatest rogue in detective fiction"),[17] in a novel and three short story collections at the turn of the century. In *Raffles* a.k.a. *The Amateur Cracksman* (1899), Hornung offers an early version of the ruthless and ostentatious Jewish plutocrat, a flashy speculator with a murky past. Reuben Rosenthall, a dealer in illicit gemstones, makes a fortune on the South African diamond fields and sets up an exotic and notorious establishment in the London suburb of St John's Wood. Here (we are told):

he kept a retinue of Kaffirs, who were literally his slaves; and hence he would sally with enormous diamonds on his shirt and on his finger, in the convoy of a prizefighter of heinous repute, who was not, however, by any means the worst element in the Rosenthall menage. (p.29)

Rosenthall (according to Raffles) is:

the most astounding brute to look at, well over six feet, with a chest like a barrel and a great hook-nose, and the reddest hair and whiskers you ever saw . . . He boasted of his race, he bragged of his riches, and he blackguarded society for taking him up for his money and dropping him out of sheer pique and jealousy because he had so much. (p.29-30)

When he challenges the assorted guests at a dinner to rob him of two prominently displayed diamonds, he is shrewdly out-witted by the ingenious Raffles.

C.L. (Catherine Louisa) Pirkis similarly places social-climbing Jews (along with "Turks, heretics and infidels" and "faddists of every description"—"a very ill-looking set") within the murkier regions of 1890s London society, in the story "A Princess's Vengeance," featuring pioneer woman sleuth Loveday Brooke (*The Experiences of Loveday Brooke, Lady Detective,* 1894). Elsewhere, the Jewish presence on the South African dia-mond fields is also noted by Hornung's contemporary George Griffith (better known in his lifetime as a writer of science fic-tion), in a series of short stories for *Pearson's Magazine* collec-tively titled *"I.D.B."* (Illicit diamond buyers). The series was reprinted in volume form as *Knave of Diamonds: Being Tales of Mine and Veld* (1899). Ikey Cohen, a "little Hebrew accom-plice," whose English "was of the oriental order, and whose tenses changed with the variations of his mental temperature," features in "The Border Gang" while Augustus Lowenfeldt, who speaks an odd mixture of Yiddish and Cockney, appears in "The Diamond Dog." Other characters with Jewish-sounding names crop up throughout the stories (e.g. Michael Mosenstein, the fashion-conscious Mrs Mosenstein, "Jossey Mo," the unfortu-nate Max Sandheim, the gullible Lowenthal, possibly even the skilled Inspector Lipinzki). They are all inhabitants of a rough-and-tumble world where robbery, violence, intrigue and shady deals are the norm ("as long as there are diamonds there'll be I.D.B.s of some sort"). There are no Reuben Rosenthalls here, and Griffith's Jews are rendered relatively inoffensively—although it might well be argued that merely depicting such a profusion of Jews engaged in illicit activity leaves Griffith open to censure. (According to historian Marcia Leveson, legislation to control Illicit diamond-buying was widely scorned in South Africa, and "the trade" was regarded as something of a "gentle-man's crime"—so long as it was practised by non-Jews. Not so if practised by Jews. Leveson notes that the clash "between the heroic Gentile—often the detective investigating I.D.B. . . . . and the evil Jew" became a key construct in turn-of-the-century South African fiction.[18] Griffith's stories are among the more innocuous.)

By the early 1900s (maintains Colin Holmes), the word "Jew" was in widespread use in England as a form of "opprobrium" or "reprobation," most frequently associated with crafty dealing or extortionate moneylending. By emphasising the Jewishness of individuals who attained or sought wealth in South Africa, Hornung and Griffith echoed populist claims that wealthy Jews were in control of the colonial economy. Rubinstein notes a temporary upsurge in "Liberal-radical" antisemitism in England during the Boer War period; at one point, the Trades Union Council formally condemned the war as being fought primarily in the interests of "cosmopolitan Jews." Rubinstein believes this was probably the only time in modern British history that a nationally representative body passed such "an explicitly antisemitic resolution."[19] Negative connotations were reinforced by allegations of credit trading in South Wales during a period of extreme economic misery, while Alderman and Rubinstein concur that the high-point of Edwardian and post-Edwardian antisemitism was the claim of Jewish involvement in two major Government scandals—the Marconi and Indian Silver affairs.[20] In the first instance, allegations were made that four ruling party M.P.s had benefited substantially from a contract awarded to the Marconi Co. to construct a chain of wireless stations throughout the Empire. Two of the M.P.s were Jews, Sir Rufus Isaacs and Herbert Samuel; the English head of the Marconi operations was Isaacs' brother Godfrey. In the second case, a deal to provide five million pounds to the Indian government led to claims of a conspiracy to enrich a Jewish financial firm which had close links to the British government. As it eventuated, neither of the scandals had any long-term repercussions on the careers of the Jews involved, although the allegations found ready acceptance among the "Jew-conscious," like the outspoken G.K. Chesterton. (I should note that Rubinstein argues against the traditional perception that the Welsh Riots of 1911 were primarily antisemitic in motivation, and he believes that critics of the Marconi affair were more intent on punishing

Lloyd George than on deriding the "Jewishness" of either Herbert Samuel or the Isaacs brothers.) The polarisation of French public opinion over Captain Dreyfus' guilt or innocence—and the attendant prejudice—fuelled some speculation in England.[21] Interestingly, LeRoy Panek has suggested that *l'affaire Dreyfus,* revolving as it did around a "hot public issue and a figure of great sentimental potential," was a key influence in the development of the spy novel at the hands of Willian Le Queux and E. Phillips Oppenheim.[22]

Hostility at this point defined Jews according to two general and encompassing sets of images: as wealth-holder, with excessive often sinister influence on international markets, the press and society; or as poor immigrant, prone to fast practice or even criminality, similarly addicted to money, self-serving (or "clannish") and unpatriotic.[23] According to veteran historian Solomon Grayzel, assertions of the "international character of Jewish business" derived from the importance throughout Europe of the Rothschild dynasty. Ignored by antisemites was the reality that, even at the height of the family's influence in the mid-nineteenth century, Jewish bankers *per se* represented only a small proportion of the international money network. Grayzel emphasises also the failure of antisemites to acknowledge the Rothschilds' consistently ardent patriotism towards their countries of residence. (The English branch of the dynasty was instrumental in Britain gaining control over the Suez canal, for instance.)[24] Rich Jew images were reinforced by the high profile of such figures as German-born Sir Alfred Mond or Sir Ernest Cassel, the latter a good friend of Edward VII. Poor Jew images reflected pockets of discontent at the mass immigration of non-acculturated, overly visible refugees from Eastern Europe.

In both cases, the Jew was, by definition, essentially alien and un-British, a point of view endorsed by extremist propagandists Arnold White and Joseph Bannister, who gained attention in the early years of the twentieth century with their warnings about Jewish manipulation of the press and finance.[25] Hilaire Belloc and to a lesser extent G.K. Chesterton subsequently campaigned against the corrupting influence of Jews in public life, promoted the myth of Jewish conspiracy to achieve world domination, advocated a form of *apartheid* and stripping of Jews' civil rights, and endorsed emigration to Palestine. A controversy over the conscription of unnaturalised East End immigrants during World War I produced rumblings in some quarters about the loyalty of Jews in general.

Critics are notably divided over the claims of Arnold Bennett's *Grand Babylon Hotel* (1902) to be an early variant of the crime novel. Steinbrunner & Penzler note that it "contains much pure detection," while Barzun & Taylor declare that anybody who calls it a detective story "is in need of psychiatric care."[26] Regardless, millionaire moneylender Sampson Levi can be cited as the first, or one of the first, in a long line of powerful Jewish magnates who would populate detective stories and novels. The "great stockbroker of the 'Kaffir Circus,'" Bennett informs us:

was a rather short, florid man, dressed like a typical Hebraic financier, with too much watch-chain and too little waistcoat. In his fat hand he held a gold-headed cane and an absolutely new silk hat—for it was Friday, and Mr Levi purchased a new hat every Friday of his life, holiday times only excepted.

Levi is known, "down Throgmorton Street way," as "the Court pawnbroker" because, he explains, "I arrange loans for the minor, second-class Princes of Europe. I'm a stockbroker, but my real business is financing some of the little Courts of Europe" (p.92-99).

Other financiers, albeit they are acting on more modest scales than the Rothschild-style Sampson Levi, appear in the work of Baroness Emmuska Orczy. Best remembered today for her Scarlet Pimpernel books, the Hungarian-born baroness also made a substantial contribution to the early annals of detective fiction with three colourful investigators, Skin'o'My Tooth, Lady Molly of Scotland Yard, and most importantly, the Old Man in the Corner. Among "the first and greatest of all 'armchair detectives,'" the Old Man appeared in three short story collections; his modus operandi was to ponder and solve complex cases brought to him by a young female newspaper reporter, without ever leaving his chair in a London tea-shop. In "The Regent's Park Murder" (originally published in the *Royal*

Magazine 1901; collected in *The Old Man in the Corner*, 1909), the Old Man—we never learn his name—solves the murder of gambler and moneylender Aaron Cohen. It transpires that the obdurate Cohen had died because of his decision to foreclose on a debt rather than allow his debtor more time to repay. Ungrudging in his admiration of the murderer's ingenuity, the Old Man in the Corner clearly has little sympathy for the victim. Aaron Cohen is a relatively mild prototype for what was to become a villainous staple among Orczy's successors.

Unscrupulous and unattractive lawyer Patrick Mulligan, nicknamed Skin'o'my Tooth, investigates the disappearance of a young nursery governess in the Orczy story "The Inverted Five" (*Windsor Magazine* 1903; collected in *Skin'o' My Tooth: His Memoirs by His Confidential Clerk,* 1928). In the process, he exposes a respected, albeit overindulged plutocrat, Sir Leopold Messinger, as the leader of a cocaine smuggling network. Despite his title and "all that he has done for England," Messinger is "not altogether English." Large, stout, florid, his black hair carefully brushed across his cranium, he dresses in perfectly cut tweed and sports a big cigar. One of his associates, believed to be a relative, is a "well-dressed, youngish man of somewhat foreign appearance" named Horatio Dreyfus! Dreyfus is found on a seat in Hyde Park, "with a silken cord tied tightly round his throat."

In the short story "A Castle in Brittany," featuring Orczy's third series investigator, Lady Molly, another money-lender named Abraham Rubinstein precipitates a greater crime when he threatens to expose fraud perpetrated by a young aristocrat (*Lady Molly of Scotland Yard,* 1910). Elsewhere, in the course of investigating a mysterious disappearance, the quick-thinking Lady Molly masquerades as the distinctly plebeian Mrs Marcus Stein, wife of a hotelier living "at his Majesty's expense." To transform herself into the flashy Mrs Stein, Lady Molly acquires hair of "the yellow-reddish tint only to be met with in very cheap dyes" and her face is "plentifully covered with brick-red." She sports a purple cloth coat and skirt "of a peculiarly vivid hue," while "the shrill rasping voice which she assumed" echoes "from attic to cellar" ("The Man in the Inverness Cape," *Lady Molly of Scotland Yard*).

William Le Queux produced more than 100 novels about the secret service and international intrigue, as well as a number of more "orthodox" crime stories, from 1891 until his death in 1927. A tireless "Germanophobe," he was convinced that war between Britain and Germany was inevitable and his warnings were seemingly vindicated by the outbreak of hostilities in 1914.[27] Le Queux's concerns extended to doubts about the influence of Jewish financiers on Anglo-German relations. He did, in fact, pinpoint an awkward reality confronting the British Jewish community at the time. Particularly after Sarajevo, as Vivian D. Lipman has noted, Anglo-Jewry had close familial links with Germany through such magnates as Cassel and Sir Edgar Speyer (both involved in British-German financial collaboration), shipowner Albert Ballin and Lord Rothschild (both of whom tried to effect rapprochement between the two nations). Rothschild went so far as to appeal to Lloyd George, and the proprietor of the *Times,* Lord Northcliffe, in a quest to maintain British neutrality, a stand which elicited furious accusations from that newspaper's influential editor Wickham Steed that Jews were pro-German. At the same time, a somewhat bewildered Anglo-Jewry found itself linked through the *Entente Cordiale* with France to a wartime alliance with Czarist Russia from which country a substantial proportion of the community had fled as refugees.[28]

One of Le Queux's earliest spy novels, *A Secret Service* (1896), examines the persecution of Russian Jews after the assassination of Czar Alexander II, and includes a sympathetic Jewish revolutionary among the characters; later books contain less generous, and more predictable, accounts of Jews working undercover in attempts to undermine British National security (*Spies of the Kaiser,* 1909; *The Catspaw,* 1917, for example).[29] In "A Run with Rosalie," one of a series of detective short stories about the elusive criminal Count Bindi di Ferraris and his driver (*The Count's Chauffeur*, 1907), a nouveau-riche "Jew banker from Turin" and his wife are duped by jewel-thieves. Significantly, the victims are portrayed much less sympathetically than are the thieves who make off with their valuable diamond necklace. Mrs Jacobi (referred to simply as "the Jewess") is "stout, vulgar [and] overdressed . . ." and prone to fawn on royalty.

Bearing more than a passing resemblance to both Orczy's illusory Mrs Stein and Le Queux's Mrs Jacobi, although more sinister than either, is Madame Wachner in *A Chink in the Armour* (1912) by Mrs Belloc Lowndes. "Plain, almost grotesque in appearance," addicted to "common, showy clothes," seemingly kindly but "certainly rather vulgar," Madame Wachner is prominent among visitors to a French gambling resort. Although Lowndes never says so explicitly, I presume that Madame Wachner is intended to fit the Jew-parvenu image; where Monsieur Wachner is said to be Viennese, his wife describes herself as "'une vraie cosmopolitane' . . . a true citizeness of the world." She is ultimately brought undone by her passion for pearls, and revealed as a blackmailer and murderess; interestingly, one of her victims, the "tall, dark, almost swarthy" Madame Wolsky from Poland, is also suspected of being "a citizeness of the world."

Romney Pringle, a charming rogue, patterned on Hornung's Raffles, made a specialty of giving other crooks their comeuppance in a series of short stories by Clifford Ashdown for *Cassell's Magazine*. In "The Assyrian Rejuvenator" (reprinted in *The Adventures of Romney Pringle*, 1902), Pringle, in his guise as literary agent, is on the trail of the shady secretary of a patent medicine distribution company. The secretary, Harry Jacobs, absconds when things "hot up." "Clifford Ashdown" was the pseudonym of two medicos, John James Pitcairn and (R)ichard Austin Freeman; the latter subsequently attained much more lasting fame, under his real name, as creator of "the greatest medico-legal detective of all time," forensic scientist Dr John Thorndyke.[30] Freeman (1862-1943) introduced Thorndyke in *The Red Thumb Mark* (1907) and continued to chronicle his superman's investigations throughout the Golden Age. Along the way, he did not hesitate to provide readers with an array of criminous or otherwise socially deviant secondary Jewish characters.

Freeman was a wholehearted disciple of the Eugenics movement, and even published a book *Social Decay and Regeneration* (1921) in which he contemplated the selective breeding of "superior humans." Rubinstein has described him as "a thoroughgoing racist and xenophobe," noting that Jews appear gratuitously in nearly half of the Thorndyke stories. In

"The Moabite Cipher" (*John Thorndyke's Cases*, 1909), for instance, Adolf Schonberg, an underworld habitue with an address in Soho, is described as "a very typical Jew of the red-haired type"; a neighbour delineates Sconberg more bluntly as "a blooming Sheeny, with a carroty beard and gold gig-lamps!" (Members of Schonberg's gang communicate in code, using an ancient Semitic alphabet.) Moneylender Solomon Gordon, a "Scotsman" who hails from Palestine, is "putting the screw" to young artist Thomas Elton in "The Missing Mortgagee" (*The Great Portrait Mystery*, 1918; reprinted in *The Famous Cases of Dr Thorndyke*, 1929). Gordon is induced to change clothes with his victim before plunging to, a not undeserved, death over a clifftop; Elton disappears leaving the police to assume that the corpse is his. Described variously as a "human spider," a "vampire" and a "blood-sucking parasite," the unsavoury Gordon's horizons are bounded by greed. ("Money first, for its own sake, and then those coarser and more primitive gratifications that it was capable of purchasing.") In "The Stolen Ingots" (*Dr Thorndyke's Case Book*, 1923), the English agent of an international gang of smugglers is "a small seedy man," with beady eyes and a "strongly Semitic appearance." (Realising that the "game is up," he flees along a wharf as if he has the Philistines at his heels.)

Less offensively, Solomon Lowe, "a typical Hebrew of the blonde type—good-looking, faultlessly dressed . . . ," enlists Thorndyke to investigate a major robbery, in "The Anthropologist at Large" (*John Thorndyke's Cases*). The home of Lowe's art-collector brother Isaac has been burgled. Isaac, according to his brother, "is a Jew, and he has that passion for things that are rich and costly that has distinguished our race from the time of my namesake Solomon onwards." (Drawing adroitly on his knowledge of "racial characteristics," Thorndyke traces the crime to a Japanese resident of London's Limehouse district.) A Hatton Garden diamond merchant is the murder victim in "The Case of Oscar Brodski" (*The Singing Bone*, 1912), while Jewish art-dealer Lionel Montague, of the firm Montague & Salaman, is chloroformed and robbed of a valuable diamond necklace in "A Fisher of Men" (*Dr Thorndyke's Case Book*).

The Dr Thorndyke chronicles apart, Freeman wrote a number of criminous short stories featuring either Shuttlebury Cobb or the Raffles-like Danby Croker. In the lighthearted "The Brazen Serpent" (*The Exploits of Danby Croker,* 1916), the "hero," recently escaped from prison, colludes with Judith Lyon, the comely but crafty daughter of a London art-dealer, to dupe the usually astute Mr Jacobi, a collector. "Now, for sheer, repulsive ugliness," observes Croker, "commend me to an ugly Jew. On the other hand, there are Jews who to the best favoured Gentile are as gold brocade to a faded wallpaper." The opulent Judith is clearly a prime example of the latter—an alluring and unscrupulous adventuress, "tall, shapely, gorgeous, red-haired, with a face and figure that would have sent Solomon flying to the nearest register office." She emerges triumphant, sporting a new sealskin coat, at the end of the exploit.

Jewish criminals, great and small, likewise appear in the work of the enormously popular and prolific Edgar Wallace, known in his day as the "king of the Thrillers." Wallace published his first mystery novel and best-known work, *The Four Just Men,* at his own expense in 1905. Among the colourful characters inhabiting his vision of turn-of-the-century London is Billy Marks, a petty pickpocket and frequenter of Soho, who comes to a bad end under a train at Victoria Station. Two decades later, Wallace would feature a much more prominent member of the criminal classes (Mo Liski, "the biggest of the gang leaders and an uncrowned emperor of the underworld") in *The Mind of Mr J.G. Reeder.* (See chapter 3.) Wallace has been described as a "passionate conservative" who did not hesitate to characterise Germans as "Huns" and "decadent apes" during the Great War. In fairness, however, Symons cites a general lack of antisemitism in his writing, particularly if compared to other highly popular figures like Buchan, McNeile, Le Queux or Horler; certainly the portraits of Billy Marks and Mo Liski are *relatively* inoffensive.[31]

In *The Triumphs of Eugene Valmont* (1906), which details the exploits in Paris and London of a senior French detective, author Robert Barr tells us in passing that a fabulously valuable necklace had been safely and promptly delivered back to the French authorities by none other than "a young captain of artillery, to whom its custody had been entrusted"—Alfred Dreyfus! Barr speaks nostalgically of Paris in the early 1890s: "Every one was well off and reasonably happy, a marked contrast to the state of things a few years later, when dissension over the Dreyfus case rent the country in twain" (p.2-3). The case is cited frequently as the prime example of Gallic Jew-hatred run rampant. Court-martialled and found guilty of having sold military secrets to the Germans, Captain Dreyfus was imprisoned at French Guiana amid claims that his behaviour exemplified the Jewish propensity for treachery. When subsequently the authorities refused initially to re-open the case despite proof that incriminating evidence had been forged, the issue of Dreyfus' guilt or innocence, and to a marked extent, his Jewishness, divided public opinion. Dreyfusards like Emile Zola found themselves ranged against such bastions of conservatism as the Catholic newspaper *La Croix* which launched an all-out attack on the Jews. Dreyfus was ultimately exonerated and reinstated following a confession by the real traitor, Esterhazy, but not before the world had glimpsed the frightening depth of French antisemitism. In England, throughout the affair, which lasted, in all, from 1894 to 1906, there was a smattering of far-right support for the "Jews' plot" viewpoint, notably within sections of the Catholic Church press; Rubinstein contends, however, that 99% of British newspapers were pro-Dreyfus, as was the overwhelming majority of mainstream public opinion.[32] (One can only speculate on the extent to which the traditional British national dislike of the French may have impacted on the general willingness to accept that Dreyfus was a victim.) Another fictional reference to the affair occurs in A.E.W. Mason's first detective novel, *At the Villa Rose* (1910).

Already widely known as a playwright and author of historical novels, Mason may well have found in the detective novel (as Symons suggests) "an outlet for dark imaginings that had no place in dashing historical romances like *The Four Feathers*."[33] Inspector Gabriel Hanaud of the Paris Surete has been dubbed "the first official policeman of importance in twentieth-century fiction," and his first case, arguably, "the first twentieth century detective novel of artistic worth."[34] It is also highly unusual for its time in its acknowledgement that antisemitism was widespread in France following Dreyfus' vindication. In *At the Villa Rose,* Hanaud and his off-sider/chronicler Ricardo come to the aid of a beautiful English-woman suspected of murdering her wealthy employer. In the course of the investigation, Hanaud has dealings with a bizarre judge who is obsessed by the Dreyfus case and has suspicions of pervasive Jewish conspiracy:

Into the light eyes of M. Fleuriot there came a cold bright gleam. He took a step forward. His face seemed to narrow to a greater sharpness. In a moment . . . he ceased to be a judge; he dropped from his high office; he dwindled into a fanatic. "She is a Jewess, this Celia Harland?" he cried. (p.31)

Justice Fleuriot is disappointed when told that the girl is not Jewish; Hanaud is clearly embarrassed by the man's prejudice. Besnard, the commissaire de police, confides:

he is a good judge, M. Hanaud—quick, discriminating, sympathetic, but he has that bee in his bonnet, like so many others. Everywhere he must see *l'affaire Dreyfus.* He cannot get it out of his head. No matter how insignificant a woman is murdered, she must have letters in her possession which would convict Dreyfus. But you know! There are thousands like that—good, kindly, just people in the ordinary ways of life, but behind every crime they see the Jew. (p.31-32)

A more qualified conception of the Dreyfus case came from G[ilbert] K[eith] Chesterton, best remembered today for his 50-odd short stories featuring the commonplace but intuitively gifted little Catholic priest, Father Brown. (Ellery Queen once ranked Father Brown, along with Sherlock Holmes and Edgar Allan Poe's pioneering Auguste Dupin, as the three greatest detectives in literature.)[35] Bryan Cheyette notes that Chesterton had expressed outrage over the case and had sympathised deeply with Dreyfus as "individual victim" at the turn of the century. Subsequently, after coming under the influence of the wildly eccentric Hilaire Belloc and, significantly, not long after the Marconi scandal, he changed his position and expressed his inability to reach a "final verdict" on the incident. "The Duel of Dr Hirsch" (*The Wisdom of Father Brown,* 1914) reflects the author's uncertainty.[36] When Dr Paul Hirsch, a French Jewish scientist, is accused of passing military secrets to the Prussians, he warns that "there is going to be another Dreyfus case" with public opinion bitterly split. Whilst deliberating on Hirsch, Father Brown muses:

Well, I never understood that Dreyfus case . . . I know (though it's not modern to say so) that human nature in the highest places is still capable of being Cenci or Borgia. No, what puzzled me was the *sincerity* of both parties . . . I mean the persons of the play. I mean the conspirators, if they were conspirators. I mean the traitor, if he was a traitor. I mean the men who *must* have known the truth. Now Dreyfus went on like a man who *knew* he was a wronged man. And yet the French statesmen and soldiers went on as if they *knew* he wasn't a wronged man but simply a wrong 'un. I don't mean they behaved well; I mean they behaved as if they were sure.

Brown judges Dreyfus to have been both innocent and guilty—worse than guilty, in fact, because he knowingly allowed his actions to divide France. He applies the same judgement to Dr Hirsch, and uncovers an ingenious impersonation and a one-man conspiracy to attain "personal glory."[37]

Man of letters—essayist, novelist, poet, journalist and polemicist—and larger-than-life, Chesterton (1874-1936) was enormously popular in the first third of the twentieth century ("a spouting volcano of fire-dazzling words who appears to have left mounds of dead ashes," according to H.R.F. Keating).[38] Today he is recalled for a relatively small number of works which contain elements of the detective story and, as much if not more, for his eccentricities, particularly his outspoken espousal of radical political causes, and his determined, and oft-reiterated, antisemitism. Unsurprisingly, given his preoccupation with the Jew as perpetual alien, Jewish images surface throughout his fiction. *The Man Who Was Thursday* (1908), which Steinbrunner & Penzler term "an allegorical novel disguised as a detective story," has been described elsewhere as the "nightmare of a man who fears Christians are really Jews, or *vice versa*."[39] The non-crime novel *The Ball and the Cross* (1910) describes a Jewish shopkeeper-*cum*-pornography dealer who, we are told, has "little respect for humanity," while *Man Alive* (1912) features Moses Gould, a "small, resilient Jew" who has survived pogroms:

swaggering on short legs with a preposterous purple tie, [Gould] was the gayest of godless little dogs; but a dog also in this, that however he danced and wagged with delight, the two dark eyes on each side of his protuberant nose glistened gloomily like black buttons. (p.32)[40]

Chesterton was a "gung ho" enthusiast of the detective genre, who would serve appropriately as foundation president of the prestigious Detection Club. Father Brown, however, tended to rely, from the outset, far more on psychological inspiration than traditional deduction for his solutions. As time went on, the Brown stories contained less and less formal ratiocination, serving more and more as "a springboard for Chesterton's religious philosophy."[41] The short story "The Queer Feet" (*The Innocence of Father Brown,* 1911) is set at the exclusive Vernon Hotel in Belgravia; the hotel's owner, Lever, has made "nearly a million out of it, by making it difficult to get into." Father Brown is called in to minister to an ailing employee.

One of the waiters, an Italian, had been struck down by a paralytic stroke that afternoon, and his Jewish employer, marvelling mildly at such superstitions, had consented to send for the nearest Popish priest. With what the waiter confessed to Father Brown we are not concerned . . . but apparently it involved him in writing out a note or statement for the conveying of some message or the righting of some wrong . . . between the office and the cloak-room was a small private room without other outlet, sometimes used by the proprietor for delicate and important matters, such as lending a duke a thousand pounds or declining to lend him sixpence. It is a mark of the magnificent tolerance of Mr Lever that he permitted this holy place to be for about half an hour profaned by a mere priest, scribbling away on a piece of paper.

Father Brown utilises Lever's "holy place" to avert a crime and to extract a confession from arch-criminal Flambeau. Cheyette places a (Roman Catholic) religious interpretation on the story, suggesting that it depicts the triumph of "Christian reasoning" over "spiritual confusion." By hearing his confession, the priest saves the soul of Flambeau and enables the criminal "to enter the spiritual realm of christendom"; the Jew Lever, by contrast, "reverts to racial type and, as the story progresses . . . speaks with a 'deepening accent' and his skin, 'a genial copper-brown' is turned into a 'sickly yellow.'" (Cheyette argues further that Jewish characters in later Father Brown stories increasingly embody "spiritual confusion.")[42] In "The Purple Wig" (*The Wisdom of Father Brown,* 1914), Israel Green, who has "risen very rapidly, but from very dirty beginnings; being first a 'nark' or informer, and then a moneylender," becomes solicitor to a duke and defrauds him out of his estate. At the beginning of the same short story, a newspaper editor's substitution of the word "alien" for "Jew" in a set of proofs would seem to underline Chesterton's belief in the essential otherness of Jews.

Chesterton continued to chronicle the detections of Father Brown and other sleuths, like Horne Fisher and Mr Pond, well into the Golden Age, and included a relatively late reprise of the international Jewish conspiracy motif in *Four Faultless Felons*; I look at his work in further detail in the next chapter. Another major contributor to pre-1920 detective fiction, E.C. Bentley, deserves a passing mention here for apparently endorsing the myth of Jewish domination of international finance in his celebrated *Trent's Last Case* (1913). When magnate Sigsbee Manderson dies, precipitating a stock-market crash, Bentley tells us that a well-known French banker commits suicide on the steps of the Bourse, surrounded by a "raving crowd of French Jews" (p.6).

E. Phillips Oppenheim was, like Le Queux, a producer of spy and mystery fiction on the grand scale, his output stretching from the 1890s until the mid 1940s. John Buchan once dubbed him, perhaps satirically, "the greatest Jewish writer since Isaiah"; however, I have been unable to locate any evidence otherwise to suggest that Oppenheim was Jewish. Possibly he could claim Jewish ancestry through his father, a London leather merchant. (His mother's maiden name was the very un-semitic Budd.) Biographer Robert Standish notes that, as a young man living at Leicester, Oppenheim was active in the parish church.[43] Having once speculated that a major criminal was likely to be a "son of Israel," in the early espionage treatise *The Mysterious*

Mr Sabin (1898), he gave readers a full-fledged, and unequivocally Jewish, international mastermind in a connected sequence of detective short stories, *Mr Laxworthy's Adventures* (1913). In "The Secret of the *Magnifique*," investigating hero Laxworthy encounters the Marquis Lefant, the "greatest power in the diplomatic world," who reportedly brought about war between Russia and Japan, and once stopped Britain declaring war on Germany. Lefant is tall, "with black hair streaked with grey, a face half Jewish, half romantic, and skin like ivory." His involvement in the proliferation of powerful torpedoes is exposed in the course of the story. ("They say he has English blood in his veins. If so, he has been a sorry friend to his native land," observes Laxworthy.)

The spy and adventure story, or thriller, favoured by Oppenheim and Le Queux and hugely popular during the early decades of the century, shares many commonalities with the so-called pure detective story of the era; they are often grouped together by bibliographers, analysts and critics. Another contributor to that sub-genre, whose work spanned several decades, attracted an enormous readership, and undoubtedly influenced Golden Age practitioners, warrants a brief examination here (and in the next chapter). Diplomat, peer, politician, sometime Governor-General of Canada, biographer, publisher and lawyer, John Buchan (1875-1940), is best-remembered today for his light fiction, particularly the series of adventures featuring the fearless Richard Hannay. Keating unhesitatingly places the most famous, *The Thirty-nine Steps* (1915), in his "top ten" listing of founding fathers of the crime novel; the book is also included among the Haycraft-Queen cornerstones.[44] It could well be argued that the novel and its successors—as well as books by H.C. McNeile and Sydney Horler—gave new impetus to the Jew-as-villain stereotype in popular fiction.

Gina Mitchell notes that the threat of social disruption, and the embodiment of that threat as conspiracy theory, are hallmarks of the Buchan books. As early as 1900 and *The Half-hearted*, he claimed that a "gang of Jew speculators and vulgarians" was in process of corrupting Britain.[45] The concept of racial, or "mixed breed," inferiority is also implicit throughout. In the short story "The Grove of Ashtaroth" (*The Moon*

Endureth, 1912), the central character, Lawson, is possessed by a pagan goddess when he builds a house in a remote part of Africa. His susceptibility is blamed on his pedigree: while his mother was a blonde Anglo-Saxon from the English midlands, his grandfather had been a synagogue-frequenting antique-dealer in a Brighton back street. "Ashtaroth was the old goddess of the East," muses the narrator. "Was it not possible that in all Semitic blood there remained transmitted through the dim generations, some craving for her spell?" In the course of the story, Lawson's appearance changes until he looks curiously semitic and, in his degenerate state, he proves extraordinarily successful in financial speculation.[46]

In *The Thirty-nine Steps*, American secret agent Scudder alerts Hannay to an attempt by powerful Jews to bring Russia and Germany into conflict.

The Jew is everywhere, but you have to go far down the backstairs to find him. Take any big Teutonic business concern . . . if you're on the biggest kind of job and are bound to get to the real boss, ten to one you are brought up against a little white-faced Jew in a bathchair with an eye like a rattlesnake. (p.11-12)

In Scudder's view, the willingness of Jews to align themselves, as either capitalists or anarchists, with international espionage, has its motive in their desire for revenge after three centuries of persecution.

Stafford notes that, in the novel, the senior Foreign Office representative Sir Edward Bullivant warns Hannay against a too ready acceptance of Scudder's claims. ("He had a lot of odd biases . . . Jews, for example, made him see red. Jews and high finance" [p.101].) Stafford suggests that such disclaimers are often overlooked by critics of Buchan's depiction of Jews; even so, he concedes that the Hannay novels "assign Jews to a different universe to that of the English gentleman."[47] Hannay might treat Scudder's views with mild scepticism, yet he declares Jews to be "at the back of most German enterprises" in *Greenmantle* (published during the war, in 1916). A Portuguese Jew turns out to be a German spy in *Mr Standfast* (1919). By defining Jews as revolutionaries, and therefore, "dangerous and disruptive politi-

cal influences" (argues Mitchell), Buchan was departing somewhat from "the traditional Jewish stereotype in English fiction
and drama" and providing the prototype for scores of subsequent
fictional Jewish radicals.[48]

A number of the so-called forerunners of the Golden Age
continued to contribute steadily during the heyday of the genre,
i.e. in the interwar years; Buchan, Wallace, Chesterton, Oppenheim, Bentley, Mason, Freeman, even Conan Doyle, all
remained active, although honours in the field were won primarily by newcomers (or apparent newcomers). One writer, J.S.
Fletcher (1863-1935), extremely popular on both sides of the
Atlantic during the 1920s and 1930s, had actually been publishing for 20 years without much distinction before he hit the big
time with *The Middle Temple Murder* (1919). To conclude this
chapter, I will look briefly at one of Fletcher's earlier books, *The
Perilous Crossways* (1914), a rollicking whodunit which draws
on a colourful cast of characters, including Anglo-Indian civil
servants, country gentry, suspicious newcomers of independent
means, gipsies and a couple of Hindus. (The book bears a passing resemblance to Wilkie Collins' *The Moonstone*.) Following
the discovery of a corpse on a rural golk links, suspicion falls on
the local squire who appears to be engaged in "fishy" business
dealings with "a vulgar and oily Jew of a particularly objection-
able type" (p.72).

Isidore Barcovitch styles himself a "financial gent" and has
the dubious distinction of being one of the most unprepossessing
and sinister Jewish moneylenders to be found in any pre-1920s
crime or mystery novel. He makes his first appearance over a
seemingly conspiratorial luncheon at the exclusive Romano's in
London.

He was a person of apparently from fifty-five to sixty years of age; a
big, fleshy man whose suit of grey tweed seemed to have been made
for him when his bulk had loomed less considerably on his immediate
surroundings. His iron-grey hair had an inclination to curl, his under-
lip was undeniably pursy, his nose was large and bulbous and disposed
to hook itself on to the protuberant lip. He was one of those men who
make much play with their hands when they talk, and it was conse-
quently an easy thing to see that his thick, stubby fingers were liberally

ornamented with diamond rings. There was another diamond in his shining silk cravat and he wore a gold chain across his ample paunch which might at a pinch have served as cable to a small boat.

"If I am any judge of physiognomy," remarked Herbert when he had looked his fill, "I should say that the gentleman is certainly of Hebraic extraction."

"Right," answered James Maury. "He's a Jew, a Levantine Jew . . . But let's talk of something else than these swine . . ." (p.33)

We learn subsequently that Barcovitch is "a smart rogue" indeed:

His transactions are many and various . . . He is a Jew of the Levant, but he has lived in many countries and cities—London, New York, Cape Town, Mel-bourne. A man who had known him in America told me that he went to that country to sell cheap jewellery. When he had made money in that way . . . he expended his capital in more profitable transactions. When I first knew him in Calcutta he lived in the Eurasian quarter of that city, and had a big business in small loans. He had the reputation of being a hard, a grasping man, who dealt harshly with the people who fell into his clutches . . . now he does not call himself a moneylender any longer, but a financial agent. (p.96-97)

Apart from his shady financial dealings, he is suspected of having been involved at one time in piracy and white slavery. He fades from the scene, presumably to flourish elsewhere, long before the novel's *denouement*, leaving the culprit to be struck down by a deadly Indian snake.

Barcovitch is clearly an unsavoury being, and Fletcher pulls no punches in describing him. Having spotted him on a train leaving London, an irate first-class passenger is moved to make the startling observation: "There ought to be a law against those sort of chaps travelling with ladies and gentlemen. The cattle-truck's more their place . . . he'll poison the air of Mickledene . . ." (p.35). To find his equal elsewhere in detective literature, we need to move on to the Golden Age.

2

Golden Age Norms:
Jewish Stereotypes 1919–1939

Negative depictions of Jewish characters, or unnecessary slurs or asides about Jews and Jewishness, increased markedly during the Golden Age. Dilys Wynn maintains that "the number of gratuitous insults dangled upon Jews in these books quite exceeds the reprimands, slights and minor indignities suffered on anyone else."[1]

At one level, this increased frequency paralleled the massive upturn in popularity (and publishing) in the genre, the expansion of lending libraries, and technological breakthroughs which enabled publishers to produce *more books more cheaply* as "fodder" for an avid mass readership. According to Robert Graves, detective and mystery stories, conforming to set rules and patterns and populated by familiar stereotypes, dominated "lowbrow reading" in the interwar years; from the mid 1920s, thousands of books were produced annually, on both sides of the Atlantic, to meet the demand.[2]

At a deeper level, of course, the incidence of antisemitic references in books and stories of this period reflected international and national trends. The impact of Bolshevism and the acceleration of anti-Jewish fervour throughout Europe after the Great War coalesced with reinvigorated manifestations in Britain of dislike and fear of Jews—at all levels of society. Popular complaints at alleged Jewish vices had a long tradition; what was new in the 1920s and 1930s was the "sheer volume of such accusations." ("Antisemitism was in the air, an unmistakable tang," Malcolm Muggeridge once wrote about the 1930s.) At times verbal or written insults were underscored by subtle discrimination socially or in education and employment.[3] Renewed stereotypes were given credence and, inevitably, surfaced again and again in the literature of the masses during its heyday.

In his New Year's message for 1937, the Archbishop of Canterbury expressed concern at the growth of anti-Jewish hostility in Britain, warning that "unless it is checked it may spread." "I trust that we may be spared the shame of giving any sort of encouragement to the discreditable prejudice which has led to the cruel persecution in other countries, and especially Germany, of the race to which our Saviour in his human life belonged," he continued.[4] The following year, Board of Deputies press officer Sidney Salomon also expressed deep disquiet at epidemic antisemitism on the Continent and its disturbing manifestations at home. Quoting Lloyd George's view that Jew-hatred had "no basis in reason," he highlighted the fundamental inconsistency of the antisemite. (If a Jew were rich, he was by definition "a bird of prey"; if he were poor, he was "vermin"; if he gave freely, he was prompted by self-interest; if not, he stood accused of avarice.) Salomon elucidated the conceptions with which British Jews were most frequently and persistently obliged to contend: (1) that the Jews were an international force intent on controlling world affairs through finance; (2) that Jews were Bolshevists; (3) that refugee Jews were over-running the professions. (Coupled with this were exaggerated claims of Jewish numbers in Britain. In fact, Jews amounted to no more than 0.69% of the population.); (4) that Jews had divided loyalties (and, by extension, were ultimately "aliens"); (5) that Jews controlled the press and chain-stores. (In the 1930s, 75% of English newspapers were controlled by three conglomerates, none of which included any Jews, while Jews directed only 21% of chain-store trade.); (6) that Jews were promoting British involvement in war so as to revenge themselves on Hitler.[5] Kushner identifies a number of other related images which held sway with sections of the British public in the interwar and war years. For instance, he suggests a modern variant on the mediaeval concept of the "Jew-Devil," rooted in the motif of Jew-as-Christ-killer and tied in with notions of sorcery or sinister sexual power, as a recurring literary stereotype. As much in vogue as ever were variations on the centuries-old Shylock image, either as financier and unscrupulous dealer or, during World War II, as black marketeer.[6]

Richard Thurlow suggests that the insulated English middle classes were particularly receptive to Jewish conspiracy fantasies. For a Britain burdened with industrial problems, deeply anxious about the collapse of the old Europe, fearful for the future and still cut to the heart by the loss of a substantial percentage of its youth in the Great War, Jews continued to serve as inevitable scapegoats. At one level, belief in Semitic plotting echoed concern at the seemingly disproportionate number of Jews prominent in the Russian Revolution of 1917. Indeed, there were claims that German and Russian Jews had actively instigated the overthrow of Czar Nicholas in a bid to help the German war effort.[7] Both Colin Holmes and Sharman Kadish note an element of truth in this Jew-Bolshevik linkage. Some Jews were certainly important in the lower levels of party machinery during and after October 1917, and a small number of Jewish radicals took their places in Lenin's first government; Lev Davidovich (Leon) Trotsky was people's commissar for foreign affairs, and subsequently for transport and military affairs, under Lenin (he was ultimately expelled by Stalin and assassinated whilst in exile); the two best-known women revolutionaries of the period were Emma Goldman and Rosa Luxemburg, both Jews (Goldman was expelled from America during the "red scare" of 1919, Luxemburg was murdered by German soldiers the same year); closer to home, British Jews, usually Russian-born, were active in the foundation and running of the Communist party in Britain. Even so, notes Kadish, these Jews were unrepresentative of the Jewish community/communities as a whole. A "reading of the Jewish press reveals that the influence of 'Jewish Bolshevism,' particularly in the East End, was vastly overestimated."[8]

Doubts about Jewish loyalty or patriotism were reinforced by the dissemination of the notorious *Protocols of the Learned Elders of Zion*. Based on a satire which had targeted the French emperor Napoleon III, this pernicious forgery was manufactured in Paris by a Russian secret agent in the 1890s, and summarily promulgated throughout Europe by antisemitic interest-groups. It purported to reveal plans by an international Jewish cartel to take over the world. The book found a considerable following in Britain after the Great War, particularly within influential sections of the Tory press, most notably the *Morning Post.* Although discredited in 1921, and widely refuted as a blatant fake (by the *Times,* for instance), the *Protocols* remained a handy propaganda tool for early far-right groups like the "Britons," the Imperial Fascist League or the "Nordic League." The Nazis continued to endorse its claims in the 1930s, the B.U.F. drew liberally on it, and the book has since continued to be marketed by lunatic-fringe groups all over the world.

Founded in 1919, the "Britons Society," and its off-shoot "Britons Publishing Company," which issued the first of 85 editions of an English-language translation of the *Protocols* in that year, claimed that Jews were, at one and the same time, disproportionately represented in the banking industry and prominent in the Bolshevik party. Completely disregarding the inherent ludicrousness of any co-operation between two such extremes, the "Britons" played on irrational fears of a "twin-edged communist and capitalist assault"; the "dialectical contradiction of a Bolshevik and bankers' alliance was mystically explained away as the consequence of a diabolical plot," writes Thurlow.[9] Led by Henry Hamilton Beamish, the organisation linked conspiracy theory to pseudo-scientific notions that Jews were racially inferior to Englishmen (on the evolutionary ladder), sentiments which were endorsed by Arnold Leese and his Imperial Fascist League in the late 1920s. Adopting, and distorting, the eugenics research of biometrician Karl Pearson, the I.F.L. concluded that Jews were mentally and physically debased and should therefore be rejected as immigrants. Both Beamish and Leese advocated resettlement of Jews, possibly at Madagascar, Leese going so far as to contemplate mass sterilisation and murder.[10] (Not surprisingly, he apparently ended his days in an asylum.) Although both the "Britons" and the I.F.L. were marginal "ratbag" organisations, appealing only to extremists, they articulated and disseminated propaganda and paved the way for the much more influential, and seemingly credible, British Union of Fascists in the 1930s.

Dorothy L. Sayers sniffed at the notion of an international Jewish conspiracy in *Murder Must Advertise* (see Chapter 3 of this study), but a number of her contemporaries were more credulous. The perception that a "natural sympathy" existed between revolutionary Communism and world Jewry clearly gained some credence—at least until the mid 1920s.[11] Chesterton, notably, fantasised an attempt by two South American Jewish revolutionaries, Mendoza and Alvarez, to disprove the power of miracles—and, by extension, Christianity—in the surreal story "The Resurrection of Father Brown" (*The Incredulity of Father Brown,* 1926). (Naturally, the priest foils their plot.) In *The Man Who Knew Too Much* (1922), in which gentleman detective Horne Fisher solves a series of unpublicised crimes, Chesterton sneers at politically powerful moneylenders, like Sir Isaac Hook, Sir Francis Verner or "nosey Zimmern," creditor to "half the Cabinet," and describes a firm of murderous Jewish plutocrats as being "as big as the bank of England."

Even though he acknowledged early on that the *Protocols* were a forgery, the persistent theory of a union between Jewish money and Jewish revolutionaries clearly continued to strike a chord with Chesterton. Father Brown exposes collusion between wealth-holders and Bolsheviks, ostensibly on opposite sides over an industrial dispute, in "The Ghost of Gideon Wise" (*The Incredulity of Father Brown*). Jacob P. Stein, one of a trio of millionaires "concerned with arranging for a coal lock-out, and denouncing it as a coal-strike," has a permanent smile "rather like a permanent sneer." (He ends up strangled in his opulent Roman bath.) John Elias, one of "the triumvirate of those who would have been very glad to turn the lock-out into a strike—and the strike into a revolution," is a "cosmopolitan wire-puller" with "a taste for absinthe." He speaks with a "faintly lisping drawl." Both Father Brown and a journalist covering the industrial dispute are struck by the similarities "in face and mind and manner" of the two Jews ("the millionaire might have disappeared down a trap-door in the Babylon hotel and come up again in the stronghold of the Bolshevists").

By the 1920s, according to Cheyette, Chesterton's "earlier distinction between 'rich and poor' or 'orthodox and broad' Jews" had "elided in the all-embracing context of 'Semitic trouble.'" It is the "racial interconnection between poor Jewish communists and rich Jewish capitalists that is of profound importance and transcends all class and religious differences."[12] In "The Loyal Traitor," one of four novellas published as *Four*

Faultless Felons (1930), Loeb, an immensely affluent pawnbroker, provides the wherewithal and premises for the shadowy "Brotherhood of the Word," a group bent on revolution in the small European kingdom of Pavonia. (The Brotherhood is investigated by the king's astute financial advisor, Isidor Simon.) Chesterton subsequently targeted Jews and the "red menace" briefly in his Prologue to the Detection Club's collaborative novel *The Floating Admiral* (1931). Among the international sailors hanging around an opium den near the Hong Kong docks is "a little swarthy Jew, who was born in Budapest but had lived in Whitechapel." The Jew strikes up:

in piping tones a song he had heard there: "Every nice girl loves a sailor." And in his song there was a sneer that was some day to be seen on the face of Trotsky, and to change the world. (p.9)

Given the evidence from his detective stories, as well as a host of journalistic references to Jews in England,[13] it would seem indisputable that Chesterton was highly antisemitic, particularly following the Marconi scandal. It is interesting, therefore, that some debate exists as to the true nature of his anti-Jewish sentiments. Colin Watson links Chesterton unequivocally with "other equally famous and equally psychotic authors" like Buchan; Colin Holmes and recent biographer Michael Ffinch similarly declare his antisemitism to be unquestionable.[14] Chesterton's first biographer Maisie Ward, by contrast, was quick to point out that "some of [his] best friends had been Jews," while Michael Coren argues that his statements were not necessarily racist. Rubinstein suggests that Chesterton is difficult to come to terms with because of his love of paradox; he was one of the first people outside Germany to condemn Hitler, he was unmoved by the *Protocols*, and he was, to all intents and purposes, a Zionist. According to Ward: "He wished for the Jewish people the peaceful possession of a country of their own, but he demanded urgently that they should no longer be allowed to govern his country. Marconi still obsessed him." Rubinstein makes the point also that: "Essentially [Chesterton] was a curious mixture of Christian (i.e. Catholic) patriot and English patriot; the Jews were undesirable and alien because they were neither . . . The Catholic triumphalist strand in Chesterton's attitude was just as important as his English nationalism. This distinguished him from most post 1880 antisemitism which was, increasingly, purely 'racial' in nature."[15] In the short story "The Curse of the Golden Cross" (*The Incredulity of Father Brown*), he (as the little priest) expounds on the men who built Britain's parish churches and named its towns and roads, and disputes the claim that the same men might have burned Jews for their religion. In response to the argument that mediaeval Jews suffered persecution, he declares:

It would be nearer the truth . . . to say they were the only people who weren't persecuted in the Middle Ages. If you want to satirise mediaevalism, you could make a good case by saying that some poor Christian might be burned alive for making a mistake about the Homoousion, while a rich Jew might walk down the street openly sneering at Christ and the Mother of God.

Of course, Chesterton lived and wrote before World War II. Rubinstein quotes Margaret Canovan who has written insightfully: "To radicals like Chesterton, the economic and political power of the Jews all over the Western world seemed as secure and unchallengeable as does that of America now, and the idea of a Final Solution seemed as incredible then as the destruction of America now. The jokes about pork and noses, which we read as bullying taunts against the weak, were often meant by their writers as brave gestures defying the mighty."[16] In his autobiography, Chesterton considered it odd that he should be regarded as an antisemite, but he remained convinced of the essential otherness of the Jew:

I do not believe that a crowd on the race-course is poisoned by mediaeval theology; or the navvies in a Mile End pub misled by the ethnology of Gobineau or Max Muller; nor do I believe that a mob of little boys fresh from the cricket-field or the tuckshop were troubled about Marxian economics or international finance. Yet all these people recognise Jews as Jews when they see them; and the schoolboys recognised them, not with any great hostility except in patches, but with the integration of instinct. What they saw was not Semites or Schismatics or capitalists or revolutionists, but foreigners; only foreigners that were not called foreigners. (*Autobiography,* 1935, p.75-77)

Above all, Chesterton declared himself fundamentally opposed to attempts to disguise "otherness" through assimilation. "A Tall Story" (*The Paradoxes of Mr Pond,* 1936) articulates the view that Jewish assimilation exacerbated antisemitism during the Great War. When a German spy named Levy attempts to change his name to Schiller (because "there'th a lot of prejudith againth my rathe"), he is admonished:

Why the dickens do you people do it? . . . I know you had nothing to do with burning the Louvain Library or sinking the *Lusitania.* Then why the devil can't you call yourself Levy, like your fathers before you—your fathers who go back to the most ancient priesthood of the world? And you'll get into trouble with the Germans, too, someday, if you go about calling yourself Schiller. You might as well go and live in Stratford-on-Avon and call yourself Shakespeare.[17]

Cheyette notes that this position "is entirely consistent with Chesterton's championing of distinctly inentifiable Jews, as opposed to indistinct 'Jewish cosmopolitans.'"[18]

The "rat-faced," half-Jewish Boris Ivanovitch is a member of a Bolshevik gang intent on revolution in post-Great War London in Agatha Christie's *The Secret Adversary* (1922). In *The Double Florin* (1924), one of the earliest books by the prolific John Rhode, a Bolshevik plot produces a general strike in England; a prominent tool of the plotters is a sinister Islington pawnbroker named Lazarus Hirschbein. A group of "Bolshie" terrorists, involved with a shady Jewish moneylender in a Roumanian oil deal, dispatches the moneylender when he "rats" on them, in *The Five Flamboys* (1929) by Francis Beeding. Richard Keverne's *The Shadow Syndicate* (1930) features Anna Marks, an infamous radical, "notorious throughout the world as the most intransigent of revolutionaries." Presumably patterned by Keverne after real-life revolutionary Rosa Luxemburg, Anna Marks' "hand and mind was against every government":

Even Moscow received her with suspicion, though they paid her well. Anna Marks was almost a myth. Nobody seemed to know how she came and went, but nearly always where there was industrial trouble Wild Anna would appear.

It was said that she had doubles . . . Only a short time ago Eade had read of a strike meeting in Detroit at which the woman had spoken, with disastrous effect to law and order, but there she had been billed as Maggie Lee, though it was reported the audience knew the moment she began speaking that she was Wild Anna. (p.236-37)

Elsewhere, the Bolshevik-Jew connection is highlighted by John Buchan in *Huntingtower* and *The Three Hostages*, and by H.C. McNeile in the Bulldog Drummond stories.

In *Huntingtower* (1922), the pro-socialist John Heritage expresses admiration for the Bolsheviks but concedes that there are "too many Jews among them" (p.35). *The Three Hostages* (1924) pits Richard Hannay and McGillivray of Scotland Yard against an international criminal network ("wreckers on the grand scale, merchants of pessimism, giving society another kick downhill whenever it had a chance of finding its balance, and then pocketing their profits" [p.46]). More than once Buchan links such disruption to world Jewry. "Think of it," cries the much-travelled Dr Greenslade, "All the places with names like spells—Bokhara, Samarkand—run by seedy little gangs of communist Jews . . . Europe is confused enough, but Asia is ancient Chaos" (p.11). McGillivray echoes Greenslade's concern:

A large part of the world has gone mad . . . The moral imbecile, he said, had been more or less a sport before the War; now he was a terribly common product, and throve in batches and battalions . . . You found it among the young Bolshevik Jews, among the young gentry of the wilder Communist sects . . . (p.23)

Prominent among the characters in *The Three Hostages* is Julius Victor, "one of the richest men in the world," an American banker who conducted Britain's financial business in 1914-1918 and was once described as "the whitest Jew since the apostle Paul." Victor, whose daughter is one of three children of prominent figures kidnapped "as hostages against the future," is an essentially decent being; even so (observes Mitchell) he remains "a Jew characterised by his association with money and secretive political activity."[19]

Julius Victor and Macandrew in *The Prince of the Captivity* (see chapter 4) deviate from the Buchan norm by being relatively sympathetic Jews. By and large though, such portrayals are offset by "references—either casual or in detail" to derogatory characteristics (a thug in *Mr Standfast* [1919] has "a nose with a droop like a Polish Jew") or to "Semitic" machination (Jews, hand-in-hand with the "unsleeping" communist enemy, are said to be lurking behind "respectable bourgeois" fronts, in *Huntingtower* [p.79]).[20] Elsewhere in *The Three Hostages*, Buchan describes a "dishevelled Jewess, wearing sham diamond earrings" who fronts a bogus business north of Oxford Street, and a furtive Jew in a dyed beard, obviously up to no good, who materialises fleetingly at the Wellesley Club.

Buchan, in common with H.C. McNeile and Sydney Horler (for Horler, see below), contrasts the "Britishness" to the core of his heroes with the cosmopolitanism of his bad guys. "It is the essential foreignness of his villains which is used as the key component in the construction of an overall stereotype of villainy," writes Mitchell.[21] McNeile takes the premise a step further. Like Buchan, he is concerned intimately with conspiracy theory—indeed, he is the more paranoid, adamant that "foreigners . . . always, through jealousy, want to bring England to her knees." Foreign characters, according to this point of view, are—by definition—villains: evil Germans, murderous Russians, fraudulent Italians. ("Dagoes begin at Calais.")[22] Typical of his attitude and approach is this description of a seedy waterfront bar in the adventure novel *Jim Maitland* (1928):

seated at tables round the room were a dozen or so of the sweepings of every nation—Greeks, English, Germans, Chinamen—temporarily united in the common bond of watching an ex-Balliol man giving an imitation of a dog at the order of a swarthy-looking Dago sitting at a table by himself. (p.26)

Apologists for John Buchan, like Gertrude Himmelfarb and his son Alastair, have argued that the corps of characters in the

Hannay series, and his other spy/crime novels, reflected the reality of the dispersion of Jews "in all walks of life." Alastair Buchan once suggested that critics confused author and material, and that his father was, in fact, "the prisoner of a genre and a set of characters from whom he can depart only at the cost of failing to meet the demands of a clamouring public."[23] Richard Usborne excuses Hannay *et al* as "slightly antisemitic, but no more so than was polite in any author in the pre-Hitler period."[24] Mitchell acknowledges Buchan's interest in Zionism and that he once contributed a lengthy condemnation of the persecution of Russian Jews to the *Spectator,* warning that *Judenhetz* was dormant in all northern nations. Nonetheless, the man's private correspondence tends to confirm the judgement that he was a moderate antisemite in real life.[25] There is no such leeway in the case of McNeile (1888-1937). Best known as "Sapper," creator of Bulldog Drummond, McNeile is an unqualified racist, determined to highlight the innate superiority in all things of the Englishman. Poorly written though they are (John Atkins calls him "indisputably the worst of all the popular writers . . . and also the most distasteful"),[26] his novels tapped a hugely responsive public. "He glorified, in peacetime, the comradeship, leadership and bravery of the days in the trenches," and appealed directly to a "powerful middle class yearning for law and order." (*The Final Count*, published in 1926, the year of the General Strike, went into 40 editions in 25 years.)[27]

Jews conform to well-established formulae throughout McNeile. *The Final Count,* for instance, endorses the view that the Russian Revolution had been a Jewish conspiracy (a sentiment propounded earlier in the decade by the *Morning Post,* which had dubbed the Bolshevik regime "the government of Jewry").[28] A gifted scientist is driven mad by fear that his potentially lethal invention might fall into the hands of Russia, "ruled by its clique of homicidal, alien Jews." Elsewhere in *The Final Count*, Drummond and two friends congregate at a low-life Peckham pub; Toby Sinclair V.C. and John Stockton disguise themselves respectively as a "nasty looking little Jew clerk," complete with lisp, and a "mechanic with communistic tendencies" (*Bulldog Drummond: His Four Rounds with Carl Peterson*, 1967, p.809, 814, 958).

Mitchell cites the "supposed racial inferiority" of the Jew as a "striking contribution" to McNeile's "overall structure of villainy . . . Repeatedly they are depicted as weak, unhealthy, cowardly, financially and sexually parasitic."[29] Isaac Goldstein, a moneylender in *The Island of Terror* (1931) is a small, obese coward, who has no qualms about charging interest at 100%. Emil Dressler, in the same novel, combines lending on a large scale with blackmail and involvement in the white slave trade. He is sightless, with a high-pitched voice ("almost like a woman's").[30] In *The Black Gang*, a group of communist conspirators encompasses a foreign agent, a number of working-class agitators, and a couple of Jews. The conspirators are referred to, collectively, as "specimens," "a loathsome breed," "little worms" and so on.[31] The Jews are singled out for retribution and whipped "to within an inch of their lives" as punishment for their "method of livelihood" (*Bulldog Drummond: His Four Rounds with Carl Peterson*, p.276).

Not surprisingly, Mitchell sees a resemblance between McNeile's stereotypes and ideas central to Nazi ideology.[32] Eric Ambler once claimed that McNeile's books intensified class hatred in fiction; he found particularly disconcerting *The Black Gang* in which Drummond and his cohorts parade as a private strong-arm squad, dress in masks and black shirts (!), and personally seek out and discipline leftists, trade unionists and "Bolshie" Jews, all with the tacit endorsement of Scotland Yard. Watson goes further, cautiously speculating on possible indebtedness to Bulldog Drummond of Mosley and the British Union of Fascists. "Fascism sprang, in Britain as elsewhere, from frustration caused by economic chaos and political ineptitude. That same frustration had made readers' minds receptive to tales of improbable heroics." It is undeniable that McNeile's world vision strongly resembles the Fascist world view, i.e. that both capitalists and Bolshevists wish to undermine Britain, and are prepared to work hand in hand towards that end.[33]

Far to the right of the Jew-Bolsheviks described by Keverne, McNeile, Buchan, *et al,* are magnates whose business dealings impact on the fate of nations. Sir Herman Isaacstein is intent on exploiting the oil resources of Herzoslovakia in Agatha Christie's *The Secret of Chimneys* (see Chapter 3 of the current study). The financial genius Berglund schemes to smash the League of Nations so that he can "make a bundle" on fluctuating stock markets in Francis Beeding's *Six Proud Walkers* (1928), while Albert Wertheim, one of the three biggest men in Europe, has no qualms about bringing his country to the brink of war so long as he is able to further his business interests, in another Beeding book, *The Three Fishers* (1931). Graham Greene, who interspersed his serious novels with a number of mass-appeal "entertainments," featured the megalomaniacal Sir Marcus in *A Gun for Sale* (1936).[34] Sir Marcus, whose business concerns encompass steel mills and brothels, manipulates the fate of nations and threatens to engulf the world in war:

Sir Marcus had many friends, in many countries; he wintered with them regularly at Cannes or in Soppelsa's yacht off Rhodes; he was the intimate friend of Mrs Cranheim. It was impossible now to export arms, but it was still possible to export nickel and most of the other metals which were necessary to the arming of nations. Even when war was declared . . . the British Government would not forbid the export of nickel to Switzerland or other neutral countries so long as the British requirements were met first. (p.115-16)

Sir Marcus is "a very old, sick man with a little wisp of white beard on his chin resembling chicken fluff" ("a man almost without pleasures; his most vivid emotion was venom, his main object defence"):

He gave the impression that many cities had rubbed him smooth. If there was a touch of Jerusalem, there was also a touch of St James, if of some Central European capital, there were also marks of the most exclusive clubs in Cannes . . . He bowed with the slightly servile grace of a man who might have been a pawnbroker to the Pompadour . . . Everyone knew a lot about Sir Marcus. The trouble was, all that they knew was contradictory. There were people who, because of his Christian name, believed he was a Greek; others were quite as certain that he had been born in a ghetto . . . an enterprising journalist who once tried to write his life found extraordinary gaps in the registers . . . There was even a gap in the legal records of Marseilles where one rumour said that Sir Marcus as a youth had been charged with theft from a vistor to

a bawdy house. Now he sat in the Edwardian dining-room . . . one of
the richest men in Europe. (p.106-07)

Harold Fisch maintains that Greene reactivated the Jew-
Devil literary archetype in Sir Marcus, and that *A Gun for Sale*
is an allegory.[35] The old man receives his "just deserts" when he
is gunned down by one of his hired assassins.

Closely allied to images of the Jew as international conspir-
ator are images of the Jew as disloyal, unpatriotic, clannish and
always a foreigner, dedicated either to self, the enemy, or world
Jewry, rather than to his country of residence (i.e. England).
"These Jews stick together like leeches," observes the Hon Freddie Arbuthnot (Dorothy L. Sayers, *Strong Poison,* 1930, p.152),
while Jewish characters in Agatha Christie's *Three Act Tragedy*
and *The Secret of Chimneys* are seen as un-English and therefore
suspect. The genial, urbane, Polish-born Dr Bauerstein turns out
to be a German spy in Christie's *The Mysterious Affair at Styles*
(1920), as does the "sleek and smooth" Dr Custrin in Valentine
Williams' *The Return of Clubfoot* (1922).[36] Mrs Abrahams, a
leading society figure, uses her friendship with Cabinet minis-
ters to ensure that she can transmit sensitive information back to
Germany with impunity, in E. Phillips Oppenheim's *Aaron Rodd
Diviner* (1920). (Her name is crossed off an official list of suspected collaborators, "at the special instructions of a highly
placed personage" [p.191-93].) Henry D. Steinletter, representative of "the greatest German-American banking firm in the
world," is also part of "the great Teutonic espionage system" in
England, in another Oppenheim book, *Ambrose Lavendale
Diplomat* (1920, p.278). The fair-haired Dr Gregory, in G.K.
Chesterton's "The Moderate Murderer" (*Four Faultless Felons*),
"comes from Germany, though he often passes for English." "A
stormy petrel," who once offered his talents to the government
of mythic Polybia, Gregory "has a pretty rotten reputation." A
young girl who meets him unexpectedly while out walking in
the moonlight realises in a flash that he is "no more German
than an Englishman": "And though she had no antisemitic prejudice in particular, she felt somehow that there was something
sinister in a fair Jew, as in a white negro" (p.42, 45-46).

Mr Steinz, a chiropodist and hairdresser in Henry Wade's *The Dying Alderman* (1930) is described wryly as "a Saxon, naturalised to a super-British subjection" (p.145).

The most popular (i.e. most frequently recurring) Golden Age images are (predictably) negative renderings of the Jew as financial individual—either as financier and banker, moneylender, dealer, commission agent, fence or lowly pawnbroker. Aside from Christie's Sir Herman Isaacstein, Anthony Berkeley Cox's Pleydell and Sir Julius Hammerstein, or Sayers' Sir Reuben Levy (for all of whom see Chapter 3 of this study), the upper echelon of powerful Jewish financiers includes Leopold Hessel, who conspires with another man to kill a fellow-banker in Henry Wade's *The Duke of York's Steps* (1929). Hessel has "the dark eyes and sensitive hands, but none of the more exaggerated features of his race"; the murder is seen to be the logical end-product of past mistreatment. "He had had a devilish time in the war," we are told, " 'German Jew' and all the rest of it. His one idea was to get his own back—he was quite unscrupulous—and unreasonable as to how he did it and who he did it to" (p.346). Isidor Simon, the banker who serves as financial adviser to the King of Pavonia in G.K. Chesterton's "The Loyal Traitor" (*Four Faultless Felons*), is a "slight, refined little figure with straight, grey hair and a hooked nose rather large for his attenuated features . . . only when he carefully fitted a pair of tortoise-shell goggles, did his eyes seem suddenly to stand out and come to life; as if he were a monster who put his eyes on and off like a mask" (p.202). Simon joins with the Pavonian chief of police to thwart a revolution. At one point in the story, he disputes the claim that Jews can be misers:

Avarice is not a Jewish vice; it's a peasant's vice, a vice of people who want to protect themselves with personal possessions in perpetuity. Greed is the Jewish vice: greed for luxury, greed for vulgarity; greed for gambling; greed for throwing away other people's money and their own on a harem or a theatre or a grand hotel or some harlotry—or possibly on a grand revolution. But not hoarding it. That is the madness of sane men; of men who have a soil.

"How do you know?" asked the King with mild curiosity. "How did you come to make a study of Jews?"

"Only by being one myself," replied the banker. (p.204-05)

The same story pits Simon against a pawnbroker, Loeb, who "lives at the corner of the Old Market, in the poorest part of the town. He's a Jew, of course, but not so much disliked as some Jews of his trade . . . The result of our inquiries points to the man being quite incredibly rich, all the more because he lives like a poor man" (p.204). Loeb is active, or appears to be, in inciting revolution in Pavonia.

Born in a Polish or Roumanian ghetto, and having ruthlessly clawed his way to financial heights by "putting the screw on his victims," Angus McGuffie (real name Shadrach Lowenstein) is "rolling in money," owns a handsome villa on the Isle of Wight, and dabbles in shady deals with international terrorists. Unfortunately for him, he is murdered by disgruntled former cohorts in the opening chapter of Francis Beeding's *The Five Flamboys*.

Movie magnate and financier, Maurice Steinberg, is a suspect in the slaying of a rising American film producer (and ensuing killings) in Henry Holt's *The Mystery of the Smiling Doll* (1939). Born in Poland, and brought to England as a child, the enigmatic Steinberg is "a solid business man, who plays the game of finance for the fun of it" and is interested only "in assets." He can be merciless or unexpectedly generous in business, depending largely on whim:

He will take a rich man's scalp without the tiniest flicker of emotion on that set white face, but when he knows some poor devil has his back up against the wall and is gasping for his last financial breath, he is as likely as not to call the whole deal off.

"There is something about his cold, calculating eyes and dead white skin that has always made me shiver," confides one of the women characters, whereas the investigating hero observes: "I find it very difficult to read his real character, especially, perhaps, because of his alien origin" (p.49-51, 160). Another money-man, "well known . . . in the [British] film world," is Otto Goldstein; Goldstein and his office—off Regent Street—are mentioned by Freeman Wills Crofts in the 1935 Inspector French case, *The Crime at Guildford*.

Isidore Cohen, a moneylender who appears in the short story "A Matter of Luck" by Henry Wade (*Policeman's Lot,* 1933), is portrayed with the standard lisp and referred to (by the author) as "the Jew." Interestingly though, Cohen is a not unsympathetic figure, and he expresses disdain for those Jews who assume non-Jewish sounding surnames as a camouflage in business. Fictional examples include the aforementioned Angus McGuffie, or Messrs MacBride and MacPherson & MacDonald, who surface to collect money owing in Sayers' *Busman's Honeymoon* and Christie's *The Murder of Roger Ackroyd,* respectively. A similar sentiment is expressed about the elusive Israel Levinsky in W. Stanley Sykes' *The Missing Moneylender* (1931):

I will say this for him—he doesn't call himself Griffith Jones or Angus Macallister, like most of them do. He doesn't even hide himself behind the name of a company. A Jew as a Jew is all right, but a Jew who pretends he is a gentile is a nasty bit of work. (p.12)

(Presumably, such comments would have been applauded by G.K. Chesterton). *The Missing Moneylender,* which was very popular in its day, enjoying four hardback printings and twelve Penguin paperback impressions between 1936-1945,[37] refers briefly to the alleged temperamental duality of the Jew (i.e. the combination of East and West, "emotionalism" and "rectitude"). When Isaac Levinsky, brother of the missing man, is interviewed by the police:

The emotional side of his nature prevailed so strongly that the initial part of the interview was quite useless, but just as the inspector's patience was reaching its limit, the curious duality of the visitor's race became evident and the lamenting Oriental changed into the cool-headed Western business man. (p.45)

An openly Jewish businessman expresses contempt for his two highly acculturated business rivals, one of whom has gone so far as to convert, in Graham Greene's *Stamboul Train* (1932). "I never trust a Jew who has turned Christian," declares Myatt of one competitor (Eckman). The other is "very bluff and cordial. Very English":

[B]ut the nose betrayed him, the nose which had been straightened by an operation and bore the scar. The hostility between the open Jew and the disguised Jew showed itself at once in the conjurer's smiles, the hearty handclasp, the avoidance of the eyes. (p.240-41)[38]

To return, specifically, to the Jewish "financial individual" —Oppenheim's *Aaron Rodd Diviner* is a connected sequence of detective/adventure stories, in which a down-at-heels solicitor joins forces with a neo-American thrill-seeker, a young poet with a flair for self-advertisement, and the requisite beautiful young female associate, to track down missing diamonds. The search brings them into contact with a gallery of opportunistic Jews, most prominently, gem merchant Abraham Letchowiski and Mrs Abrahams, a German spy (mentioned earlier). A "picturesque looking object—patriarchal, almost biblical," and "a familiar feature of the dingy marketing thoroughfare," Letchowiski runs a questionable business in Mile End Road. He "hoards gold and loves it as though it were his own lifeblood" (p.122-23, 245). Letchowiski's equally self-interested and acquisitive granddaughter, Rosa ("a fierce, strong young Jewess"), also active in the family firm, is portrayed by Oppenheim as typically flashy and over-dressed: scarlet-lipped, exposing "at least twelve inches of silk-clad limbs," sporting loudly squeaking patent shoes, and evincing a passion for gaudy jewellery. In the course of events, Rosa sets her sights on a young watchmaker, Ed Levy, who (it turns out) is one of the amateur adventurers working undercover. Unlike her grandfather (who swears "before the God of my fathers that you shall marry none but a Jew"), the predatory Rosa has no qualms about badgering the unmasked Levy into marriage ("I like you better than any of the Jews I know"); rejected, she shrewdly puts the family business first and betrays her former beau. Rosa's younger brother ("a remarkable, cross-eyed youth") has inherited his grandfather's business acumen (as well as the old man's lisp); a "beatific smile" spreads over the boy's face at the prospect of earning a "little commission" tending the shop in the elder Letchowiski's absence (p.123-24, 224, 231-32, 236, 246).

In *The Sloane Square Mystery* (1925), Herbert Adams plays rather effectively on reader expectations by offering up Joe Levy, an allegedly ruthless and unscrupulous moneylender, referred to by an eminent barrister as a "wretched Jew," who is believed to have driven at least one impoverished nobleman to suicide. In a neat twist, Levy turns out to be simply the front man or nominee in moneylending schemes masterminded by the unpleasant aristocrat who (deservedly) becomes the murder victim. American writer Leslie Ford who, under the pseudonym David Frome, wrote a determinedly "English" series of stories and novels featuring Mr Pinkerton, details the slaying of a sup- posedly Jewish moneylender in *The Man from Scotland Yard* (1932). (The dead man is, in fact, a Scotsman.) An unfortunate woman character in the book is described as being "in the hands of the Jews . . . You know the sort. People that lend a thousand pounds and charge you seven hundred interest, and then go to your husband and he pays it" (p.24, 152). Isaac Feldman, owner of a dingy little second-hand clothes store and pawnshop, is a suspect in the murder at an East End public library of an unpop- ular local councillor (Josephine Bell, *Death on the Borough Council,* 1934). Feldman is honest but mean, and is regarded as "making a profit out of death and misfortune" (p.89). The "Shy- lockian" intractability of the silky-voiced Ambrose Hardstein, "a tough nut . . . who generally wants overweight with his pound of flesh," precipitates a desperate killing in Leonard Gribble's short story "The Case of Jacob Heylyn" (1937).

Herbert Adams tackles Jewish financial realms again in his unusual *The Old Jew Mystery* (1936). "Old Jew" is the name of a dice game, currently in vogue with vistors to Old Jew House, a trendy, albeit predictably shady, gambling den near Maidenhead, run by the mysterious Mr Kolle. The game itself is described as a variation on "lending one another money at extortionate inter- est"; at the centre of the board, representing the pool, is the painted figure of "a typical Shylock." Among habitues of the venue is Bella Basoot, who has "the fair opulent loveliness, the blue eyes and long dark lashes, sometimes seen in girls of mixed blood in the East" (p.39, 57, 60). At one point in this rather eccentric mystery, an old man speculates on the likely descen- dants of the lost tribes of Israel:

The Jew is the seed of Abraham . . . but Jacob had twelve sons and Judah—the Jew—was but one of them. Where are the rest? Jacob gave his chiefest blessing to the children of Joseph—a double portion. *They* were to be blessed above all others. *They* were to inherit the earth and to hold the gates of the enemy.

In the old man's view, the Briton, "through whom all the world was to be blessed," was undoubtedly the brother of the Jew (p.211).

It is a short leap in Golden Age fiction from the ambiguities of "Old Jew House" to Soho and the Jew as criminal or inhabitant of the multicultural ("mixed-breed") underworld. Interwar writers persisted in ignoring statistical evidence which completely refuted the myth that Jews veered disproportionately towards criminal activity. In 1935, of 14,729 men and women charged with indictable offences in England, only 134 were Jews, out of a Jewish population of 350,000. Of 400 Jews who passed through Brixton Prison, then a "sorting-house," in 1936, 156 were there for debt or maintenance payment arrears, and a further 38 were "bound over" or placed on probation. Writing in the 1930s, Sidney Salomon maintained that the tendency of "a section of the press" to note the religion of a person up on charges only if that person were a Jew contributed to the popular misconception of Jewish affinity to lawbreaking.[39]

Fictional Jewish villains, by contrast, run the gamut of criminality, depictions of their nefarious activities and livelihoods often, and frequently, overlapping or blending with other stereotypes (embezzling financiers, pawnbroking "fences," burglarious Bolsheviks, dope-peddling megalomaniacs, and so on). At one extreme is underworld czar Mo Liski who appears in Edgar Wallace's *The Mind of Mr J.G. Reeder* (1925), that writer's most lasting contribution to the detective short story (according to Keating and Symons). Liski, who draws close on 15,000 pounds a year from racing, a nightclub and the drug trade, is:

a small, dapper man who wore glasses and looked rather like a member of the learned professions—apart from a weakness for jewellery. Yet he ruled the Strafas and the Sullivans and the Birklows, and his word was law on a dozen racetracks, in a score of spieling clubs and innumerable establishments less liable to police supervision. (p.106)

"Joseph," leader of "the most dangerous lot of criminals London has ever harboured" is hunted by the police and by his arch-enemy, a maniacal art-collector, in E. Phillips Oppenheim's *The Treasure House of Martin Hews* (1929). A master of disguise, Joseph is equally at ease as a bloodthirsty East End thug or as a refined and wealthy West-Ender, exploiting his social facade "in search of places to rob." He is ruthless and brutal, yet he abides by his own code.

That's where Joseph's honest [declares a former associate]. He'd swing himself before he gave a pal away. So would every one of them [his gang]. They're mostly Jews. They're as wicked as you like. They're up to any dirty trick. They'd stab you in the back as soon as look at you, but they'd stand torture sooner than turn informer. (p.101)

Oppenheim populates the gangland setting with a number of obviously Jewish characters, including spurious plutocrat Ruben Sams, Joseph's commission agent Isaacs, and his former "moll," Rachel. Code of honour notwithstanding, Joseph proves merciless in vengeance; his final encounter with Rachel leaves her with hair and brows shaven and her legs mutilated.

In Graham Greene's *Brighton Rock* (1938), the evil Colleoni is deceptively mild in appearance. First spotted by the reader in the Great Lounge of the Cosmopolitan Hotel, flanked by two bitchy "little Jewesses," he resembles any other "rich, middle-aged Jew returning to the Cosmopolitan after a rich concert at the Pavilion." In the course of the novel, Colleoni plays Mephistopheles to the young thug Pinkie, and ultimately leads him on to catastrophe.[40] "You can't stand against Colleoni," a detective warns a small-time operative, "it will be Colleoni who'll have the alibis. No one's going to fake you an alibi against Colleoni" (p.63-66, 68).

At the other end of the scale are Barney, a pudgy and cowardly East-end thief (in Valentine Williams' *The Secret Hand*, 1918),[41] Phil Abrahams, a small-time thug (and member of Joseph's "consortium"), who takes a lethal bullet in a gangland skirmish (*The Treasure House of Martin Hews*, p.19), and Bertie Marks, a "shabby, sloppy bird-of-passage," who maintains a seedy flat in pre-voguish Chelsea. As it eventuates, Marks is one of the disguises adopted by Simon Templar ("The Saint") in order to infiltrate the London underworld (Leslie Charteris, "The Man Who Was Clever," *Enter the Saint,* 1930). More middle-of-the-road are the immaculately attired Percy Neamore and the "frenchified" Derek Holmes. Ostensibly a turf accountant, the former prospers in the employ of a sinister Oriental gangster. (Something about Neamore suggests "money or diamonds," observes his creator [J.S. Fletcher, *The Mysterious Chinaman,* 1923, p.84].) Holmes (born Dirk de Heems), an unsavoury "city gentleman" who has the business skill of his Dutch-Jew father, disappears in the midst of a financial scandal just before 1914, and resurfaces a decade on as a member of a gang of smugglers (Richard Keverne, *Carteret's Cure,* 1926, p.102, 110, 126). Nathan Goldschmidt, erstwhile leader of a group of small-time stand-over men, fixes boxing matches in Herbert Jenkins' comic *Malcolm Sage Detective* (1921).

One writer who made a specialty of the Jewish criminal (at varying social levels) was Sydney Horler (1888-1954). Read today, Horler's writing has the dubious distinction of being the most glaringly offending body of work produced by any of the writers under consideration. Even McNeile looks relatively restrained beside him. (Disconcertingly, Horler ranked with McNeile as one of the bestsellers of the era). The novels reflect the man. An outspoken homophobe, unashamed misogynist and dedicated political conservative, he revelled in "Britishness" and (like McNeile and Buchan) suspected or despised all things foreign. He had, and expressed, particular aversion to "stinking Italianos," "fanatical Huns" and "Fu Manchu-style megalomaniacs," but his world view encompassed dishonest Frenchmen, avaricious Swiss and "absurd Americans."[42] Typical of his output is *Miss Mystery* (1928). Set in Monte Carlo (traditional Phillips Oppenheim territory), the book is populated with exiled royals, statesman, celebrities, and all-powerful financiers, rubbing shoulders with notorious women, blackmailers and craftsmen crooks. A renegade White Russian nobleman, Baron Veseloffsky, heads a polyglot criminal commune which includes "blood-maddened" Bolshies (one of them a grotesque hunchback) and a gigantic, gorilla-like Asiatic henchman.

Horler's sales (an estimated two million volumes by the early 1930s) suggest that his insular views were shared by a large number of readers. Although "sly," notes Colin Watson, his references to Jews "invariably [have] that self-congratulatory tone used by people who believe they are saying something agreeable to their hearers."[43] The swarthy-looking Jacobson is a member of a well-dressed Soho gang in *Wolves of the Night* (1931). Jacobson purports to be a bucket-shopkeeper. ("His real activities are best not stated," warns Horler). Known contemptuously, even to his cohorts, as "Jewey," he rightly predicts trouble ahead for the gang (p.107-11).

Nighthawk (a cut-rate version of Charteris' "The Saint") "goes round robbing crooks, taking on cases which the police have been powerless to touch." In *The Return of Nighthawk* (1939), he takes on a crusading project: the destruction of a wealthy and highly successful criminal organisation. Financed by a mystery money-man, the gang is led by the extraordinarily unattractive Marius Abrahams, "a crook of undoubted ability . . . and many specialties," among them blackmail and insurance fraud (p.10, 22). Also in the gang is the immaculately dressed (by Savile Row) Felix Goldman, a skilled confidence-trickster who makes an art of parting foolish women from their securities. Both he and Abrahams are entirely self-serving, cowardly, and quite prepared to sell out each other or anyone else in sight. Nighthawk ensures they receive their well-earned comeuppance.

Where negative Jewish stereotypes are often routinely employed by writers who probably could not be described as being antisemitic *per se,* Horler's unsavoury Jews reflect his personal point of view and accord with the man's pathological dislike of virtually anyone who does not match up to his ultra-British ideal. In his 1933 memoirs, he protests about having to share a holiday spot with Jews:

The choicest collection of Hebraic types I have yet seen (even in New York) was to be observed; what it is about Bournemouth that attracts these pronouncedly Asiatic-looking Jews I do not know.[44]

An unequivocally unpleasant man, and a less than mediocre literary stylist (Panek judges his work "egregiously bad" and

Stafford declares him "among the worst" of the thriller-writers of his time), Horler would continue to peddle his racist nonsense throughout World War II.[45] (As we shall see, he subscribes to wartime slanders of Jew-Nazi collaboration and Jewish profiteering in his 1940s titles).

In Gerald Verner's *White Wig* (1935), police investigating the shooting of a passenger on a London bus trace the suspect to Marroc's, a seedy nightclub. The music there is provided by a "raucous negro orchestra that had brought to civilisation the screaming melodies of their jungle home"; Marroc, the proprietor, is "a fat, greasy man, with more than a touch of the tarbrush in his blood"; the patrons represent a heterogeneous collection of humanity—nocturnal negroes, Chinese, and "fat Jews with dirty and jewel-laden hands, who gulped quantities of lager beer and leered at the painted women who languidly walked back and forth in the arms of their partners" (p.57, 59-60).

Ostentatiousness (particularly in the matter of jewellery) epitomises the vulgarity frequently associated with the Jewish *parvenu*, and manifestations of it recur throughout the Golden Age. Tony Kushner has written:

Having escaped from the East End . . . the Jew-boy is transformed, but not beyond recognition. He may or may not have lost his lisp en route, but in the process he had acquired even more diamonds for his podgy fingers, along with some bright plus-fours and patent leather shoes. The *nouveau-riche* Jew may have entered Hampstead but he was "of any nationality save English."[46]

In addition to Rosa Letchowiski, Mo Liski, Percy Neamore and other over-dressed and overly-adorned individuals already noted, Shadrach Lowenstein in *The Five Flamboys* is:

the last in the world to give himself away—except, of course, in his clothes. For the apparel doth proclaim the man. Shadrach was always very carefully dressed, in striped trousers, black coat, butterfly collar, grey tie with a good pin in it—rather too good a pin, the diamond a trifle too large . . . And white spats, of course. Rings on his fingers and spats on his toes. (p.9)

Barney Morris' clothes fit him "a shade too well," their colour scheme "a shade too complete for perfect taste" (Francis Grierson, *The Yellow Rat,* 1929). Isaac Levinsky in *The Missing Moneylender,* by contrast, has assimilated more skilfully:

He was a dapper little man of unmistakeably Jewish appearance, neatly and quietly dressed. In all things he avoided the ostentatious flashiness which is a failing of some of his race: heavy gold watch-chains and pointed, patent-leather boots were conspicuous by their absence. In their stead were an inconspicuous and severely unornamental silver wrist-watch and plain black shoes; but it was typical of their owner that the watch, owing to the quality of its works, had cost more than most gold ones, and the shoes were made to order by a high-class Gentile pirate whose exorbitant charges were only excused by his supreme reputation as a craftsman. (p.45)

Elsewhere, Carleton Myatt sports silk pajamas, a Savile Road suit and a fur coat in Graham Greene's *Stamboul Train* (1932). His business rival, Eckman, who has assimilated completely and makes a big show of having converted, keeps a chained Bible by his lavatory: "Large and shabby and very 'family' amongst the silver and gilt taps and plugs, it advertised to every man and woman who dined in his flat Mr Eckman's Christianity" (p.7, 19). Olga Kohn's choice of crested blue writing paper ("as supplied by Mr Selfridge's fancy counter to the nobility and gentry") alerts Lord Peter Wimsey that she "was obviously not educated at Oxford or Cambridge" (Dorothy L. Sayers, *Have His Carcase,* 1932, p.295-96). Another Olga, the Russian beauty in Ethel Lina White's *An Elephant Never Forgets* (1937), is "a fair Jewess, with plaits of golden hair and a famished intellectual face, which was subtly cheapened by the meretricious fur coat she wore" (p.21).

Several writers, in the 1920s, target the nouveaux-riches, according to the premise that some Jews acquired wealth through speculative ventures or unfair profiteering in the Great War. The obnoxious German-born Isaac Heidelberger wrests away the country estate of an unfortunate and respected aristocratic family in *The Dream Detective* (1920) by Sax Rohmer (author of the intensely xenophobic Fu Manchu series). Dornford Yates' *Berry and Co* (1920) successfully foil a determined bid by the immensely wealthy Mr Dunkelsbaum to buy up the country home of another impoverished aristocrat. Dunkelsbaum (Yates informs us) is "a terrible fellow . . . Strictly neutral during the war, but managed to get over a million out of cotton, which he sold to the Central Powers at a lower price than Great Britain offered before we tightened the blockade." Like McNeile's heroes, Yates' ardently Empire-building Berry and Boy Pleydell do not hesitate to take matters into their own hands, systematically harassing and humiliating the profiteer and his Yiddish-speaking lawyer, thereby ensuring the triumph of "the squirearchy."[47] In *Carteret's Cure* (which revolves around smuggling on the Suffolk saltmarshes), a discontented local landowner, crippled by war and taxes, is outraged by sighting another would-be "country gent":

"It does make me sick [he complains], to see the country teeming with illiterates, with so much money they don't know what to do with it. I had some fellow here last summer, with a Jew nose and a German name, asking if I'd like to sell the Grange to him, if you please. The impudent beast came up here in a huge car and said he liked the look of the place, and money was no object. I set the dogs on him."

"Then I'm almost sorry for the profiteer," Carteret laughed. (p.52)

Without exception, the most offensively-conceived nouveaux-riches in any of the material surveyed for this study are the Samuelsons in H.C. McNeile's short story "Rout of the Oliver Samuelsons" (*The Saving Clause*, 1927). Clearly intended as a comic tale, along the lines of the ever-popular Wodehouse, the story is only of marginal detective interest. It revolves (like the scene in *Berry & Co,* described above) around a scheme to rid the English countryside of an unpleasant family. The Oliver Samuelsons, who have made their fortune in the patent medicine industry, are, we are told repeatedly, "an altogether beastly family":

And, let it be clearly understood, beastly is the *mot juste* . . . it is a doubtful point as to which of the five was the most unpleasant. In fact, the generally accepted theory was that it was whichever you happened to be with last. But they rolled in money—positively rolled in it . . . Now far be it from me to suggest that there is any reason why the vendor of patent medicines should not be quite as charming a person as anyone else . . . The cause of their beastliness was not that: it was simply them. If Mr Samuelson had been the Archbishop of Canterbury, or a stockbroker, or even an author, he would still have been beastly. And the same applies to the rest of them.

The implication is clear: the Samuelsons are "beastly" simply because they are Jews. At no point does McNeile provide us with any real evidence as to their "awfulness"—all he offers are their aspirations to rise beyond their humble beginnings, and their transparently "Jewish" name. The family's defeat at the hands of a group of typically McNeile-style "young Britishers" fails dismally as comedy, and the fact that most of the local gentry are in on the plot renders the story and its premise all the more inexcusable.

Allied with references to Jews as usurer, criminal or vulgarian, are frequent and unflattering portraits of them as physically unattractive or inferior, repellent, gross, even grotesque—portraits which recall Fletcher's Barcovitch or Chesterton at his most paranoid. One of the most offensively conceived is Sir Herman Isaacstein in Agatha Christie's *The Secret of Chimneys* (for detail, see Chapter 3 of this study). While such descriptions lose some of their generalised nastiness in the course of the interwar years, they remain a feature throughout the 1930s and into the war years. By way of just a few examples: Sax Rohmer's Heidelberger (who makes an unlamented murder victim) is "large and oily, with huge coarse features and a little black moustache that had been assiduously trained in a futile attempt to hide a mouth that had well befitted Nero" (*The Dream Detective,* p.41). Yates describes Mr Dunkelsbaum thus:

I have seldom set eyes upon a less prepossessing man. To liken him to a vicious over-fed pug is more than charitable. Smug, purse-proud and evil, his bloated countenance was most suggestive. There was no pity about the coarse mouth, which he had twisted into a smile, two deep sneer lines cut into the unwholesome pallor of his cheeks, from under drooping lids two beady eyes shifted their keen appraising glance . . . There was about him not a single redeeming feature, and for the brute's pompous carriage alone I could have kicked him heartily. (*Berry & Co*, p.235)

Moses Goldstein, dealer in stolen gems in Freeman Wills Crofts' *The Groote Park Murder* (1923) is "dark and oily of countenance, with Semitic features and a pair of furtive, shifty eyes" (p.66). Garbed in a tight frock-coat "which came nearly to his heels," and sporting "a stiff green skull cap," cringing second-hand dealer Demetrius Jacob presents an undeniably "queer figure" in H.C. Bailey's *Mr Fortune's Practice* (1923, p.112). Lazarus Hirschbein, a pawnbroker in John Rhode's *The Double Florin*, has a "crown of white hair . . . wide, protruding forehead, overhanging large and deeply set eye-sockets. His nose seemed to take up half the space of his face between the wide and prominent cheek-bones, and curved downwards to meet a great Square chin" (p.101). A circus acrobat, "strong but badly proportioned" is described as not quite first rate: "Each one of his movements offered an opportunity for grace which his short-legged body denied." The acrobat is referred to only as "the Jew"; presumably readers are meant to see his physical imperfection as a by-product of his racial "inferiority" (Clemence Dane & Helen Simpson, *Enter Sir John,* 1928, p.228-30). Barney Morris, the principal murderer in *The Yellow Rat,* possesses "beady black eyes set a little too close together . . . a pointed nose projected over thin lips and a narrow chin." There is a "certain rodential sleekness in his movements" [p.67]). Joseph Meyers, an unprepossessing youth with "a pale, anaemic face . . . shifty eyes, large unattractive nose" and "totally inadequate chin," known as "the Wart," is tossed overboard (to his death) in Delano Ames' *No Traveller Returns* (1934, p.5). As late as 1938, businessman Abraham Budd has astute eyes and hand-gestures that "betray his race." Budd is "a short, fat man, with a certain oiliness of skin and an air of open affability that was almost oppressive"; his suit is "on the loud side" (Georgette Heyer, *A Blunt Instrument,* 1938, [p.14, 81]). Marius Abrahams in Sydney Horler's *The Return of Nighthawk* (1939) has "yeasty-grey skin," a "huge, fleshy nose," shrewd eyes and a "rat-trap of a mouth" (p.10).

Both Evelyn Waugh and Harold Nicolson privately derided what they saw as "Jewish promiscuity" in their diaries. ("The nymphomania of East End Jewesses . . . makes me sick," declared Nicolson on one occasion.)[48] Fictional depictions of Jews as lascivious or sexually unscrupulous compound (and complement) accusations of moneyed vulgarity and physical grossness. Kushner describes the "sexual fear of Jews" as a manifestation of the Jew-devil image, noting, for instance, that accusations of Jewish involvement in white slave trafficking outlasted by decades the existence of such a trade.[49] A typical reference occurs in Daphne du Maurier's non-criminous novel *I'll Never Be Young Again* (1932): "I watched a fat Jew fumble about with a girl's breasts at the next table," observes the narrator/hero (p.143). "Sexual predators" in crime fiction include the smooth-talking Felix Goldman in Horler's *The Return of Nighthawk;* and Custrin, the Jewish-German spy who attempts to seduce the heroine, in Valentine Williams' *The Return of Clubfoot.* The elder son (and heir) of a grotesque nouveau-riche family assumes his brother's pretty governess to be fair game, and stalks her accordingly, in H.C. McNeile's "Rout of the Oliver Samuelsons." Oppenheim's Joseph exudes a powerful (and dire) sexual attraction; he may be Satan himself, declares a former lover, but "if I lived to be a hundred, he'd be my man" (*The Treasure House of Martin Hews*). On the distaff side, Joseph's ex-moll Rachel is a streetwise flapper, used to fending for herself ever since she left school at age eleven to find money for her mother's funeral. Rachel makes the most of opportunity; according to one cynic, she is "utterly devoid of morals. She has been the mistress for the moment of any man who has taken her fancy." "Blood and fire" are what Rachel requires in a man. "That's why I like Jews," she confides (p.19, 120, 151, 212-13).

Elsewhere in Golden Age novels and stories, Jews are subject to fleeting, seemingly irrelevant insults. There seems no reason why Lynn Brock, in *The Deductions of Colonel Gore* (1924), should describe a soldier recently home after years abroad as "bored to extinction by a London which seemed to him populated by Jews . . .";[50] why Philip MacDonald, in *The Mystery of Kensington Gore* (1932), should describe a man's nodding head as "a cross between an owl and an East-end Jew" (p.93); or why an otherwise likeable young aristocrat should refer flippantly to a business partnership as "Waldron, Smith and a sub-Aryan called Cohen" in Cyril Hare's *Suicide Excepted* (1939, p.154). (The last remark, while not unduly offensive and undoubtedly in character for the speaker, still seems unnecessary, particularly given the book's late publication date.) Surely only the writer's deep-seated neuroses can have prompted G.K. Chesterton to sneer:

How absolutely characteristic of the little Jew to have a little champagne, but very expensive; and to have black coffee after it. Ah, he understands health better than the health faddist does! But there's something blood-curdling about these cultured Jews, with their delicate and cautious art of pleasure. Some say it's because they don't believe in a future life. (*Four Faultless Felons*, p.214-15)

Unsurprisingly, the insults, slurs and negative characterisations found routinely in crime and detective fiction as the position/image of the Jew became more and more tenuous, were duplicated in the written word elsewhere. By way of a few examples:—T.S. Eliot, Ezra Pound, D.H. Lawrence and Wyndham Lewis are all notable for the antisemitic content of their prose and poetry.[51] Novelist Evelyn Waugh's mutterings against "appalling little Jewish oiks" in his diaries are formalised in his delineation of schoolmaster Augustus Fagan in the 1928 novel *Decline and Fall*. (The character draws his name from Trollope's Melmotte and Dickens' Fagin.)[52] For every rounded exploration of the Jewish condition (such as the moderately popular *House of Prophecy* [1925] by Gilbert Cannan, *Mr Skeffington* [1940] by Elizabeth von Arnim, or even James Joyce's *Ulysses* [1922]), there were tired recapitulations of the Jew-as-alien theme (Dorothy Richardson's *Deadlock* [1921]), or the off-the-record sneers of so-called highbrows like Virginia Woolf. As a young writer, Daphne du Maurier was not above sprinkling short stories like "Mazie" and "Fairy Tale" (*Early Stories*, 1955) with disconcerting references to Jews, while her 1933 novel *The Progress of Julius* charts the life-story of a singularly unsympathetic Jewish entrepreneur. Modern readers of Anthony Powell's *Afternoon Men* (1931) finds the author's asides on Jews as off-putting as other aspects of his general snobbishness. Even children's literature was not sacrosanct. Richmal Crompton, creator of the immensely popular William Brown, featured her youthful protaganist in a dubious short story "William and the Nasties" (1934). The Outlaws (William's gang) play at being Nazis and harrass Mr Isaacs, the elderly sweet-shop owner they believe is giving them short measure. Crompton clearly thought better of the story in the light of World War II, and it disappeared from reprints of *William the Detective,* the 1935 collection in which it first emerged in book form.[53]

John Galsworthy was forced to conclude that the Jew could never cease to be an alien within certain upper echelons of British society—because of the flaws and constraints inherent in that society—in his thoughtful play *Loyalties* (1922). It is refreshing to note therefore that at least one of the most enduring writers of the interwar period, the gloriously prolific P.G. Wodehouse, refused signally to extract cheap laughs at the expense of Jews. Any discussion of Wodehouse in this context entails its own problematic: throughout his later life the writer was forced to combat accusations that he had deliberately collaborated with Germany in a couple of radio broadcasts when he was living in occupied France. Regardless, none of the very few Jewish characters who appear in Wodehouse stories is treated in a derogatory manner. The Cohen Brothers, clothes-dealers, appear quite harmlessly in *Mr Mulliner Speaking* (1929), for instance, and *The Code of the Woosters* (1938) pits Bertie Wooster against Roderick Spode, leader of the "Black Shorts"—a delightfully topical comic caricature of Sir Oswald Mosley. Having surveyed Wodehouse exhaustively, Kristin Thompson insists that there is "no evidence of antisemitism in [his] works or private life."[54]

Neither is the Golden Age unrelievedly negative. In Chapter 4 I look in detail at more positive depictions and descriptions during the years 1933-1945, i.e. the duration of the Third Reich and of Hitler's war against the Jews. Leading up to 1933, a number of exceptions to the general (negative) rule stand out. *Ashenden* (1928) is the sole venture into the crime/thriller field by celebrated novelist and playwright W. Somerset Maugham. A connected series of stories detailing the wartime secret service exploits of a novelist-turned-Government operative, the book is populated by a predictable array of continental exotics and foreign odd-balls, among them numerous German spies, a feared Indian agitator, a desperate Italian dancer and a White Russian adventuress. The one Jew—refreshingly—is "on the side of the righteous"; a brisk and efficient young interpreter for the British consulate at Vladivostok, Benedict renders Ashenden valuable assistance in the closing chapters of the book (p.251-54). Interestingly, Maugham has been accused of having been antisemitic. He drew on stereotype for Jewish characters in his plays *Smith* and *Lady Frederick* and, on more than one occasion, he expressed the view that Jews provoked prejudice through their behaviour. Biographer Ted Morgan discusses Maugham's ambivalence over the Jewish question and notes, by way of balance, that the writer was a good friend of Jerome Weidman and stockbroker Bert Alanson, and that he actively intervened on behalf of the interned writer Leon Feuchtwanger.[55]

Non-English "baddies" and stock foreigners are likewise a feature of Margery Allingham's early novels. For example, the chief villain in *The Crime at Black Dudley* (1929), grossly fat with heavy-lidded eyes and a broad nose, is identified as a "Hun" (p.12-13); a dapper Frenchman and a volatile Italian hold important information in *The White Cottage Mystery* (1928); and a mysterious beauty, part Italian part Teuton, serves as a famous artist's inspiration in *Death of a Ghost* (1934). Surprisingly though, and unlike many of her contemporaries, Allingham rarely singles out Jews for mention. Rubinstein points out that *The Fashion in Shrouds* (1939) features two unsavoury Greeks, a French designer and a White Russian nobleman, but makes no mention of "the minority group most likely to be encountered in London's rag trade."[56] True, an immense Jew stage-manages a punch-up and is summarily dealt with by Lugg, Albert Campion's offsider, in *Mystery Mile* (1931). However, the thug in question appears only fleetingly, as member of a cosmopolitan gang of toughs, and he is only one player in a virtual League of Nations of odd ethnics. The shadowy stereotypes in *Mystery Mile* include a dark-skinned Japanese conjurer, an evil Chinaman "in a rusty black suit," a "lanky Belfast Irishman," and a "loquacious Turk" named Ali Baba Fergusson. Even more marginal are a burglar named Abrahams, mentioned in passing in

The White Cottage Mystery (p.83), or one Isadore Levy, the partner of flamboyant art-critic Max Fustian (*Death of a
Ghost*). Levy's worry over his partner's increasing eccentricity
elicits sympathy from Inspector Oates.

There is one noteworthy exception.[57] In *Look to the Lady*
(1931), Allingham deliberately defies stereotype in her portrait
of jeweller Israel Melchizadek. An old friend of Campion, his
family business in "that ancient and slightly gloomy section of
the city which is called Poultry" has been patronised "by all the
best people since the first George, don't you know." Campion
and Val Gyrth, heir to a priceless chalice, enlist Melchizadek's
assistance in creating an undetectable dupicate of the heirloom
(so as to avert a likely "heist"). He is "one of the most striking
looking old men" Gyrth has ever seen.

Mr Israel Melchizadek was that miracle of good breeding, the refined
and intellectual Jew. Looking at him one was irresistibly reminded of
the fact that his ancestors had ancestors who had conversed with Jeho-
vah. He was nearing seventy years of age, a tall, lean old fellow with a
firm delicate face of what might well have been polished ivory. He was
clean-shaven and his white hair was cut close to his head . . . His voice
had a luxurious quality which heightened the peculiar Oriental note of
his whole personality . . . The boy was conscious of little shrewd black
eyes peering into his face, summing him up with unerring judgement.
In spite of himself he was impressed. (p.123)

The very reverse of the stock crafty Jewish dealer ("He
came forward with outstretched hand"), Melchizadek justifies
Campion's good opinion by shrewdly identifying the chalice to
be other than original.

In the following chapters, I note the more balanced references to Jews in the writing of Allingham's peers, Ngaio Marsh
and (on occasion) Christie, Sayers and others. Philip MacDonald
(writing as Martin Porlock) also underlines Jewish astuteness in
his comic but acceptable portrait of Morris Rosenklotz in the
justly-praised *X versus Rex* (1933). When a serial killer dispatches a succession of policemen, one of the corpses is discovered in a zinc gravel bin by the shrewd 13-year-old schoolboy.
(Master Rosenklotz has "a colossus of a nose" and "two small

and black and very shiny buttons which never omitted to see anything worth seeing" [p.189]). A neat twist, probably anticipating reader prejudice, distinguishes Henry Wade's short story "The Three Keys." Levi and Berg, partners in a Hatton Garden diamond firm, are described by their gentile partner as "thoroughly decent fellows" although "Jews"; unexpectedly, it is the gentile—not the Jews—who is found guilty of defrauding the business (*Policeman's Lot,* 1933).

Certainly one of the most sensitive delineations in any fiction of the period is that of the cultivated Sir Simon Flaquer, who appears as solicitor to the doomed Mrs Paradine in Robert Hichens' *The Paradine Case* (1933). Flaquer, "like many Jews" is an ardent lover of music and the theatre, and a devoted family man. Married to "a beautiful Viennese Jewess" (also "tremendously intelligent and . . . tremendously kind"), he knows all the important Jews in London, and has innumerable non-Jewish acquaintances. He is "valued for his extraordinary astuteness and discretion by many members of the English aristocracy" [p.20]. Despite a lifetime in the law, Sir Simon:

had not become a hardened cynic, although he had become an exceedingly sharp and wary man of the world. Like many Jews, he had a sentimental side, though as a rule he carefully concealed it. (p.192)

Flaquer's daughter Judith is "almost as acute as her father":

A radiant cosmopolitan who would be at home anywhere except perhaps in the Ghetto . . . Israel has made her what she is yet she secretly laughs at Israel . . . She's a Bird of Paradise who's managed to make friends with the London sparrows. (p.61)

Although indubitably a crime novel, which traces the circumstances surrounding, and solves the mystery of a man's death, *The Paradine Case* differs substantially from the run-of-the-mill detective story of the period in the depth and breadth of its characterisation. Hichens is clearly fascinated by the "assimilated/acculturated Jew" and his descriptions of the Flaquer family are a refreshing contrast to the stereotypes found in formula literature of the interwar years. It is probably not stretching the point too far, though, to suggest that Sir Simon and the beautiful and clever Judith draw on the centuries-old literary combination of elderly Jew and personable daughter. (Enormously popular with Edwardian readers who made his mawkish *The Garden of Allah* into a publishing bestseller, Hichens gave readers another multi-dimensional Jewish figure, Dr Meyer Isaacson, in his 1909 novel of passion and poison, *Bella Donna*.)

The Golden Age of detective fiction enshrined a number of already well-worn stereotypes, most of them variants of the traditional "Shylock" construct. Writers of interwar detective stories and thrillers offered increased and intensified images of Jews as moneyed vulgarians, plutocrats with criminal or megalomaniacal propensities and ambitions, gangsters and more minor villains, grasping dealers, greedy moneylenders, dishonest tricksters, etc., along with newer manifestations of the Jew as threat-to-the social order. The Jewish traitor, usually in German employ, Communism-inspired terrorists, and updated renderings of Capitalists bent on international domination (towards a somewhat cloudy world "Jewish" end), overlapped with, and grew out of, earlier images, in response to post-war turbulence and uncertainty. Fears of alleged Jewish power found a degree of sublimation in the unflattering description of characters' physical appearances or in allegations of their sinister sexual powers. Evocations of Jewish criminality ignored official statistics confirming the *under-representation* of Jews in criminal activity, although (in fairness), fictional Jews tended to be lower-echelon participants in "underworld goings-on" more frequently than they were criminal masterminds. Rarely, even among such clearly prejudiced commentators as McNeile, Horler, Oppenheim or Freeman, were Jewish characters accounted responsible for the capital crime of murder. Among the very few exceptions were Grierson's Barney Morris, Wade's Hessel, and R. Austin Freeman's Maurice Lyon, an antiques-dealer who kills to obtain a precious artifact, in the short story "The Seal of Nebuchadnezzar" (*The Puzzle Lock,* 1926). Still, underlying the majority of formula fictional representations of the Jew in the interwar years, there continued the motif of the Jew as outsider, never quite one of us, ultimately always self-serving, dedicated to other Jews rather than to the host country.

Of course, there were some changes to these images (and formulae) as the Crime and Detective genre itself evolved, and as a rethinking of the position of the Jew in society—and, by extension, in fiction—was evident during the later years of the Golden Age. Occasional exceptions occurred even earlier. The Flaquers in *The Paradine Case,* the dealer Melchizadek in *Look to the Lady* and instances in the 1920s output of Agatha Christie, all foreshadowed the more widespread revaluation of Jewish stereotyping following the rise of Hitler. Before moving on to look at those changes, a more detailed examination is warranted of the treatment of Jews by three of the most important crime-writers of the period.

3

Three Golden Age Case-studies:
Christie, Sayers and Cox

As case studies of the nature and extent of Jewish caricature in Golden Age detective fiction, it is illuminating to examine representations and allusions to Jews in the writing of three
of the leading contributors to the genre. The pre-eminence of the
first two can hardly be disputed. Agatha Christie (1890-1976),
creator of Miss Marple and Hercule Poirot and one of the most
popular, and best-selling, authors of all time, produced 66 full-
length mysteries over half a century; few would query H.R.F.
Keating's description of her as "beyond doubt the First Lady of
Crime."[1] Less prolific, but more widely admired for her skill as a
writer, both in her time and now, Dorothy L. Sayers (1893-1958)
remains enduringly popular as the creator of Lord Peter Wimsey.
My third choice, Anthony Berkeley Cox (1893-1971), may be a
more controversial one. Relatively unknown today, and reprinted only intermittently, Cox has been judged, nevertheless,
one of the most significant and influential figures in the history
of the Crime novel by such analysts as Julian Symons and
LeRoy Panek.[2] As Anthony Berkeley, he created the entertain-
ingly fallible sleuth Roger Sheringham who featured in a series
of light-hearted full-length puzzles, most notably *The Poisoned
Chocolates Case,* in the interwar years, while as Francis Iles, he
pioneered the "inverted" crime novel with the classic *Malice
Aforethought* and *Before the Fact.*

Most of the descriptions and passing references to Jews in
Christie's interwar output can be cited as typical of Golden Age
writing—although, true to form, she could, and did, confound
reader expectations with more sensitive allusions at times.
Sayers, similarly, occasionally balanced recurrent negative
stereotyping with more thoughtful portrayals. The least guilty of

the three in this regard, the "maverick" Cox worked deliberately against cliché in several instances; at other times, his remarks could be as disconcertingly regressive as those of his peers. Some attention has been paid by scholars to Jews in the work of Christie and Sayers. In Christie's case, the most solid analysis of the topic is by Gillian Gill in her excellent *Agatha Christie: The Woman and Her Mysteries;* Janet Morgan has also examined what she refers to, tactfully, as "Agatha's unsophisticated generalisations about Jews and Jewishness" in her authorised biography, Robert Osborne has gone so far as to highlight specific examples from the novels and stories, and Robert Barnard has touched on the subject in *A Talent to Deceive*.[3] The complex question of Sayers' alleged antisemitism is discussed, to a greater or lesser extent, by James Brabazon, Janet Hitchman, Nancy-Lou Patterson (in her important article for the *Sayers Review*), Philip L. Scowcroft, and—in passing—by Jessica Mann and Catherine Kenney.[4] Rubinstein also examines both writers briefly.[5] To date, my own study of Cox contains the only prior mention of Jews in that writer's work.[6]

Gill has observed that "a kind of jingoistic, knee-jerk antisemitism colours the presentation of Jewish characters" in Agatha Christie's novels of the 1920s and 1930s, and that in this regard, Christie is every bit "as unreflective and conventional as the majority of her compatriots." Jews appear regularly—if marginally—in almost all the early books, commencing with Christie's very first novel, *The Mysterious Affair at Styles* (1920), and in most instances, the depictions conform to the stereotypes I highlighted in the previous chapters. "One can be fairly sure that any Jewish character [in early Christie] will be ridiculed, abused or rendered sinister," maintains Barnard.[7]

Dr Bauerstein is urbane, charming and attractive to women. Unsurprisingly, therefore, when circumstances place him among the house-party at Styles he proves less than popular with the other males in the household. Even though he is a distinguished poisons expert, Bauerstein is never a serious suspect in the murder investigation; predictably (the novel was written and set during the Great War), he turns out to be an enemy agent. Christie leaps intriguingly beyond stereotype on one occasion, however: When a jealous husband confronts his seemingly infatuated wife with "I've had enough of the fellow hanging about. He's a Polish Jew, anyway," the exasperated spouse counters, "A tinge of Jewish blood is not a bad thing. It leavens . . . the stolid stupidity of the ordinary Englishman" (*The Mysterious Affair at Styles,* p.127, 139). Osborne perceptively finds an implication in the book that Bauerstein's "Jewish cleverness" might well be just as unacceptable to his insular English peers as his spying activity![8]

Also involved in espionage is the much less attractive, indeed, rat-faced, Boris Ivanovitch, who appears in *The Secret Adversary* (1922) as a member of a ruthless gang of Bolsheviks revolution-bent in London. He resurfaces in *The Mystery of the Blue Train* (1928) when his unsavoury activities encompass involvement in the theft of the priceless Heart of Fire ruby. "In an Empire where rats ruled, [Boris] was the King of the rats," writes Christie.

His face gleamed white and sharp in the moonlight. There was the least hint of a curve to the thin nose. His father had been a Polish Jew, a journeyman tailor. It was business such as his father would have loved that took him abroad tonight. (*The Mystery of the Blue Train,* p.1)

The most offensively depicted of any of Christie's Jewish characters is the financier Sir Herman Isaacstein in *The Secret of Chimneys* (1925).[9] (Gill calls the portrait "hard to forgive.")[10] An otherwise likeable, lightweight quasi-Ruritanian extravaganza which melds elements of the whodunit on to the adventure tradition of Buchan or Anthony Hope, *Chimneys* is infected with a buoyant generalised snobbery and racism ("Any name's good enough for a dago" remarks one of the cast of "bright young things"), but its chief slurs are reserved for the representatives of high finance ("Hebraic people. Yellow-faced financiers").[11] The sinister Isaacstein, who is intent on plundering the oil resources of the troubled European region of Herzoslovakia, is physically repellent (with "a fat yellow face, and black eyes, as impenetrable as those of a cobra. There was a generous curve to the big nose and power in the square lines of the vast jaw"). Lord Caterham, the Wodehousian peer who plays host to the lethal house-party which dominates the action of *Chimneys,* objects strongly to Isaacstein's non-British name and refers variously to the financier as "Ikey Hermanstein" or "Nosystein." His daughter, the novel's heroine, is no more cosmopolitan in outlook—she has no qualms about dubbing their guest "Fat Ikey" (*The Secret of Chimneys,* p.16, 17, 22-3, 77, 98, 155).

Just as Bauerstein and Boris are Christie's rendering of stereotypical international Jewish double-agents, Isaacstein is her version of the stock sinister Semitic financier, intent on manipulating international markets and events for his own nefarious ends. Elsewhere, at least in her pre-1940 writing, Christie's Jewish characters conform to a range of well-worn stock types, and often exemplify the equation of Jewishness with financial dexterity. Dr Sheppard wryly suspects a "Semitic strain" in the ancestry of two Scottish gentlemen, MacPherson and MacDonald, who come to the financial aid of a lady-in-distress in *The Murder of Roger Ackroyd* (1926, p.174). The energetic Tommy and Tuppence, in their guise as Blunt's Young Detectives, lunch at the "Blitz" and note the presence there of the usual array of girls in short skirts and wealthy Jewish profiteers (*Partners in Crime,* 1929, p.74). Bond Street art-dealer Jim Lazarus (judged "a Jew, of course, but a frightfully decent one") is reportedly "rolling in money" (*Peril at End House,* 1932, p.44). Gifted impressionist Carlotta Adams (based on Ruth Draper), who features in *Lord Edgware Dies* (1933), might be an eminently shrewd young woman, but her love of money proves to be her downfall (p.11-12). Rebecca Arnholt, described as "a very notorious Jewess," is heiress to the vast Rotherstein banking empire (*One Two Buckle My Shoe,* 1940, p.42-43, 155).

On other occasions, Christie targets the Jew-parvenu. The "really smart" rub shoulders with ladies of the evening, "portly foreigners" and "opulent Jewesses" at a seedy Soho night-club in *The Seven Dials Mystery* (1929, p.67). Lady Roscheimer, "a fat Jewess with a penchant for young men of the artistic persuasion" appears briefly in the short story "Harlequin's Lane" (*The Mysterious Mr Quin,* 1929). The "extremely rich and extremely musical" Dortheimers keep a box at Covent Garden in the interests of inviting "young men with prospects" to keep company with unmarried daughter Rachel. Rachel's "long Jewish nose" is wont to quiver "with emotion" on such occasions, we are told

(*Lord Edgware Dies,* p.91). Another titled Dortheimer, Lady Naomi, "as hard as nails" where money or jewellery are concerned, flirts outrageously with Jules, a gigolo dancer at an extravagant ball she is hosting. Her husband, Sir Reuben, is similarly dazzled by Jules' partner, the exotic Sanchia ("The Case of the Distressed Lady," *Parker Pyne Investigates,* 1934).

Conceptions of the "Jew-as-alien" colour Christie's description of Oliver Manders, a young playboy, and suspect, in *Three Act Tragedy* (1935). There is "something very un-English" about the young man, observes Mr Satterthwaite, and Manders is playfully derided as a Slippery Shylock by one of his friends (p.26, 28). Elsewhere, we are informed that while London hairdresser M. Antoine's only claim to being "foreign" seems to be a Jewish mother, his employees do not hesitate to refer to him as "Ikey Andrew" (*Death in the Clouds,* 1936, p.106).

More positive depictions of Jewish characters do surface in Christie from time to time. The negative rendering of the underworld figure Boris Ivanovitch is balanced, to an extent, by the character of Demetrius Papopoulos, jewellery expert and antiques dealer, in *The Mystery of the Blue Train.* The venerable Papopoulos sails close to the wind legally, his "exquisite discretion" having carried him through several "very questionable transactions," but we are assured that he has a certain "nobility of aspect." Years earlier, Poirot's intervention had saved Papopoulos from ruin and the old man now recognises that he owes a debt of honour to the little Belgian sleuth:

"I believe that I am right in saying, Monsieur, that your race does not forget."

"A Greek?" murmured Papopoulos with an ironical smile.

"It was not as a Greek I meant," said Poirot.

There was a silence, and then the old man drew himself up proudly.

"You are right, M. Poirot," he said quietly. "I am a Jew. And, as you say, our race does not forget." (*The Mystery of the Blue Train,* p.9, 10, 158)

In due course, Papopoulos, assisted by his Junoesque daughter Zia, provides Poirot with the vital clue which enables him to solve the Kettering case. The Papopoulos/Zia combination seems to be a minor, twentieth-century manifestation of the "elderly Jew with beautiful daughter" image.

Sir Montagu Corner, one of several Jewish characters in *Lord Edgware Dies,* is treated a little more sympathetically by the author than are his fellows. A prominent London host and *bon vivant,* Corner has "a distinctly Jewish cast of countenance, very small intelligent black eyes . . . a carefully-arranged toupee," and an affected manner. He waxes loquacious on Japanese prints, chinese lacquer, Persian carpets, the French Impressionists, modern music and Einstein's theories, when interviewed by Poirot, but essentially, he is a warm, harmless and extraordinarily knowledgeable eccentric (*Lord Edgware Dies,* p.102-04). In *Cards on the Table* (1936, p.177), a solicitor is referred to approvingly as "very alert and Jewish."

Jews rarely seem to intrude into the worlds of Miss Marple or Tommy and Tuppence Beresford, Christie's subsidiary series sleuths. The more cosmopolitan Poirot appears to enjoy contact with a broader, multicultural cross-section of humanity and, interestingly, appears to have no animosity towards Jews as Jews. Papopoulos, we are told, is an associate of many years standing. Likewise, Poirot regards Joseph Aarons, theatrical agent and walking encyclopaedia of the dramatic profession, as an "old and faithful" friend. Aarons appears in three novels and a short story in the 1920s. Beholden to the sleuth for assistance over the "little matter of a Japanese wrestler," he helps Poirot and Hastings locate the young actress Dulcie Duveen (the future Mrs Hastings) in *Murder on the Links* (1922, p.167-68). In *The Big Four* (1927, p.194) Poirot recruits him to help identify and locate a master criminal who is a former actor. Poirot, in turn, comes to Aarons' aid in the story "Double Sin" (1929; *Poirot's Early Cases,* 1974). *The Mystery of the Blue Train* reveals Aarons to be a likeable and down-to-earth devotee of plain, home-style English *cuisine:* he declares his passion for a good Porterhouse steak, steak and kidney pudding, apple tart and a tankard of "something worth drinking" ("anyone can have your French fallals and whatnots, your ordoovres and your omelettes and your little bits of quail"). Aarons has little time or inclination for romantic upheaval: "A woman should be calm and sympathetic, and a good cook," he declares (p.221-23).

Another, apparently longstanding, friend of Poirot is Solomon Levy, an amateur criminologist, who occasionally passes mutually enjoyable evenings sparring with the famous sleuth over the rights and wrongs of tantalising unsolved crimes (*Hallowe'en Party,* 1969, p.21-22). Elsewhere, Poirot's qualified admiration for Dr Bauerstein (he dubs the doctor "a very clever man" albeit "a Jew—of course") contrasts markedly with the one-eyed response of the upright, uptight, arch-conservative Captain Hastings (Poirot's "Watson") in *The Mysterious Affair at Styles.* (Hastings immediately and instinctively distrusts Bauerstein [p.18, 127].) Similarly, the shrewdness of art-dealer Jim Lazarus in offering more money than seems warranted for a painting excites Poirot's interest in *Peril at End House.* Lazarus' sleekness again alienates the insular and unimaginative Hastings (p.44, 138). Christie allows Poirot one irritating lapse: the perceptive Belgian applauds the shrewdness of Carlotta Adams in *Lord Edgware Dies,* but predicts correctly that her "Semitic ancestry" (synonymous here with greed) will be her undoing (p.11-12).

Christie's most sensitive and complex rendering of Jewish characters occurs in her non-crime novel, the romantic *Giant's Bread* (1930), published under the pseudonym Mary Westmacott. Gill calls the book, and its portrait of the talented Sebastian Levinne and his family, the "best key" to Christie's attitude towards Jews.[12] Overwhelmingly wealthy, physically unattractive, and "alien" within the upper-class social stratum they occupy on one hand, the Levinnes are portrayed at the same time as essentially decent, generous, kind-hearted and perceptive beings. In the course of the novel, indeed, Sebastian attains to being something of a romantic hero. One of the chief strengths of *Giant's Bread* is Christie's account of the family's qualifiedly successful struggle against prejudice as they seek to integrate into "good society," a struggle which encompasses joining the Church of England (*Giant's Bread,* p.85-88).

For many years Christie accompanied her archaeologist husband Max Mallowan on his annual "digs" in the Middle East, and they became well-acquainted with Dr Julius Jordan, the German Director of Antiquities for the Baghdad Museum. In her autobiography, Christie gives a chilling account of first becoming aware that the cultured and charming Jordan was, in fact, a zealous Nazi who was convinced that Germany's Jews constituted a danger and must be exterminated (*An Autobiography,* p.451).[13] Osborne and other analysts suggest that the incident, which apparently occurred shortly after publication of her glaringly offending *Lord Edgware Dies* in 1933, was a salutary experience for the writer and heralded a change of attitude on her part to the use of random antisemitic slurs and remarks.[14] Barnard claims that, from that point on, "offensive references to Jews cease in her books," although this is not quite accurate.[15] Certainly, from the mid 1930s, Jewish characters of any description became more of a rarity in Christie. Rubinstein notes, for instance, that instead of portraying the exotic and Machiavellian Mr Shaitana as a stock "wealthy, sinister Jew," she makes him a shadowy figure of indeterminate nationality, possibly Syrian, Levantine, Portuguese, Argentinian, Greek, or "some other nationality rightly despised by the insular Briton" (*Cards on the Table,* p.11, 21-22).[16] *N or M* (1941) and *One Two Buckle My Shoe* touch sympathetically on refugees from Nazism, including Jews, and the evils of British Fascism respectively. However, there are still a couple of disconcerting lapses.

It seems unnecessary, for example, for the young heroine, on trial for murder in *Sad Cypress* (1940), to draw attention to the prosecuting lawyer's "Jewish nose" (although her description of him as a "horrible man" is understandable given the poor girl's predicament [p.227]). Isaac Morris, a "shady little creature" with "thick Semitic lips," is a dope-pedlar and low-life "jack of all trades" who makes all the arrangements for assembling and isolating the ten victims in *Ten Little Niggers,* retitled *And Then There Were None* in more politically correct times. Captain Lombard, himself a distinctly unsavoury character, observes of Morris: "that was the damnable thing about Jews, you couldn't deceive them about money—they *knew.*" Morris is dispatched early in the piece with a well-deserved overdose of barbiturates (*Ten Little Niggers,* 1939, p.8, 184).

Least defensible is the portrayal of the lisping Madame Alfrege, the owner of a London dress shop in *The Hollow* (1946). "A Whitechapel Jewess with dyed [henna red] hair and a voice like a corncrake," Alfrege is altogether unsympathetic-grasping, snobbish, vitriolic and raucous. She employs and bullies the well-connected heroine Midge Hardcastle in the hope that she will thus attract a better class of customer to her "ethtablishment." When Midge becomes engaged to her suave "Mr Right" in the course of the novel, she celebrates by, at last, "being rude to Madame Alfrege" (p.127, 205-06, 211).

Janet Morgan records that, following World War II, Christie's U.S. publisher Dodd Mead, began receiving objections to the antisemitic references in her books, and that *The Hollow* prompted a formal complaint by the Anti-Defamation League. Subsequently her literary agents ensured that similarly offensive remarks did not appear in future publications, and Dodd Mead was granted permission to delete references where necessary.[17] (It is worth noting that there is no reference to Madame Alfrege in Christie's 1952 dramatisation of *The Hollow.*) Although "foreigners" continued to be targeted by the writer from time to time, most strikingly, the household of international eccentrics in *Hickory Dickory Dock,* with one minor exception Jews ceased to figure negatively in Christie's work from that time on.

The exception—innocuous enough but gratuitous even so—occurs in *They Came to Baghdad* (1951). Victoria Jones, the novel's bright young heroine, is a typist with the London firm of Greenholtz, Simmons & Lederbetter. She entertains her co-workers with a convincing but unflattering imitation of the tight-fisted Mr Greenholtz's wife:

"Why do you say we not have that Knole settee, Daddee?" she demanded in a high whining voice. "Mrs Dievtakis she have one in electric blue satin. You say it is money that is tight? But then why you take that blonde girl out dining and dancing—Ah! you think I do not know—and if you take that girl—then I have a settee and all done plum coloured and gold cushions. And when you say it is a business dinner you are a damn' fool—yes—and come back with lipstick on your shirt. So I have the Knole settee and I order a fur cape—very nice—all like mink but not really mink and I get him very cheap and it is good business—."

Unluckily for Victoria, Greenholtz overhears her too-accurate imitation of his wife and Victoria is summarily dismissed (p.17-19, 103). Other post-war Christie characters who are clearly Jewish are Mrs Jacob Samuelson, who appeals to Poirot in connection with the kidnapping of her adored Pekinese in *The Labours of Hercules* (1947, p.26-28); Dr Isaacs of Bethnal Green, who arrives too late to save the unfortunate Rex Fortescue in *A Pocketful of Rye* (1953, p.8); the eminent, if unscrupulous, artifact-collector, Sir Reuben Rosenthal, in *The Labours of Hercules* (p.219-22); Mr Soloman, the elderly, fish-faced proprietor of a dingy bookshop near the British Museum, in *The Clocks* (1963, p.112-13); and learned Hebrew scholar Dr Weissgarten in *At Bertram's Hotel* (1965, p.108-09). None of them is portrayed, or referred to, in an offensive or questionable manner.[18]

Given the counterweight of positive Jewish images and references in Christie's writing (particularly in *Giant's Bread*), it is difficult not to agree with Gill and Morgan that the writer's prejudice emanated more from ignorance and an unblinking conformity to the normative views of the English middle class than to any deep-seated personal animosity to specific Jews. "Agatha mirrored in her books the attitudes of her class and generation," writes Morgan.[19] Considered chronologically, the Jews in her early books suggest she subscribed to whatever anti-Jewish myth was most in vogue at the time: for instance, the urbane continental unmasked as a German spy in *The Mysterious Affair at Styles* (written during the war), the Bolshevik Boris in *The Secret Adversary* (written at the height of post-revolutionary "red" scare-mongering), the internationally active Isaacstein in *The Secret of Chimneys* (written not too long after publicity about the *Protocols* had peaked). More flippant than malicious, if none the less offensive for that, Christie's negative descriptions of Jews or stereotypical, so-called, Jewish traits can be classified as "of the stupidly unthinking rather than the deliberately vicious kind."[20] More often she sees Jews as "different" or "alien" than "dangerous," and with that in mind, it is worth noting that none of her Jews ever turns out to be the culprit. Indeed, Barnard and Gill both make the important point that Christie uses Jewish stereotypes most effectively as "red herrings"; she manipulates the readers by anticipating and appealing to their own prejudices, and thus cunningly misleads them. The sinister Isaacstein does *not* commit murder at Chimneys, for instance; nor is prime suspect Oliver Manders the culprit in *Three Act Tragedy.* Indeed, he ends up exhibiting many characteristics of the stock romantic hero. Mosgorovsky, the shady Russian Jewish proprietor of a Soho night-spot, and the Mata Hari-like Babe St Maur ("her real name's Goldschmidt or Abrameier") turn out to be talented international agents working for the "good guy" British Government in *The Seven Dials Mystery* (p.63, 178-79). Nor, to Christie's credit, when plotting an international conspiracy aimed at world domination or destruction, as in *The Big Four, Passenger to Frankfurt* or *The Secret Adversary,* does she invoke the Jewish master-criminals so popular with her peers.[21]

As with Agatha Christie, the crime fiction of Dorothy L. Sayers contains a surprisingly large number of gratuitous slurs against Jews—and, similarly, the books contain other more complex depictions. There are references to Jews in all but two of her novels.[22] Barnard has observed that Sayers herself was much more intellectual, and perhaps more intelligent, than Christie, although, sadly, "her intelligence failed her a little when confronted with Bolsheviks, Jews or admirers of D.H. Lawrence."[23] Of course, Sayers (again like Christie) was also a product of her time and class. Add to this the ingredient of her personal, and passionate, fealty to mainstream Christian Orthodoxy, which certainly incorporated a degree of theological antisemitism.

Sayers' allusions are generally as fleeting and peripheral as those made by Christie, sometimes even more so. In *Clouds of Witness* (1926), for example, Inspector Parker interviews a salesgirl in a French jewellery store. For no discernible reason, Sayers tells us that the girl in question had "just finished selling an engagement ring to an obese and elderly Jew" (p.129). In *Gaudy Night* (1935), a temporarily insolvent young nobleman owes money to the "children of Israel," and must choose either to blow his brains out, "try Levy again" or swallow his pride and appeal to Lord Peter Wimsey. ("He's my uncle," the Hon Saint-George confesses to Harriet Vane, "and a dashed sight more accommodating than the Jewish kind" [p.178, 193, 195].)

Clues found at a crime scene in *Unnatural Death* (1927) suggest that there may be an "East End" connection to the abduction and murder of a young woman. Wimsey deduces that a garish cap found near the body was "sold by a gentleman of the Jewish persuasion, resident of Stepney." The cap smells strongly of "California Poppy." Footprints at the scene point to a man with narrow feet, wearing "the long-toed boots affected by Jew-boys of the louder sort." Chief Inspector Parker makes an alternative, and no less offensive, deduction from the clues, hypothesising that "the long-toed gentleman was a nigger . . . Nigger taste runs rather to boots and hair-oil. Or possibly a Hindu or Parsee of sorts" (p.237-39). As it turns out, both speculations prove to be wrong.

Just as tiresome is this description of the elderly victim of a jewel robbery in *The Nine Tailors* (1934): "She's got a stack of money and the meanness of fifty thousand Scotch Jews rolled into one" (p.113). Clarence Gordon, "a stout little gentleman with a pronounced facial angle," is a travelling salesman for a ladies-wear firm in *Five Red Herrings* (1931); he provides police with clues to the murder of an artist. As Janet Hitchman has observed, there is absolutely no reason why Sayers should have portrayed Gordon as Jewish or why, except in pursuit of a particularly "cheap laugh," his dialogue should be riddled with "lispths."[24] Like Gordon, the theatrical agent Rosencrantz is introduced as apparent comic relief in *Have His Carcase* (1932); complete with accent (on the order of "The vorm is a good vorm . . . as Shakespeare says"), Rosencrantz tries exuberantly to induce Wimsey to take up the stage ("It 'ud go vell, eh? . . ."). Olga Kohn, a mannequin on Rosencrantz's books, is dismissed by Lord Peter as "a Russian Jewess . . . not precisely out of the top drawer"; Miss Kohn has a surly "Semitic-looking" fiance, Mr Simons, who glowers at Wimsey from the sidelines (p.296-99, 306). In the same novel, Harriet Vane dances with a gigolo in order to extract information; quite unnecessarily, Sayers tells us that the suave Mr Antoine is "rather surprisingly, neither Jew, nor South-American dago, nor Central European mongrel, but French . . ." (p.83). In the short story "Striding Folly" (1939, collected in *Lord Peter,* 1972), the shadowy Mr Moses, erstwhile employee of Chen & Gold, manufacturers of electrical fittings, is an accomplice in the murder of an unpopular rural property-developer. (Scowcroft calls the chess-playing Moses the only actual "bad" Jew in Sayers' fiction.)[25]

More prominent among Sayers' *dramatis personae* is the "financial individual," MacBride, "a brisk young man, bowler hatted, with sharp black eyes that seemed to inventory everything they encountered," who breaks in upon the Wimseys' domestic tranquillity in *Busman's Honeymoon* (1938). Far from being Scottish, MacBride's native accents are identified ("apart from a trifling difficulty with his sibilants") as "pure White-chapel." MacBride arrives inopportunely, shortly after Harriet and Lord Peter have discovered that their rural retreat comes complete with their landlord's corpse, and he wastes little time on social niceties. ("Has he [the dead man] got the money on him?" he demands singlemindedly.) A second, equally unlike-able moneylender, subsequently bursts in on the Wimseys while they are having dinner. This "stout, elderly Hebrew," Mr Solomons, representative of the firm of Moss & Isaacs, is intent on repossessing the recently deceased man's furniture before MacBride beats him to it (p.105, 107, 116, 306-08). In the stage version of *Busman's Honeymoon* (1936), written prior to the novel in collaboration with Muriel St Clare Byrne, Sayers bluntly describes MacBride as "a brisk young Cockney Jew, with eyes that see everything and a regrettable tie" (p.322).

More positive Jewish images surface elsewhere in Sayers. His banter at the expense of Olga Kohn and flashy East-enders aside, Lord Peter displays no more personal animosity towards Jews than Poirot does. In the short story "The Piscatorial Farce of the Stolen Stomach" (*Lord Peter Views the Body,* 1928), Wimsey consults a friendly diamond merchant, "rather curly in the nose and fleshy about the eyelids," but who "nevertheless came under Mr Chesterton's definition of a nice Jew, for his name was neither Montagu nor McDonald, but Nathan Abrahams. . . ." In referring to a customer, Abrahams notes: "He insisted on discount for cash," to which Wimsey responds wryly: "He was a Scotsman" (p.211, 213). (Abrahams subsequently cuts and sets Harriet Vane's engagment ring [*Busman's Honeymoon* p.24].) One of Lord Peter's London tenants, a modest second-hand dealer whose talents have enabled him to become "a damn sight richer than Wimsey," excites the sleuth's admiration. ("He's a Jew, of course, and knows exactly what he's doing" [*Busman's Honeymoon*, p.47].)[26] A destitute, aristocratic Russian youth, fleeing the Bolsheviks, is taken in and adopted by a kindly Jewish tailor and his family in *Have His Carcase* (p.71). Armstrong, a copy-chief with Pym's Publicity (the setting of *Murder Must Advertise,* 1933), is described as a brilliant but faddish man; the fact that he dislikes any lay-out which includes the picture of a Judge "or a Jew" is seen as confirmation of his foibles. In the same novel, a woman's conviction that a movement is afoot to "establish the supremacy of the Jews in England" testifies to her unreliability as a witness (p.38, 272).

Sayers' first novel, *Whose Body* (1923), contains her most extended focus on Jewish images. The plot revolves around the discovery of a naked body in a bath-tub. The "Semitic-looking stranger" is initially believed to be missing magnate Sir Reuben Levy; Wimsey proves that he is not so, and then proceeds to investigate the grisly fate of Sir Reuben. Wimsey's mother, the Dowager Duchess of Denver, recalls that the elopement and marriage 20 years earlier of the up-and-coming Levy and the highly eligible Christine Ford had caused a considerable stir:

He was very handsome then . . . in a foreign-looking way, but he hadn't any means, and the Fords didn't like his religion. Of course, . . . they wouldn't have minded if he'd pretended to be something else, like that Mr Simons we met at Mrs Porchester's, who always tells everybody that he got his nose in Italy at the Renaissance, and claims to be descended somehow or other from La Bella Simonetta—so foolish, you know, dear—as if anybody believed it . . .

By the time of his disappearance, Sir Reuben has amassed a fortune in oil, has become a leading name in the City, and is reportedly "as well loved at home as he is hated abroad." Although Levy's valet, for one, doesn't "hold with Hebrews as a rule," he makes an exception of his employer; Wimsey himself judges the magnate "pea-green incorruptible" (p.26-27, 54-56, 63).

"I'm sure some Jews are very good people," observes the Dowager Duchess:

[A]nd, personally, I'd much rather they believed something, though, of course, it must be very inconvenient, what with not working on Saturdays and circumcising the poor little babies and everything depending on the new moon and that funny kind of meat they have with such a slang-sounding name, and never being able to have bacon for breakfast.

Sir Reuben, it eventuates, has been murdered by an old rival, the eminent surgeon Sir Julius Freke. Freke, jilted by Christine Ford in favour of Levy, had bitterly resented ever since having had "his aristocratic nose put out of joint by a little Jewish nobody." In a harrowing development, Levy's remains end up in Freke's dissecting-room for use by his medical students. The students irreverently refer to the corpse as "the old sheeny" (p.55, 194, 203).

Wimsey's young friend, the seemingly empty-headed Hon Freddie Arbuthnot, strikes up an acquaintance with Levy's widow and daughter in the course of *Whose Body*. The acquaintance blossoms and Freddie and Rachel Levy marry in *Strong Poison* (1930). Freddie notes flippantly that marrying into the enormously wealthy Levy-Goldberg dynasty may be of immense benefit to his offspring but the marriage is clearly a love-match. The wedding itself takes place in a synagogue, with Wimsey in attendance as Freddie's best man (p.152-53).

Taken overall, the references to Jews in Dorothy L. Sayers' fiction conform to Golden Age norms. As offensive as the remarks often may be, they are no more so than Christie's (although Christie employs Jewish stereotypes as red herrings on occasion; Sayers never does). Given the snobberies which attend it, her rendering of Sir Reuben Levy in *Whose Body* might even be described as sympathetic. Hitchman notes that Sayers' representational prejudices extended to "niggers," servants and the working class, and the Soviet menace, and she speculates that the writer would have defended her negative racial/social images as dictated by characterisation. (Hitchman envisages Sayers insisting: "I am not voicing my *own* ideas, this is how those kinds of people [her characters] would regard Jews, Negroes or socialists.")[27] Interestingly, two articles, published by the Sayers Society in Britain, draw opposing conclusions regarding the extent to which the writer's utterances reflected her personal views. In rejecting claims that the author was racist, Philip L. Scowcroft cites the fact that most of her Jews are "excellent citizens"; he notes that Clarence Gordon and Olga Kohn and her fiance do their best to assist Wimsey and the police with their enquiries, for instance. Similarly, the persistent MacBride and Solomons are merely doing their duty by their clients. Scowcroft suggests that Sayers' over-use of the "lisp" motif in rendering Gordon's dialogue in *Five Red Herrings* is "a literary solecism" rather than "a racial sneer," and he argues that Sayers targets stereotyped Americans, Spaniards, Frenchmen (and other "dagos") as often as she does Jews. Nancy-Lou Patterson, by contrast, concludes (on the basis of her fiction) that Sayers was anti-semitic. Patterson concedes Scowcroft's point that Jews are rarely villains in the Wimsey canon, but she condemns the casualness and gratuitousness of Sayers' slurs: "Despite her extraordinary achievement . . . Sayers had her ordinary side; she had not rid herself entirely of her parsonage snobberies."[28] It is worth noting that, where references to Jews change over time in Christie, those in "Striding Folly" and *Busman's Honeymoon* are really no more acceptable than similar remarks/descriptions by Sayers a decade earlier. Indeed, it might be argued that it is "all downhill" after *Whose Body*.

Defenders of the writer have consistently pointed out that she enjoyed excellent relations with her Jewish publisher (Victor Gollancz) and literary agent (David Higham) and that she desperately wanted to marry the Russian-born writer John Cournos in the 1920s.[29] However, in light of her privately-expressed sentiments later in life, it is not easy to dismiss the anti-Jewish slurs and remarks in her fiction as being, like Christie's, due more to thoughtlessness than anything else. Following her retirement from writing fiction (in 1939), Sayers coupled scholarly research into Dante with the making of Christian polemics and wartime propaganda. In 1943 pro-Zionist Sir Wyndham Deedes and Miss L.M. Livingstone, who was active in moves to combat wartime antisemitism, both attempted to enlist Sayers' propagandist skills for their causes. Sayers bluntly doubted whether or not she was a suitable person to recruit, and in a letter to Deedes she expressed disdain for those British Jewesses who had sent their money to

America for safekeeping in 1939, Jewish children who were reportedly unable to learn "the common school code of honour," Jewish East End families allegedly failing to take their turns at fire-watching during the Blitz, etc. She was convinced that resurgent anti-semitism in Britain during the 1940s was understandable given the combination of "bombs, black-out, restrictions, rations, coal-targets, bread-targets, clothes-coupons, call-ups . . . and an influx of people with alien culture and alien standards was one imposition too many."[30]

A year later, an essay contributed by Sayers to a symposium on the future of the Jews in England was rejected by editor J.J. Lynx after complaints from a number of Jewish contributors to the project. This rejection simply reinforced Sayers' belief that no constructive *entente* could be reached between Jews and Christians in Britain given the Jews' inability to tolerate criticism.[31] It is likely that her increasing fervour for conservative Christianity underlay her conviction, by late middle age, that an inherent incompatibility persisted between Jews and the indigenes of their host nations. Patterson suggests she was influenced by G.K. Chesterton in this regard.[32] Perhaps the most caustic of all her published references to Jews occurs in "The Heirs to the Kingdom," one of the religious radio-plays she wrote during the war under the collective title *The Man Born to Be King*. Sayers pulls no punches in her description of St Matthew:

He is as vulgar a little commercial Jew as ever walked Whitechapel . . . He has oily black hair and rapacious little hands, and though his common little soul has been converted as thoroughly as that of any Salvation Army penitent, his common little wits are in full working order . . . his professional instincts are shocked by financial stupidity and appealed to by financial astuteness.[33]

Sayers' treatment of Matthew as a Cockney con-man is more extreme than anything in her fiction but there are clear echoes of the two moneylenders, MacBride and Solomons, of *Busman's Honeymoon*. This time though, her description can hardly claim validation according to the conventions and standards of low-brow detective fiction. At base, Sayers' writing, like Chesterton's, was concerned with the Jew as perpetual alien, and in her view: "nothing could alter the 'otherness' of Jews, which indeed they themselves fostered and took pride in. Having fostered it [she maintained], they could hardly object if it was commented on and sometimes resented."[34]

The sometimes ambivalent attitudes displayed towards Jews by Sayers and Christie also seem to be characteristic of Anthony Berkeley Cox (1893-1971). Cox, a highly opinionated, eccentric individual, who cloaked his personal life in mystery, produced a large number of more-or-less traditional murder-mysteries under the pseudonym Anthony Berkeley, as well as three novels and several short stories under the guise of Francis Iles. The amateur sleuth Roger Sheringham appears in most of the Berkeley books. Initially conceived deliberately as an obnoxious, gleefully fallible alternative to the detecting super-heroes then in vogue (i.e. the 1920s), Sheringham (at least in his early incarnations) makes an art of offensiveness. His attitudes towards women are particularly galling to 1990s sensibilities, and it seems consistent with his general tiresomeness that, apart from prunes and tapioca pudding, he should detest "Jews" more than anything in the world (*The Layton Court Mystery,* 1925, p.264). No further reference is made to Sheringham's prejudice until *The Silk Stocking Murders* (1928), by which time he seems to confine his intolerance to the recent immigrant: "It's the hybrid Jew, the Russian and Polish and German variety, that's let the race down so badly." By contrast, he finds what he calls "the real pure-blood Jew . . . one of the best fellows in the world" (p.17).

In *The Silk Stocking Murders,* Sheringham and Scotland Yard's Chief Inspector Moresby match wits to hunt down a serial killer who is preying on young women in London's theatre district. In the process, Sheringham enlists the assistance of the personable young sister of one of the victims, and Pleydell, the "tall, dark, good-looking" fiance of another. Roger observes that:

[T]he Jewish blood in his veins was not just a strain, but filled his veins. Pleydell was evidently a pure Jew, tall, handsome and dignified as the Jews of unmixed race often are. Roger liked the look of him at once. (p.63)

In Pleydell, Cox/Berkeley depicts a Jewish financial genius who is worlds removed from the stock yellow-faced, unscrupulous money-men generally encountered in popular fiction of the period; indeed, with Pleydell, Cox/Berkeley apears to be deliberately attacking the standard negative Jewish stereotype:

The term financier conjures up a slightly repulsive picture. It is unfortunate that financiers, in the abstract, should constitute an idea that is repulsive, but so it is. No doubt they will bear it. The ideal financier is short, stubby, with squat fingers, small eyes, no hair and a protruding stomach. Pleydell had none of these marks of the tribe; considered as a specimen of humanity he was pleasant to look on, with sharp clear features, dark brown eyes that were perhaps the slightest bit hard but only if one looked at them very searchingly, and plenty of black, crisp hair; considered as a financier, he was an Apollo. His age was somewhere between twenty-eight and thirty-five; it might have been either. Of course Roger had heard of him before the tragedy . . . Pleydell senior was of the financial rank that is known as "the power behind the throne," meaning, in these days, the power behind the party; Pleydell junior had been spoken of for some years as more than a worthy successor, with several exploits of sheer genius on the financial battlefield already to his credit. Father and son were outstanding for another reason also; they were scrupulously honest, they were behind no shady deals, and they never crushed unless they were unnecessarily attacked. (p.68)

Pleydell is such a paragon that he comes close to making even Sheringham feel a little inadequate. "I never met a Jew I liked so much before," declares the heroine Anne,"he seems as reserved and unimpassioned as an Englishman" (p.69, 158). Sheringham does manage one dig ("They'd give up everything in the world to save the life of a dying friend," he acknowledges of assimilated Anglo-Jews, "but that doesn't prevent them from asking the undertaker for a cash discount" [p.22]), but otherwise Cox's portrayal of Pleydell-as-Jew seems to be a consistently favourable one.

The twist, of course (and to pay Cox his due, it is a very clever twist which reverses, say, Christie's employment of the sinister Jewish character as red herring), is that Pleydell is ultimately exposed as the killer. Nor is he in any way a "sympathetic murderer." Many of Cox's culprits are much more likeable human beings than are their often grotesquely unpleasant victims. Pleydell proves to be a deranged "Jack the Ripper" type; once he is unmasked, his reason topples completely, the implication being that there is a very fine line between genius and insanity. "Well, well," remarks Sheringham, "it's a pity that quite the most interesting brain that any of us is likely to meet has turned out to be a bad one" (p.253). Notwithstanding Cox's unusually sympathetic rendering of a Jewish character, Pleydell ultimately stands out as one of the few Jews who turns out to be the murderer in Golden Age detective novels.

Cox renders another Jewish financier along much more "conventional" lines in a comic crime novel *Cicely Disappears* (1927), which he published under the pseudonym A. Monmouth Platts. *Cicely* is a burlesque which seems to have been inspired by Christie's *The Secret of Chimneys* (and in the seance sequence, by Mason's *At the Villa Rose*); accordingly, the house-party's guest-list includes the requisite dowagers, "bright young things," "silly asses," a famous explorer, a bluff colonel, shifty major-domo and Semitic moneylender. Sir Julius Hammerstein, "a pretty poisonous sort of blighter," with small eyes, set too close together in a fleshy red face, is almost a clone of Christie's Isaacstein. (The novel's hero refers to him as "Sir Julius Guggleheimer, or whatever his horrible name is.") In order to save her father from bankruptcy, the heroine, Pauline, is forced to become engaged to Hammerstein (p.37, 169). This time around, unsurprisingly, Hammerstein is not the killer. The fact that the butler *did* do it is a testament to Cox's particular humour.

Writing for the magazine *Time and Tide* in the early 1930s, Cox indicated that he nurtured a weakness for books about Jews. "This is not only because the Jew is an intense person, fervent in his loyalties, courageous, sincere, and a good hater . . . but he is an intelligent person, too."[35] He expressed concern in passing at the rise of Hitlerism and British Fascism in his non-fiction attack on British government (A.B. Cox, *O England,* 1934, p.22, 194), and allowed his concerns to resurface in two Anthony Berkeley novels. "I've always found Jews to be very decent fellows," declares a retired Indian civil servant in *Trial and Error,* while elsewhere in the novel, the possibility of annihilating Hitler is mooted as a means of saving German Jewry (Anthony Berkeley, *Trial and Error,* 1937, p.18, 46). Cox/Berkeley similarly pokes fun at Nazism in *Not to Be Taken* (1938). A vehemently pro-Nazi Austrian refugee, dismissed from her job as a cook because of incompetence, insists that any and every-one she dislikes or comes into conflict with must be "Chews." Outsize and ludicrously comic, she is clearly a vehicle for the author to lampoon the mindlessness of fealty to Nazism (Anthony Berkeley, *Not to Be Taken,* p.134-38). Yet in the same period, a ruthless newspaper tycoon, Isidore Fisher (ne Fischmann), is described as "a nasty piece of work . . . As nasty as they make 'em . . . American German Jew, with a dash of anything else unpleasant thrown in" (*Trial and Error,* p.66). An Englishwoman, highly respected for her astuteness, expresses the view that the majority of German-speaking refugees in the country must be covertly pro-Nazi (*Not to Be Taken,* p.100-91). Cox's last published story "It Takes Two to Make a Hero" (signed Francis Iles), which appeared during World War II, contains the following inexcusable passage:

He didn't care much for the occupant of the shop either. In fact it gave him quite a nasty jar, as he was hesitating outside the door, to see a fat little Jew squatting behind the counter like . . . a kind of frog, you know, and watching him with beady bright eyes that never winked.

While the references to Fischmann (in *Trial and Error*) and the Jewish tobacconist (in the short story) might be explained away as embodying the values and views of the fictional characters making the statements, and while the refugee reference (in *Not to Be Taken*) must be placed in context of everydays fears about impending war with Germany, they are surprising and ultimately unnecessary, particularly in light of the sensitivity displayed on the subject elsewhere by Cox. It is worth noting that in a reprint of "It Takes Two to Make a Hero" ("The Coward," *Ellery Queen's Mystery Magazine,* 1953), the sinister frog-like Jew becomes merely a "fat little man" without detriment to the story.

From the evidence available, it seems that Sayers, alone of the three writers discussed in this chapter, harboured strong personal feelings regarding Jews as a group in twentieth-century England; Christie subscribed to popularist misconceptions/prejudices of the time (as did Cox to a lesser extent), but Sayers' cultural conservatism seems to have been compounded by her increasingly one-eyed passion for Anglican Orthodoxy into an actual dislike of Jews. All three writers were political conservatives and solidly middle class, and that background (and their generally narrow personal visions) is reflected in their fictional treatment of foreigners, servants, radicals, gays, women (in Cox's case), Jews, and other outsiders. It may be significant that the three were foundation members of the Detection Club in 1929; the organisation formulated a fair-play code of practice for writers early in its existence and, in doing so, sought to institutionalise the genre's orthodoxies including, implicitly, standardised approaches to rendering stock, two-dimensional characters in puzzle-stories.

The majority of references to Jews in Sayers and Christie, and a small number of like references in Cox, conform unequivocally to the Golden Age norm. At the same time, there is a degree of ambivalence in their work. Certainly the slurs, cheap laughs and unnecessary insults are there, and are often hard to excuse. Yet, just as Sayers and Cox diverged readily from the Detection Club's fairplay code in their writing, on occasion the rendering of Jewish characters in the writing of all three transcends the Golden Age and can hold surprises.

4

Lingering Stereotypes
and Shifting Attitudes
1933–1945

A growing revisionism was apparent in the depiction of Jews in crime and detective fiction from the early 1930s, specifically from 1933. Clearly a number of factors came into play, among them the maturing of the genre. As the staple detective novel evolved from the Golden Age puzzle into the more complex book-length study of the criminal mind, it seems likely that writers, and some readers, increasingly rejected the use of stock, one-dimensional character-types. In laying down "the rules of the game" in 1929, Ronald Knox warned writers against the use of such hackneyed, outmoded plot devices as the sinister Chinaman or the hitherto undiscovered poison; the Oath of the Detection Club, founded by Cox and Sayers circa 1928, similarly called upon candidates to "observe a seemly moderation" in employing gangs, conspiracies, Chinamen or super-criminals.[1] A delightfully potent Superintendent Wilson short story by G.D.H. and Margaret Cole, "A Lesson in Crime," suggests that by that time (1933), the more discerning public may have become saturated with *Protocols*-inspired myths of Jewish conspiracy. Mystery writer Joseph Newton is murdered in a railway carriage by a disgruntled reader who berates the former for not even troubling to make his stories plausible. Among the shortcomings of Newton's latest crime novel, *The Big Noise*: "you introduced three gangs, a mysterious Chinaman, an unknown poison that leaves no trace, and a secret society of international Jews high up in the political world" (*A Lesson in Crime and Other Stories*, 1933).[2]

Of far greater significance than any desire to transcend cliché, however, was the impact of international events (most importantly, the institution of the Third Reich and the course of Hitler's war against the Jews) on the perceptions and preconceptions of many writers. Rubinstein cites the striking instance of R. Austin Freeman. Previously "obsessed by Jews, who appear throughout his earlier stories and novels as anarchists, villains, and organisers of London's criminal underworld," Freeman becomes more circumspect during the 1930s (a group of degenerate artists in the 1939 book *The Stoneware Monkey* does *not* include Jews, for example) and he does an "about-face" in his final novel. A benign solicitor named Cohen saves the life of Dr Thorndyke's laboratory assistant Polton in *Mr Polton Explains* (1940). Freeman afficianados see this as his way of making amends "in light of Hitler"; Rubinstein suggests that, "like many essentially humane Englishmen who were antisemites, Freeman was apparently cured of this disease when faced with endorsing Hitler's enormities."[3]

Something similar seems to have occurred with both John Buchan and E. Phillips Oppenheim. Although the late Buchan opus *A Prince of the Captivity* (1933) runs true to form in depicting a disreputable pawnshop owner who wears a skull-cap and is "rarely sober," as well as a woman who has a dread of moneylenders ("soft spoken people with Scotch names and curved noses . . . [who] take no denial"), the novel redeems itself with the intensely patriotic Macandrew, a leading figure in the British secret service. Buchan tells the reader:

It appeared that his real name was Meyer, and that he was a Belgian Jew, who had long foreseen the war and had made many preparations. Adam discovered one day the motive for his devotion to the British cause. The man was an ardent Zionist, and the mainspring of his life was his dream of a reconstituted Israel. He believed that this could not come about except as a consequence of a great war, which should break down the traditional frontiers of Europe, and that Britain was the agent destined by God to lead his people out of the wilderness . . . Adam read [in Macandrew's eyes] the purpose which makes saints and martyrs. (p.59)[4]

Buchan was publicly sympathetic to the Zionist movement, became friendly with Chaim Weizmann, and even served as chairman of the Parliamentary Palestine committee in the early 1930s. Cheyette suggests that he (and Macandrew) visualised Zionism as "a major force for the restoration of a British Imperial order after the anarchy of the First World War," and that, in *A Prince of the Captivity,* it was presented as "the obverse of Scudder's 'Jewish world conspiracy' in *The Thirty-nine Steps*."[5]

Nearly three decades after rendering the international mastermind Lefant in *Mr Laxworthy's Adventures,* Oppenheim gives us the contrasting Leopold Benjamin, and addresses the plight of continental Jewry, in his late thriller *Last Train Out* (1941). Although Oppenheim's time-line is slapdash in places (he seems slightly premature in lamenting "a perfect affliction of the Gestapo here amongst us," for example), the result remains a commendably exciting book. Major Charles Mildenhall, English soldier and adventurer, visits Vienna just prior to the *Anschluss* and becomes acquainted with the beleaguered Benjamin, banker, art-collector, philanthropist, "lover of the human race" and "the most important Jew in the city." "Our race becomes less and less popular as the days go by," confides Benjamin who is in imminent danger of arrest or worse. ("Vienna, alas, is greatly changed.") He disappears in the course of a formal dinner, managing first to ensure that his priceless art collection eludes the Nazis.

Mildenhall is immediately assumed, by Benjamin and other characters, to be fundamentally decent—by virtue of his nationality. "I know, too, that you are an Englishman, and that the English have always been the protectors of any persecuted race," he is told. When he revisits a transformed Vienna, this time just after Britain's declaration of war against Germany, he justifies their expectations by helping victims of the Nazis to safety (in the nick of time, as it turns out). The book's finale finds Benjamin alive and well in Paris.

All the Jewish characters in *Last Train Out* are portrayed sympathetically. In addition, Mildenhall finds himself aided along the way by several non-Jewish humanitarians appalled at the upsurge of antisemitism in their beloved Vienna. One of them, the down-to-earth wife of an American diplomat, tells him (and we can speculate that she is voicing her creator's own point of view):

The Austrian Nazis are getting stronger every day. It really is alarming, Charles. We are expecting the Germans to cross the frontier at any moment and I can't imagine what will happen then. I don't particularly care for Jews, Charles, but some of them are quite delightful people and they are being treated brutally . . . You must admit that this Jew-baiting, for a civilised nation, is a filthy affair. (p.6, 9, 10, 12, 19, 35)

Other writers similarly found their complacency "nudged" by ominous trends on the continent, and some tacitly acknowledged that their own prejudices might need reassessing. As early as 1932, Graham Greene expressed alarm at increasing levels of antisemitic activity in Europe in his *Grand Hotel*-like *Stamboul Train*. Forced to brook the sneers and insults of travel staff from the moment he boards the Channel ferry, the vulgar (but not altogether unsympathetic) businessman Myatt recognises correctly that obtaining a sleeping compartment to himself on the Orient Express will cost him more trouble and money than usual—"because he [is] a Jew" (p.17). The situation worsens the further Myatt penetrates into Europe. A surly guard spits to show his contempt, mutters "remarks about Jews under his breath," then suddenly becomes brutal. Striking at Myatt with the butt of his rifle, the guard snarls, "Go away, you Jew!":

in the small hungry eyes shone hatred and a desire to kill; it was as if all the oppressions, the pogroms, the chains, and the envy and superstition which caused them, had been herded into a dark cup of the earth and now he stared down at them from the rim. (p.206-07)

Anthony Berkeley Cox (who so cunningly misdirected readers with his attractive, gifted and likeable financier Pleydell in *The Silk Stocking Murders*) published a heartfelt (and heavy-going) critique of interwar Britain, *O England,* in 1934. In *O England,* Cox makes passing reference to the deterioration of Germany and comments on topical European concerns. Conceding that Britain had been the most civilised major power in the world, he lamented that "just in the last two years, we find one great nation reverting to hooliganism and mediaeval Jew-baiting, another submitting to an out-of-date autocracy . . ." (p.22). Later in the book he discusses Fascism at home:

The trouble and danger of Fascism is that it is so extreme. After all it is neither necessary to worship the really childish theory of economic nationalism, as the Fascists do, nor to be ready with praise of any country but one's own like the anti-national type of British Socialist. Nevertheless the middle ground is never the spectacular one, and we must expect Fascism to go on gaining ground for a time in this country. There are very powerful interests behind it, financial and other, as we have seen in the recent British Fascist denunciation of the Jews—a really inept piece of psychology, in view of public feeling here upon events elsewhere. (p.194)

Cox was referring here to statements made by the leader of the most recent development in organised British Fascism. The 1920s groups, the "Britons" and the I.F.L., had operated within a narrow orbit and had enjoyed little support. Whereas Lebzelter believes they were significant in providing "a niche" and "political home" to those "who shared a fanatical hatred of the Jews," as well as a base for the ongoing circulation of antisemitic literature and propaganda, Rubinstein uses meeting attendance figures to prove that the organisations, and others of their ilk, were "literally unknown" to 999 persons out of 1000. By contrast, the British Union of Fascists, established in 1932 and led by Sir Oswald Mosley, was much better organised and more influential. (Lebzelter judges the B.U.F. "the only group among radical right organisations in Britain which succeeded in attracting wide public attention and some mass support.")[6] Seeking to provide a remedy for unemployment during the Depression, Mosley (a former Labor Government minister who had not previously demonstrated any overt anti-Jewish prejudice) peddled a familiar Jew-behind-the-scenes motif, and consciously manipulated Jewish conspiracy claims, in order to increase the B.U.F.'s popular appeal. ("Behind the Communist or Socialist mob is the alien Jewish financier supplying the 'palm-oil' to make them yell," he once wrote.) Some response was forthcoming from London's East End although Thurlow concludes (as did Cox at the time) that Mosley's antisemitism was, in the end, counterproductive.[7]

Cox predicted little future for Fascism in Britain, but, possibly in a nod to Mosley's flair for publicity, he accepted that it would "probably give us some trouble before it is done" (p.195).

In reviewing Sinclair Lewis' anti-totalitarian novel *It Can't Happen Here,* for the *Daily Telegraph* the following year, he cautioned that Lewis offered an object-lesson "even for us Islanders." Although Lewis' novel targeted American political corruption specifically, Cox saw clear parallels with happenings closer to home. "Lewis does not exaggerate," he declared. "Not a single development [in *It Can't Happen Here*] . . . but has its true counterpart in Germany and Italy."[8]

Cox/Berkeley's 1937 novel *Trial and Error* opens with a symposium at which a group of middle-class men engage in an after-dinner discussion about altruistic killing ("for the good of humanity"). In the course of conversation, one speaker suggests that the assassination of Mussolini would be of immense benefit to humanity. Another suggests eliminating Hitler: "Mussolini's played out already, in my opinion. Hitler's the real menace." Another participant disagrees, suggesting that dictators represent merely the mouthpiece of a movement. "Wiping out Hitler wouldn't necessarily destroy Hitlerism. These movements have to play themselves out" (p.18). The topic arises again elsewhere in the novel. Assassinating Hitler might make matters even worse for the Jews, it is argued. "Hitler isn't nearly so impossible as his successor might be. And the same applies to Mussolini and Stalin." The speaker acknowledges that the killer of Huey Long may have done more for America than Roosevelt but "that was an isolated case. The movement collapsed with Huey Long's removal. Hitlerism wouldn't collapse if Hitler were killed" (p.46).

As I noted earlier, Cox/Berkeley satirised the ridiculousness of Nazism in his portrayal of the cook Maria Pfeiffer in *Not to Be Taken*. (Pfeiffer dismisses all and sundry as "Chews.") In the same book, Mrs Perriton, an elderly pillar of rural British common sense, expounds shrewdly on Germany while simultaneously voicing reservation about the refugee situation. She maintains the existence in London of an embassy-endorsed organisation which kept track of every German expatriate in England. "It's not worth any German's while not to be [a Nazi]," Mrs Perriton declares. When a refugee housemaid disappears from the Dorset village setting, she is convinced that the girl has been ordered back to Germany. Mrs Perriton believes it a great mistake to "rag" any German: "The Germans have no sense of humour about themselves. It makes me doubt very much whether they can really come from the same stock as ourselves." In her view, ideologues like the missing Mitzi are incurably one-eyed: "Show her the most sober and categorical account in a reputable newspaper of some case of persecution in Germany, and she'll say flatly: 'It isn't true'" (p.100-01).

Fictional passages like these, as well as the extracts from *O England*, testify to Cox's awareness and concern at the European state-of-play. In the previous chapter, I noted also Agatha Christie's stunned reaction to statements made by the rabid Nazi Julius Jordan, and the apparent effect his views had on sensitising her to her own fictional rendering of Jews. Christie consistently let her guard down and allowed more of her real self to emerge in the romantic novels she wrote as Mary Westmacott than in her crime fiction, and her comments (made in hindsight) on the approach of war with Germany, and the shortsightedness of Hitler's Jewish program, in *Absent in the Spring* (1943), are instructive. A self-enchanted and limited Englishwoman, returning from Bagdad to England by train in the late 1930s, shares her compartment with a cosmopolitan Russian aristocrat. Preparing to undergo a medical operation in Vienna, the worldly-wise Russian lady has placed her faith in a famous surgeon ("he is very clever—a Jew . . . They are clever doctors and surgeons, yes, and they are clever artistically too"). She predicts impending international war with the Germans, and muses on the stupidity of attempts to annihilate European Jewry. "Surely," argues Mrs Scudamore, "nobody really wants war?":

> She spoke incredulously.
> "For what else does the Hitler Youth movement exist?"
> Joan said earnestly, "But I have friends who have been in Germany a good deal, and they think there is a lot to be said for the Nazi movement."
> "Oh la la," cried Sasha. "See if they say that in three years time."
> (p.173-74)

We appear to have here an uncharacteristically politicised Christie. Indeed, the complacent, insensitive and insular Joan

Scudamore might well be seen as a metaphor for a smug and shortsighted Britain which had failed to take on Hitler, or intervene on behalf of the Jews, earlier.

Christie, like Cox, clearly found the activities of homegrown Fascists distasteful. In the Poirot novel *One Two Buckle My Shoe,* there is speculation that an extremist group is behind attempts to kill eminent financier and public figure Alistair Blunt. An arch-conservative, with enemies on both Left and Right of politics, Blunt is a self-made magnate who made his climb to power through marriage to a Jewish heiress. It is seen as unsurprising when he is targeted by the Mosleyesque "Imperial Shirts" ("they march with banners and have a ridiculous salute" [p.42-43, 155]).

The threat of continental Fascist outrages being replicated in Britain is explored by Bruce Graeme in *Impeached* (1933). The sinister Colonel Derbyshire spearheads the formation of the far-right Nationalist party. An admirer of Mussolini, he predicts great things for Germany under the Nazis: "Despite their defeat in the war, despite the collapse of their currency, despite the partition of their land . . . Germany is becoming an even greater country than she was before 1914." By contrast, Derbyshire judges Britain to be shiftless, timid and supine (p.216-17). Similar sentiments are expressed by the gullible Miss Mayfield in Nicholas Blake's *The Smiler with the Knife* (1939). A member of the "English Banner," Miss Mayfield (who is possibly modelled after the controversially pro-Hitler Unity Mitford) declares Nazi Germany to be "wonderful":

the spirit of youth and confidence and hero-worship. Sometimes I wish we could have something like it in England—not Fascism, of course, but something adapted to our national character. Get rid of all these doddering old politicians and the greasy Jews and the agitators. (p.66)

Following Hitler's annexation of Austria, and in the lead-up to *Kristallnacht,* much-loved novelist Louis Golding published an anguished polemic which warned that Nazi and Fascist influence was increasing daily in Britain:

Even the minds of agricultural labourers and farmers . . . are being poisoned by the stock anti-Jewish propaganda, such as that the "Jewish" multiple stores are the ruin of British farming . . . At select dinner parties in Mayfair . . . the conversation will be skilfully guided to the "Jewish problem," and a well-primed guest will explain why the German example deserves imitation . . . Following Herr Hitler's lead, provocative Fascist marches have been staged through Jewish quarters, and any consequent disorder has been paraded as proof of Jewish malice. ("No one else attacks us," Sir Oswald innocently declares.) The inevitable *Protocols* . . . are given all the veneration which can be spared from the *ipissima verba* of the Leader. Leaflets have been distributed advocating a boycott of Jewish businesses. Anti-Jewish scrawls are seen on blank walls and hoardings all over England. Jewish shop-keepers' windows are defaced by anti-Jewish labels (in some cases printed in Germany) . . . In the East End of London . . . individuals of Jewish appearance have been molested . . .[9]

Incursions by Mosley's "Blackshirts" into the East End alarmed more enlightened sections of the British public, despite an underlying conviction that "It can't happen here."[10] *The Smiler with the Knife* speculates on the potential of just such a group inflicting an extreme right-wing regime on England, and deals with the recruitment of Nigel and Georgia Strangeways (Blake's series sleuths) to hunt down the leader. The Strangeways are acutely alert to the seriousness of the situation; walking along the Thames embankment, a wary Georgia:

seemed to feel silent, jack-booted watchers standing outside frightened houses, figures kneeling to scrub the pavements, children coldly excluded from their familiar playgrounds, the reformer's whisper in the cafe, fear and suspicion like rheumatism fastening upon the easy intercourse of friends . . . all the vicious little tricks of modern tyranny. (p.42-43)

The fight against Fascism forms a subtext to a subsequent Blake novel, *The Case of the Abominable Snowman* (1941), set and written in the early months of the war. Rather than give himself up to justice, the slayer of a particularly odious drug-pusher chooses to make reparation by going into Germany undercover.

He proposes to "do as much damage as I can before they find me out. I have friends who will be working with me" (p.190). (The hero of another well-received crime novel, Geoffrey Household's thriller *Rogue Male* [1939], sets out to avenge the murder of his Jewish fiancee by trailing and killing Hitler!)

Notwithstanding the group's high profile at the time, Rubinstein assesses that the public impact of Mosley and the B.U.F. has been over-rated, and that the "Blackshirts" were "never anything but absolutely marginal . . . without electoral success of any kind and, almost from the first . . . 'beyond the pale.'" Endelman agrees that organised antisemitism (a la Mosley) remained on the periphery of party politics in Britain; even so, he contends that the B.U.F.'s engagement in vehement anti-Jewish diatribe may well have borne fruit in colouring the average English man or woman's perception of Jews, and in confirming doubts about Jewish morality, loyalty or trustworthiness.[11] Likewise, credence was given to Fascist-propagated rumours that the Jews were trying to plunge Britain into another war. (17% of people surveyed in November 1939 believed Britain was fighting "for the Jews.")[12] Undoubtedly the most penetrating and effective reference to home-grown Fascism and antisemitism in any Golden Age title occurs in the celebrated *Verdict of Twelve* (1940) by Raymond Postgate. Renowned as a social historian, socialist, and brother-in-law of G.D.H. Cole, Postgate (1896-1971) produced three detective novels in the course of a long and prolific career; all three are of some relevance to this study. The best known (*Verdict*) has been judged a *tour de force* by Howard Haycraft and is included in the Haycraft-Queen cornerstones listing.[13]

Postgate provides the reader with detailed biographies of six out of twelve jurors empanelled to try an elderly woman for the murder of her young nephew. Each juror brings with him/her a set of personal attitudes and histories which colour his/her reading of the evidence. One member of the panel is Alice Rachel Morris, nee Greenberg, described as "a Jewess from her too high-heeled shoes to her bright and gleaming-eyed little face, so well made-up and so anxiously deprived of all individuality" (p.69). Mrs Morris regards herself as modern and assimilated, having given up "all her racial beliefs and practices"; she is "consciously English." (Her favourite poetry, for instance, is that of G.K. Chesterton. Surely, "the happy jewelled alien men" described by Chesterton could not refer to either the Morrises or their friends? [p.69, 72]).

Given the critical context of the 1930s, however, Postgate suggests that—even in Britain—full Jewish integration has become a pipe-dream:

Half-Jews are unhappier than whole Jews: part of a nation, or a race, or whatever you choose to call it, was slowly assimilating itself to its neighbours until 1933, when it was ordered by Hitler to go back from where it came. Those who had never started on the journey were least injured, those who could no longer be Jews and might not now be gentiles were the unhappiest. (p.69)

Postgate concentrates on the contagiousness of antisemitism: "Before Hitler came to power antisemitism had been an endemic disease only in certain limited areas where Jewish commercial competition was serious. Certain American towns, the environs of Stoke Newington and Whitechapel in London, for example." Once the Nazis promulgated the Nuremberg laws, however, even their enemies became Jew-conscious.

The strongest anti-antisemite became, against his will, a Jew-smeller. Were Jews ill-mannered, rapacious, lustful and dishonest? Did they congregate in loud-voiced, ostentatious groups? He must notice them more carefully, in order to refute these silly slanders. (p.69-70)

In defending the Jews (Postgate suggests), even their advocates ceased to look on them as normal human beings:

Once a group, no matter what, is separated from the rest of society, it is by that mere fact made different, and develops at once marked characteristics of its own . . . So, since 1933, the Jews of England have become in fact more sharply differentiated from the Gentiles. They have developed more of both fearfulness and of compensating self-assertiveness. The antisemite lie has by its mere propagation brought into existence the differences on which it pretended to base itself. (p.70-71)

Alice Morris, we learn, is a widow. Out for a Sunday stroll with husband Les, she saw him attacked and killed by a gang of antisemitic East end thugs.

Before Hitler [argues Postgate] Les Morris would have passed unnoticed and unobjected-to among his fellows. No one would have considered that his shoes were too brightly-polished, his ties too loud, his green shirts too fanciful, and the checks on his black and white suit too large. (p.71)

As a juror, Alice Morris' bitter experiences predispose her to suppose the defendant guilty:

Why had her life been ruined and her husband killed? For no other reason than that murder was not punished. The arm of the law was weak: after Les had died the police had explained to her again and again that they had not got the power to arrest all the likely suspects and force them to confess. In Germany, and for that manner in the United States, the law wasn't made a fool of like that. (p.235)

In a softer mood, Alice sees unpunished killing as "too common and too near." By both sex and religion, she believes, she belongs "to the weak who need protection" (p.235).

Verdict of Twelve is a masterly and absorbing novel, highly unusual in its time for the depth of its sociological probing. In its magnificent character studies, it shows clearly the influence of Francis Iles (i.e. Anthony Berkeley Cox in his guise as pioneer of the crime novel as study of personality). In particular, Postgate renders the unfortunate Alice Morris with great compassion. In another of his crime novels, *Somebody at the Door* (1943), he redirects his sympathy to the plight of the Jewish refugee in England. When an unpleasant town councillor Henry Grayling dies shortly after leaving a train and arriving home one Friday evening, suspicion falls on his fellow-passengers. Predictably, each of the suspects has ample motive for Grayling's murder. One of them, a part-Jewish Austrian refugee Anton Mannheim, is a gifted physicist who was rescued by a secret service agent and helped to England under extraordinary circumstances. Detained in a routine round-up of aliens in 1940,

Mannheim is released only to be denounced by Grayling as a Nazi spy—not the real Mannheim at all. The only person able to prove his true identity is the secret agent, recently killed in action. Although he is exonerated of Grayling's murder, at the end of the book Mannheim's true identity remains at issue. The reader is still unsure whether or not he is who he claims to be. Postgate emphasises the tragedy of such a dilemma:

How does a man prove that he is himself? [pleads Mannheim]. I do not have the answer. In Berlin are those who know me, they are in Berlin. The young David, who rescued me, he is dead . . . So do I tell you of my books, what I wrote in them, and who published them? . . . But as you have truly said, I could copy all that from the British Museum. I tell you where I lived, and whom I knew: that, too, I might have been told by the Nazis, if I am a spy. I did not take part in politics very much: I do not know those who are refugees here. In Germany I was not the sort of person who was photographed in picture papers. (p.181)

Other crime writers who broached the refugee experience in their work were E.R. Punshon and Ngaio Marsh (as well as Anthony Gilbert, Delano Ames and Cyril Hare in books written after World War II. See Chapter 5). Punshon's *The Crossword Mystery* (1934) offers us a much more ambivalent character than Postgate's Mannheim. Nabersberg, a gold-buyer, had always supposed himself to be a "Nordic of the purest type" prior to the rise of Hitler. In a chilling passage, he recalls that, having once witnessed "a number of high-spirited young Storm troopers kicking an aged Jew into a canal, and then pulling him out to kick him in again, I gave the Nazi salute as I passed." Nabersberg is stunned when it is discovered that his maternal grandmother was Jewish, and he is forced to flee Germany. "It is unfortunate," he observes uncomprehendingly, "that the Hitler Government does not feel it can fully depend on the zeal and the loyalty and devotion of Germans of Jewish descent" (p.231-32).

Ngaio Marsh deals particularly perceptively with the experience of the refugee in a less-than-hospitable England. In *Death and the Dancing Footman* (1942), Dr Francis Hart, a noted plastic surgeon from Vienna, becomes chief suspect in a country house murder case, and is shunned by the other house-guests.

When another guest attempts suicide, however, Hart's professional instincts overwhelm his resentment, and he administers all the medical aid he can. When another character marvels at his apparent lack of concern at being labelled a murderer, Hart concurs:

You mean that I am not afraid . . . You are right. Lady Hersey, I am an Austrian refugee and a Jew who has become a naturalised Briton. I have developed what I believe you would call a good nose for justice. Austrian justice, Nazi justice, and English justice. I have learned when to be terrified and when not to be terrified. (p.209)

Hart's cool faith in British "fair play" also surprises Chief Inspector Alleyn:

Alleyn had had official dealings with aliens for many years. Since the onset of Nazidom, he had learned to recognise a common and tragic characteristic in many of them, and that was a deep-seated terror of plain-clothes police officers. (p.222)

Death and the Dancing Footman ends optimistically for Hart—if for few of the other characters. Although denounced by his treacherous wife, he is confident that "when all this is over," he will be able to resume his career. "I think in a little while there will be a need for many surgeons in England," he speculates ominously (p.276). (The book is set in early 1940.)

A New Zealander, Marsh spent lengthy periods in England from the early 1930s, and the majority of her traditional whodunits are set in London or the British countryside. She is now widely revered as one of four *grandes dames* of the classic English detective story (along with Allingham, Sayers and Christie). Marsh is unusual among Golden Age craftsmen in that her few Jewish characters are all portrayed positively (as are the native New Zealand Maori characters in her books *Colour Scheme* and *Vintage Murder*). Quite possibly she was sensitised to the plight of the Jews in Europe and problems confronting refugees by a disturbing visit to Germany in 1937. Biographer Margaret Lewis notes that Marsh was staying at the village of Belstein when she witnessed "the arrival of jack-booted officials who nailed up a notice in the square demanding the ostracism of Jews in the village." The village's elderly Jewish shopkeepers were afraid to go out and unable to sleep for fear of what might happen to them. Marsh and her companions readily took the hotelier's advice and left Germany at the first opportunity.[14]

A minor player in one of Marsh's finest books, *Death in a White Tie* (1938), is Rose Birnbaum, a reluctant debutante. Her social-climbing mother has paid out 500 pounds to have the girl "launched" into London society. Rose longs to study art; she is the granddaughter of the man who painted the famous "Jewish Sabbath," and yearns to follow in his footsteps: "He was a Jew, of course. I'm a Jewess," she tells Alleyn, crediting that background for her unusual maturity. (She is only sixteen.) In the meantime, the girl is forced to brook the racist invective of the colonel's wife paid by her mother to act as chaperon; "My dear child," snarls Mrs Halcut-Hackett, "I suppose you can't help looking what you are, but at least you might make some effort to sound a little less Soho." Rose confides in the Chief Inspector:

Yesterday she told me there was a good deal to be said for the German point of view, and asked me if I had any relations among the refugees because she heard quite a number of English people were taking them as maids. (p.168, 170)

Marsh hints that Rose will eventually realise her dream by studying with artist Agatha Troy (the future Mrs Alleyn).

More prominent among the *dramatis personae* of *Death in a White Tie* is the presumably Jewish Sir Daniel Davidson, a flamboyant society doctor and dilettante, devoted to The Arts ("with rather emphatic capitals"), "frankly theatrical and theatrically frank." Davidson, we are told, is what Disraeli might have become had he "taken to medicine instead of primroses." His desk is a modified spinet, his "overflowing" conversation is spattered with "French and Italian tags," his inkwell recalls "the days when sanded paper was inscribed with high-sounding phrases of quill-scratched calligraphy" (p.32, 108, 111). Affected but witty and personable, Davidson is an exceptionally well-delineated comic character; that he turns out to be something more testifies to Marsh's plotting skills. Elsewhere in her novels, other (probably) Jewish characters appear peripherally and occasionally, neither offensively or otherwise. A New Zealand wool-buyer in *Died in the Wool* (1945) is named Sammy Joseph, while London theatrical manager Winter Morris, keen on the phrase "Live for ever, dear boy, live forever," is present in *Death at the Dolphin* (1967, p.62) and *Light Thickens* (1982). Ben Ruby, a jocular, cigar-smoking opera-manager, appears in the 1980 novel *Photo-Finish*.[15]

Also active in the semi-bohemian confines of show business is Hyman Weingott, a theatrical agent with a comprehensive knowledge of the entertainment industry. Weingott helps the illustrious Philip Trent identify and arrest a cunning killer in E.C. Bentley's "Trent and the Bad Dog" (*Trent Intervenes,* 1938). John Dickson Carr (writing as Carter Dickson) includes a comic, cigar-smoking Jewish movie producer in the cast of *And So to Murder* (1941). Possibly patterned after Hollywood moguls like Samuel Goldwyn or Harry Cohn, the artistically-compromised but likeable Mr Aaronson suggests that the Duchess of Richmond should sit at the piano and sing (in order "to cheer the troops up") in a supposedly serious film about the battle of Waterloo![16] Rachel West, who features in Edmund Crispin's *The Case of the Gilded Fly* (1944) (and who the author informs us in passing—and for no apparent reason—is Jewish), is leading lady of an acting company and long-time, understanding mistress of a celebrated playwright. A strikingly attractive woman of 28 or so, Rachel is intelligent, perceptive and down-to-earth. A series of murders attendant on the production of her lover's latest opus at an Oxford repertory theatre compels her to revaluate her life and career.

Christianna Brand highlights (and, refreshingly, ridicules) topical antisemitic prejudice in *Heads You Lose* (1941). Among the novel's circle of suspects is Henry Gold, who:

without having the characteristic features, [is] unmistakably Jewish . . . a small, slim, ugly man, with a friendly, rather Puck-like smile that lit up his face into eagerness and gave him a quite overwhelming charm. (p.15)

Gold outrages public opinion when he marries into the rural aristocracy. The local squire expresses disbelief that the well-connected Venetia Hart should dote on "this wretched little Jew." "People all thought Henry was terribly lucky to marry me," confides Venetia:

I know they did, just because he was a Jew and not very good looking and not as up in society as some of the others . . . but if they only knew, it was me that was the lucky one . . . (p.16, 21, 133)

Brand makes a point of Gold's sentimentality and "warm Jewish heart," and through his wife scoffs at the reservations of their peers. "Trust a Jew," laughs Venetia when her husband persistently wins at *vingt-et-un*.

He always does it. It shows that it's quite right when they say that the Jews have all the money and people like Henry are responsible for the War and Mussolini and the measles epidemic and the common cold and everything else that ever goes wrong with the world . . . (p.76, 188)

The examples cited above testify to a growing sensitivity among writers of Golden Age fiction. There can be no question that the desire to move beyond overworn fictional stereotype on one hand, and perceptions of Jewish suffering within a rapidly deteriorating Europe on the other, had a far-reaching impact. From the mid 1930s, or at least 1940 on, Jews generally appeared much less frequently, and were depicted with arguably more sophistication than hitherto. ("There has been conscious suppression by all thoughtful people of anything likely to wound Jewish susceptibilities," novelist George Orwell suggested in 1945.)[17] Of course, there were numerous exceptions. I noted a couple of latter-day Christie-an lapses in the previous chapter, and old habits continued to die hard for a number of other practitioners of the craft, usually the more "plodding" among them. (In defence of some apparently insensitive writers, it is possible, of course, that some "offending" novels which appeared during or after the war may have been written considerably earlier—before the world at large became privy to the full extent of

Hitler's assault on the Jews—and their publication delayed because of wartime conditions.)[18] A few writers, who veered more towards the thriller than the full-fledged whodunit, continued to find fertile territory within updated myths of Jewish self-interest, treachery or opportunism.

Historian Tony Kushner has argued, contrary to popular belief, that the British antisemitic strands underlying the fictional depiction of Jews in the interwar years evolved and continued to operate during World War II. While he recognises the country's long tradition of philosemitism, and while he acknowledges a widespread general revulsion in Britain at Nazi methods, he maintains that concern persisted among ordinary people at the alleged power of the Jew. "The fact that Britain had no death camps in the war, and indeed little violence towards its Jewish minority, does not mean that British antisemitism should be dismissed as unimportant."[19] "There is more antisemitism in England than we care to admit and the war has accentuated it," declared George Orwell at the time.[20] The influx of immigrants post-1933 (a total of 60,000 up until 1941) promoted fears that the newcomers would wrest jobs away from economically beleaguered "battlers" and ensured perpetuation of perceptions of Jews as foreign. Colin Holmes writes that: "It was not uncommon in the popular press to find the refugees portrayed specifically as Jews in accounts which suggested that they were busily engaged in undermining society and the British way of life."[21] As "foreigners," refugees were, by implication, un-British, open to suspicions of disloyalty, even treason (including spying and Fifth column activity); 30,000 foreign nationals (most of them Jews) were interned following preliminary German war successes, and 8000 were deported to Canada and Australia.[22] Somerset Maugham was only one public figure who was convinced that the Gestapo espionage network encompassed refugee Jews.[23] A prime fictional example (and one also cited by Kushner) is Carl Mendel, art dealer, rumoured chief organiser of the Nazi spy system in Europe, and the title character of Richard Keverne's *The Black Cripple* (1941). Keverne would have readers accept the ludicrous proposition that the swarthy, enigmatic Mendel is "one of the few men, despite his obvious Jewish ancestry, whom the *Fuehrer* would always see" (p.16).

Isidore Sava, a "phenomenally successful financier," one of the richest men in the world, and a friend and confidant of the British Prime minister, is a naturalised Briton of indeterminate continental origin. He is exposed as a Fifth columnist and his country home as a base for enemy operations in Sydney Horler's *The Man Who Walked with Death* (1942). Horler categorises Sava's defection as not all that surprising:

There had been precedents enough in other countries, now all under the heel of the Hun. Sava was a naturalised British subject, of course, but what did that mean? . . . Many men in different European countries had enjoyed just as much confidence as Sava did in England, and then, at the critical moment, had thrown off the mask and disclosed themselves to be Fifth Column rats. After all, Sava had no British blood: he was a cross-breed of the most variegated type, a cosmopolitan, an international financier—and, with conditions what they were, that type could be trusted to think exclusively of themselves and to the Devil with the country which was giving them hospitality. (p.149)

Sava himself sets no store whatever by the naturalisation ceremony: "I took out naturalisation papers because it suited my purpose, but that did not make me an Englishman; I have always been an Asiatic," he declares. He cites boredom as the motive for his having turned traitor and he ultimately commits suicide, having inserted "a potent but little-known eastern drug into one of his favourite cigars" (p.175-76). A mutual antipathy exists between Sava and his chief enemy contact, Field Marshal von Keyserling of the Third Reich. Von Keyserling loathes the former's "olive-tinted face":

[T]he swine had a distinct trace of the Jew in him, without a doubt, in addition to all the other polluting blood influences; and if it had not been *lese-majeste*, he would have considered it a most humiliating thing that the Third Reich should have been willing to use such an instrument as Isidore Sava. (p.158)

The cast of characters of *The Man Who Walked with Death* also includes a German-born domestic who longs to see "her Fatherland triumphant over its traditional enemies, international

Jewry and the capitalistic plutocrats . . ." (p.58). An equally fanatical Great War veteran had long since abandoned family ("like most German aristocrats," his mother regarded "the little Austrian nobody [Hitler]" with indifference) and fiancee ("how could he think now of a girl whose grandfather had been a Jew") to immerse himself in the Nazi movement (p.85). There is also a Charing Cross Road bookseller, a "rotund, elderly Jew" named Jacobs. When requested to provide someone to catalogue Sava's library, Jacobs seizes the opportunity to pass on an assistant he dislikes, thereby being able to bring his nephew into the business and so save at least 15 shillings a week (p.127).

Bill Pronzini has contrasted the relatively restrained and civilised writing of mass-producers like William Le Queux with "the lurid, opinionated, sometimes nasty prose" of the similarly prolific Horler, suggesting that a whole book might be devoted to the latter's outrageously xenophobic, homophobic and misogynist output and personal values.[24] An unregenerate Horler continued to indulge paranoid fantasies about Jewish collaboration with Nazism in *Nighthawk Mops Up* (1944). Wilfred Abrahams, a respected town-councillor and ostensibly "a pillar of strength and security" in the coastal town of Westsea, is in fact a skilled trickster, "a man fundamentally dishonest":

Like most wealthy men in Westsea, he was connected with shipping. The company of which he was managing director, sent sailors on the high seas in dangerous boats; underfed them; underpaid them, and generally regarded them as some kind of necessary vermin. (p.67)

Unexpectedly, Abrahams is charged with fraud and serves two years in prison. He returns to Westsea in the second year of the war and, by apparently throwing himself into voluntary work, manages to regain some of his former standing within the community. In reality, he has returned bent on revenge for his prison sentence, and he willingly becomes local agent for an underground pro-Nazi gang headed by a prominent peer. For two years, Abrahams immerses himself in sabotage, stealing stores from lifeboats sent out to rescue shipwrecked servicemen, stealing food-parcels earmarked for dispatch to P.O.W. camps, and so on.

Because he was a natural skunk, and because he had covered himself with so much mud now that it was impossible for him to escape from the net which had been spread about him, Wilfred Abrahams never stopped to speculate on the enormity of the crimes he was organising; he never paused to think about the harm he was doing his country, and how he, and those who worked with him and under him, were helping Hitler, that foul enemy of all mankind, to remain longer in power. (p.74)

Forced to betray his unscrupulous associates, and terrified of the form their retribution could take, Abrahams, like Isidore Sava, elects suicide as the easiest way out.

As an extension of their "foreignness," Jews were frequently seen as primarily self-interested and, specifically, as keen to avoid the discomforts endured by the rest of the population. Kushner notes that organised Fascist groups did their best to propagate stories of Jewish participation in war profiteering, along with allegations that Jews avoided their military responsibilities, whether fire watching, war work or active service. (In fact, as in the Great War, 15% of the Anglo-Jewish community joined the armed forces compared with only 10% of the population as a whole).[25] "I see you are not in uniform, Mr Gold," sneers the unlamented Miss Moreland in Christianna Brand's *Heads You Lose*. (Gold has volunteered for active duty—and been turned down [p.16].) In the thriller *Drink to Yesterday* (1940), the first appearance of Manning Coles' Tommy Hambledon, the flashy Jacob Rosenbaum is exempted from military service because his father owns a boot factory. Rosenbaum reputedly "stinks of money" and compounds his offences by being something of a lady-killer. His luck with women causes another character to lament: "The triumphs of the Chosen race are more than my stomach can stand" (p.117, 214). (In fairness to Manning Coles, it should be noted that a second novel *Pray Silence,* also published in 1940, attacks Nazism and includes a Jewish war hero. A recurring character in the Tommy Hambledon books is Joseph Joseph, a fence for stolen goods.)[26]

Rubinstein questions the true extent of anti-Jewish "grumbling" but acknowledges that there may well have been a temporary increase in populist antisemitism during the war. (He suggests—interestingly—that a degree of "oneupmanship" may have been a factor at play here; "the Jews saw themselves, with justice, as entitled to the moral credibility of mankind for what they suffered, and were thus stealing the limelight from the British, who also saw themselves as entitled to the same thing for having 'fought alone' and suffered so much.")[27] To some degree Jews became scapegoats for the real problems of war, such as food shortages and the strain of national service.[28] Although by 1940 writers were tending to avoid clichéd big-time financiers (Horler's Isidore Sava being a notable exception), an estimated 38% of the British public still saw Jews as obsessed with money.[29] In *Drink to Yesterday* Coles subscribes to myths of Jewish financial domination in Britain (as well as exaggerated claims of Jewish immigration); a German character observes: "The English don't mind appearing stupid, but it is a pose. They are financially astute—they owe that to the high proportion of Jews in the country" (p.73).

A persistent image of the period was that of the Jew as black marketeer, an updated variant on the Great War image of Jew-as-war profiteer ("making money while our boys were away fighting"). Kushner maintains that "the identification of Jews and the black market in the war was almost as strong as that between Jews and usury in the mediaeval period." In practice, it was a topical renewal of the ever-adaptable Shylock construct.[30] In addition to the dastardly Wilfred Abrahams, Horler's *Nighthawk Mops Up* features Aaron Jacobs, a shrewd operative who has no compunction about "holding up the nation to ransom in its vital commodities in wartime." Horler pictures him as an important cog within a gigantic industry, raking in fabulous profits from the resale of goods stolen from railway stations all over the country. Good-guy secret agent "Oliver Tryst" ponders on the market-controllers:

Many, like this present specimen [Jacobs] were Jews—and he wondered how it was that the race which complained, justifiably enough, of having been persecuted throughout the centuries, should be foolish enough to provide further evidence and material for that ostracism. It must be something in the Jewish blood, he supposed, that enabled these men throughout the country to batten off the very nation which was giving them succour and security against their ferocious foe. (p.49)

Horler articulates the popular belief that (a) a highly organised black market flourished, and (b) that it was Jew-dominated. The belief was not without some factual basis, as Board of Trade and Ministry of Food prosecution figures reveal. "Jewish involvement in the black market was closely related to the proportion of Jews in the British economy," concedes Kushner, "[It] reflected not a lack of business morality . . . but a stage in the socio-economic development of Anglo-Jewry, where small business ownership was common." (The dire financial position of wartime immigrants also dictated some "shady practice.") Even so, and "on purely rational grounds," Kushner concludes, "the British public was inaccurate in accusing Jews of undue involvement."[31] True to tradition, Horler's Aaron Jacobs is described as a "wart-hog," who speaks in an "oily whisper," "wolfs" his food, and wears a grin "as unpleasant as his shifty, cunning gaze." Nobody's fool (his adversary Tryst observes of him "Trust a Jew—and a criminal Jew at that—for having his wits about him"), he draws the line at killing: "[He] was quite willing for anyone else to commit murder in the good cause, but he had a horrid vision . . . of a hangman's noose" (p.52, 54).

More conventional renderings of that old standby, the usurious moneylender, continued to get an airing. A family fallen on hard times and forced to sell off household furniture piece by piece, is still described by E.C.R. Lorac as having "gone to the Jews" in *Rope's End, Rogue's End* (1942, p.88). An elderly spinster, forced to pawn her jewellery," is treated with contempt by "the stout Jewish gentleman in spectacles" to whom she applies in Patricia Wentworth's *Miss Silver Intervenes* (1944, p.54).

Fifth column activity in provincial England in the early months of World War II is at the basis of murder within an amateur theatrical troupe in the very readable (and unjustly neglected) *Measure for Murder* (1945) by Clifford Witting.[32] This superior whodunit boasts a skilled and totally unexpected, Christie-style *volte face* in the midst of the narrative (as well as a well-drawn set of subsidiary characters); unfortunately, and rather surprisingly, in view of the book's informed commentary on Hitler Germany's preparations for war, the book also contains a cliched Jewish pawnbroker, complete with "stage accent." Witting writes:

There is an inelegant type of crudely coloured picture-postcard that can be obtained in sea-side towns and sent to less leisured, but equally broadminded, friends at home. Apart from the fat woman in the small rowing-boat, the intoxicated gentleman with a beer bottle sticking from his pocket, and the girl who had been provided by the artist with an excuse for falling backwards, perhaps the most familiar figure on these cards is the elderly Jewish pawnbroker with an enormous waistcoat, standing beneath the sign of the three brass balls. One has only to remember this representation . . . to get an instant picture of Mr Aaron Sugarman. (p.152)

Sugarman proves to be an important witness in the case at hand. Even so, Inspector Charlton, the investigating officer, suspects that the "far too prosperous old Semite" adds to his income by acting as a "fence" (p.185).

John G. Brandon's wartime books are "littered with Jewish fences" notes Kushner.[33] Brandon, a prolific "hack" who produced a large number of formula Sexton Blake books, died in 1941. Publishers Wright & Brown subsequently retitled, revised and republished several of his novels, in some cases replacing Blake with other sleuths. They did not see fit to remove offensive racial stereotypes, however. "Thus, whilst . . . Brandon [or his publishers] made the occasional comment to indicate that his novels were now in a war background, his general content of Jewish and Yellow perils differs little from . . . [writing at] the turn of the century," judges Kushner.[34] The Brandon books had traditionally included, and would continue to include, a range of unflattering depictions of blacks, Asians, continentals and Jews. One member of a gang of Soho toughs in *Mr Pennington Goes Nap* (1941) is "Barney the Conk," "a racing 'head' of Semitic origin," for instance. The London setting of *Death in Duplicate* (1945) is peopled with exotic negro dancers and inscrutable Orientals, and Isaac Levant, "a gent of Semitic origin," who is arguably the most repellent of all post-1940 moneylenders.

Known to the underworld as "Sleek Ikey," Levant has combined moneylending with a host of other unsavoury occupations (such as running a protection racket in Soho, heading a mob, drug-running) to amass a fortune. Possessed of both good looks and brains, Levant has consistently evaded the law by the use of his native guile (the police are aware that strong-arm tactics are unlikely to succeed in dealing with "the cunning brain of the Jew"), and he is regularly seen about town in the company of glamorous society women. "Wealthy and titled ladies flocked to borrow money, even on outrageous terms, from the handsome Jew, solely that they might number him among their acquaintances" (p.33-34, 71).[35] His charming exterior conceals the much more sinister inner man, of course.

From a handsome man of rather suave appearance, Levant changed into something resembling a vicious animal . . . The true soul of the Jew was bared in these seconds; a cold, deadly, slimy thing, utterly devoid of compassion; vice and greed were stamped in every line and contour of his features. (p.79-80)

The moneylender ultimately gets his just deserts, murdered by a man he had attempted to frame for another death. (Wright & Brown continued to revise and reissue Brandon novels throughout the 1950s. I look at one of the last, the glaringly offensive *Death of a Socialite,* in the next chapter.)

Finally, another wartime novel warrants attention here. Written at the end of the European conflict (and in light, presumably, of revelations of Nazi atrocities), it is something of an oddity in the way it portrays the power, potential, and apparent pervasiveness, of organised antisemitism. John Bentley, best known for *The Landor Case* (1937) featuring amateur sleuth Sir Richard Herrivell, also produced a series of imitation "hard-boiled" books, set in tough-guy America, and starring Glen Gibson, "New York's youngest and most famous attorney." One of these is *Pattern for Perfidy* (1946). Stylistically, author Bentley tries to emulate Dashiell Hammett or Raymond Chandler on the one hand; on the other, he reverses the plotline of Laura Z. Hobson's topical bestseller *Gentleman's Agreement.* In the course of investigating the collaborationist activities of a prominent journalist, and exposing a nest of saboteurs, Gibson poses as a rabid antisemite in order to infiltrate the offices of the *Christian Crusader*. The *Crusader* is a pro-Axis rag ("pro-Jap . . . anti-Jewish, anti-Russ and anti-Democratic), presided over by Gustav Meyer, former *fuehrer* of the Aryan League in America.

The action of *Pattern for Perfidy,* which takes place a few months after the bombing of Pearl Harbour, pits Gibson and the forces of good (i.e. those committed to intervention in the war in Europe) against villainous isolationists ("Roosevelt and his Jewish administration demand a national unity dedicated to the war effort. If you disagree, it's just too bad" [p.38]). Here the stock "baddies" are duplicitous Italo-Americans and U.S. born (or naturalised) Japanese and Germans. Interestingly, the description of the Fujimota Club on East Broadway echoes renderings by pre-war writers of Jewish-owned or patronised nightspots in Soho:

The sing-song of Japanese, quickly spoken in a limited number of repetitive chords, provided an obbligato for the clipped, distorted speech of Bowery folk . . . Present was a motley collection of human beings, which included faded white women, racecourse touts, near-Japanese of mixed ancestry, and pure, steel-haired, sloe-eyed Japanese, each a carbon copy of the next.

The manager is "a smooth, unctuous, middle-aged Japanese":

He wore a well-cut business suit, a buttonhole, and a wristwatch with a gold band. His sleek hair shone like polished ebony and his teeth were very white in contrast. His smile was friendly, but his eyes were cold and probing. No smile came from them. He spoke flawless, accented American, rather too correctly. (p.102-03)

World War II may have alerted Bentley to the evils of anti-semitism, but he clearly finds Japanese and Germans made-to-order, alternative "sinister foreigners."

The malignant Meyer, who believes that the *Protocols of the Elders of Zion* represent "the most staggering indictment based on factual evidence that's ever been published," dubs the Jewish question "the root cause of all evil in America." Jews are everywhere, he claims, running the Post Office, the Supreme Court and "every other thing." He aims to make people "Jew conscious":

The more they think about Jews, the better they'll realise Roosevelt and his gang are the wrong mob to be running this show. They're giving the Jews all the breaks. It sticks out a mile . . . That's the one thing that's got to be kept alive. The one flame that must be fanned and fed, subtly and constantly. Awareness of the Jew. Hatred of the Semitic race. A realisation that they're responsible for all our troubles. (p.40-42)

"Working on a chain system of seditious talk that's hard to check," Meyer's propaganda machine, at the core of which is the *Christian Crusader,* encompasses fake attacks by "Jews" on newspaper sellers. ("Stirs up feeling against them [the Jews], sells the paper and increases the number of likely recruits" [p.39].) Of course, he targets "Park Avenue as well as the Bowery" (p.119).

Different sections of the community need different kinds of appeal. In the Bronx, we talk about Jews. On Park Avenue, we call them "International bankers."

Meyer elaborates:

When you're talking about Jews, don't use the word "Jew" any more than you need. Use the term "Semitic" or just refer to them as the "Chosen People" or "Big Business." (p.43)

Pattern for Perfidy ends with the *Christian Crusader* raided and closed down and the "bad guys" agreeably vanquished by Gibson and the law. The novel, as a whole, is hardly out of the ordinary (although Gibson's emulation of the American gumshoe is entertaining; at one point he is advised by his long-suffering secretary, Nancy, to "quit playing at being a man called Spade" [p.124]). What is unusual though, is Bentley's focus on the dangers of organised Jew-hatred. Indeed, his exploration of the possibility that antisemitism has the potential to take hold and become a national problem even in the U.S.A. (and, by logical extension, Great Britain) invites comparison with Raymond Postgate's insights in *Verdict of Twelve*.

5

Jews in British Crime Fiction after 1945

In a 1945 essay, novelist George Orwell claimed that, in Britain, "anti-Jewish remarks" had been "carefully eliminated from all classes of literature" following the rise of Nazi anti-semitism.[1] As Tony Kushner has pointed out—and as the multiple examples cited in the current study underline—Orwell's assessment was hardly accurate. Certainly, many writers of crime and detective stories seem to have found the spread of Fascist ideology personally confronting and took pains, accordingly, to rethink the way they had routinely portrayed or employed Jews in their fiction. However (and as we have seen), there were a significant number of exceptions to this. Kushner quotes contemporary observers like Tom Harrisson and Alex Comfort who found that antisemitism in thrillers ("and the like") continued at a high level, or even increased, during World War II.[2]

Gina M. Mitchell is more precise than Orwell in her estimate that the war years and their immediate aftermath represented a "watershed." Noting, mildly, that "retrospective research into some of the popular fiction written before 1939 certainly supports the view that Jews were commonly despised and distrusted," Mitchell maintains that revelation of Hitler's Final Solution "focused attention" on Jews (as a group and individuals)—"Unavoidably, it confronted stereotyped ideas with historical evidence and, by so doing, also stimulated a closer examination of personally held attitudes . . ."[3] By way of example, both Mitchell and Rubinstein highlight the work of Ian Fleming whose nationalistic (even jingoistic) James Bond novels clearly belong to the Le Queux/Oppenheim/Buchan/McNeile tradition. Fleming's novels are full of villainous characters categorised by their race—Negroes, Chinese, Koreans, Balts, Germans and Russians—yet apart from two innocuous asides (one to a trade unionist in *Casino Royale*, the other to the death of a moneylender in *Moonraker*), "there are no Jewish references of any significance" in any Fleming novel. As Mitchell observes, the exclusion of the Jew-as-villain from popular/best-selling literature would suggest that "even a writer like Fleming, who relied heavily upon the established conventions of a particular genre, no longer felt that the traditional image of the Jew was appropriate for a post 1945 audience."[4]

In the years since 1945, Jews have featured infrequently in crime and detective stories; when they have appeared, their treatment by authors has borne little resemblance to that of the Golden Age. Gratuitous antisemitic remarks have disappeared and, most glaringly, so have the familiar stereotypes. There have been a few exceptions, of course. Art has reflected life again in this regard. There seems to be agreement between analysts that, while isolated antisemitic incidents have occurred and continue to do so, there has been a marked absence of deep-rooted, generalised Jew-hatred. The troubled final years of the British Mandate in Palestine (1945-1948), in particular the King David Hotel bombing and the kidnap and hanging of two British soldiers by Irgun extremists, elicited the strongest public response against Jews since the Russian Revolution (including riots in major cities and the desecration of synagogues). The period even saw the temporary re-emergence of Fascist activity under Oswald Mosley. Significantly though, such reactions were short-lived. A number of surveys have pinpointed the persistence of institutionalised discrimination against Jews: exclusion from certain traditionalist organisations or tennis and golf clubs, tacit Public school quotas, under-representation in City circles and banking, the tendency of newspapers to highlight Jewish connections to scandals, and so on. More disturbing on occasion has been the growth of anti-Zionism within the Political Left and among some student groups after the 1967 Six Day War and Israel's incursions into Lebanon in 1982. Predictably, Jews have remained targets of extreme Right-wing groups like the National Front. "There cannot be a Jew in the land who has never overheard or been at the receiving end of an antisemitic jibe," writes Stephen Brook, "[yet] whether such remarks constitute antisemitism is a moot point."[5]

Rarely have any of these factors been much more than irritants for the post-war community. As W.D. Rubinstein has noted, there has been a general increase in tolerance for unorthodox behaviour and lifestyles and a parallel diminution of one-eyed British nationalism over the past 50 years. He believes that knowledge of the Holocaust has struck a deeply responsive chord with an essentially fair-minded British public while, more prosaically, hostility towards other minorities has displaced hostility to the now well-established, and mainly middle-class, Jewish community. Brook cites blacks and Asians as much more obvious scapegoats, while deep-seated dislike of Germans, even Roman Catholics, tends to outweigh negative feelings about Jews.[6] "Britain harbours much stronger feelings against Catholics than against Jews. There's no Guy Fawkes night here for Jews."[7]

This spasmodic and isolated incidence of overt anti-semitism is reflected in occasional "regressions" by crime writers. Among the more surprising (in the light of revelations of the Final Solution) is Nicholas Bentley's *The Tongue-tied Canary* (1948), which includes a fleeting reprise of the Jew-Nazi collaboration myth. The far-fetched yarn tells of a Special Branch campaign to track down one Bruno Rankel, former P.O.W. and *post-1945* organiser of the underground Hitler Youth Movement. At various points in the narrative, the Buchanesque investigator trails a suspect described as "Jewish looking" ("his teeth were rotten, the whole lot of them; unusual for a Jew, and there was no doubt at close quarters, that that's what he was"); encounters (for no apparent reason other than "atmosphere") "a thin middle-aged Jewish woman who seemed burdened with sorrows" in a shady Soho restaurant; and ultimately engages in a physical tussle with an elderly Jewish woman-member of a Nazi gang! (p.32, 85, 209, 215, 220).

Occasional evocations of the Jew as moneylender/usurer continue to surface for more than a decade after 1945. An apparently unregenerated Freeman Wills Crofts (admittedly a writer described by Symons as "humdrum") unashamedly dispatches the unscrupulous Ben Isaacs in the unimaginatively-titled "Case of the Avaricious Moneylender" (*Murderers Make Mistakes*, 1947). "If ever a man deserved his fate, Isaacs had done so," writes Crofts; it turns out that he had been "bleeding" his killer for years (p.83). Ten years on, a (presumably Jewish) pawnbroker, Lew, has traded for years "without a complaint," notwithstanding his habit of overcharging on interest, in Margery Allingham's *Hide My Eyes* (1958). (Lew disappears from his Deban Street premises, leaving his office in a mess and a bloodstain on the floor.) The assumption that Jewish moneylending frequently complemented a wider financial interest resurfaces in *Meet the Picaroon* (1958) by John Cassells (a pseudonym of W. Murdoch Duncan). Ludovic Saxon, a.k.a. "The Picaroon," is a cross between Raffles and Charteris' "The Saint," equally at ease on either side of the law, and boasting an intimate knowledge of London gangland which renders him invaluable to Scotland Yard. One of Saxon's associates is a shrewd pawnbroker:

Moshe Lipski was old and bearded, ancient as the tribes of Israel themselves. A black skull cap covered his shock of grey, frizzy hair, and his long beard was streaked with white. He was peering at something which he held in the palm of his yellow hand, and he did not raise his head as the door opened. Instead he said, "Sixteen shillings I giff you. More than that I rob myself."

The little man who stood in front of him yelped. "Sixteen bob. 'Ave an 'eart, Moshe. That there ring was my grandmother's" . . .

"Sixteen shillings," the old man said in a weary voice. "Of all the perishin' Ikes in London, Moshe, you're the worst. Make it a quid an'—."

"Sixteen shillings," said the flat voice. The old man turned away. (p.28)

Lipski lives in dingy premises in Stague Street which belie the success of his pawnbroking business—itself a camouflage for an even more lucrative involvement in jewellery smuggling.

Moshe Lipski had again fixed his jeweller's glass to his eye to examine the ring he had accepted. "Sixteen shillings," he said. "To do this I am a fool. No one else giffs more than twelve, but always it iss the same. I will die a pauper. By the God of Abraham I mean it to you."

The Picaroon smiled in the darkness. "Moshe, you're a fake and a fraud. There can't be twenty men in London wealthier than you are."

Moshe Lipski shrugged. "Now you mock me," he sighed. "It iss the way of the world." (p.31)

Lipski has a reputation for thoroughness: "When old Moshe handled a job nothing ever came unstuck at the last moment" (p.9). So he is more than disconcerted when one of his couriers, Li Jacobs, is murdered by an underworld czar whilst carrying the priceless Chenault emeralds from Dover to Antwerp. "There are risks," concedes "the old Jew," hinting that criminous activity was rather easier in the "good old days." "The Customs, the police. Then there are the gangs. They are active just now. They put 'Young Harry' down only three weeks ago, and Mankiwitz" (p.8). Also active in the milieu inhabited by Saxon, Lipski and Li Jacobs, is a shady firm of commission agents, Kullman & Stein (formerly Morris, Meynell & Stein), reportedly prepared to "buy or sell almost anything there's money in" (p.102).

Publishers Wright & Brown, who continued to provide readers with "new" titles (i.e. heavily edited, updated and otherwise revised versions of earlier books) by the late John G. Brandon for two decades after his death, issued the multiply offensive—indeed, Sydney Horler-like—*Death of a Socialite* as late as 1957. The novel features a singlemindedly homicidal Japanese drug baron, Nagato Myako, who systematically double-crosses and exterminates his former partners in crime. Brandon pulls no punches in his description of the sinister Myako ("All these yellow characters have the name of being tricky and the last War taught us a thing or two about this particular man's race," ventures an investigating police-sergeant), but his racial reservations transcend the orient. Myako's cohorts include Lisa d'Aragon, a beautiful adventuress from Brazil (she "unquestionably [has] coloured blood in her veins"), a prosperous merchant from Rotterdam ("a typical Dutchman in type and countenance, with light-coloured eyes, fair hair and carrying fat to the point of obesity"), Aaron Lee ("a particularly unpleasant specimen of the gangster tribe . . . believed by most to be a full-blooded gipsy"), and three unsavoury Jews, Isadore Granfeldt, Ike Shaumberg and Barnet Sempel. The well-heeled and socially prominent Granfeldt is found ("in full evening dress") in Duke Street, shot through the temple; East End thug Shaumberg ("wizen-faced,

under-sized, flashily-dressed" and "vicious-looking") is strangled horribly by his former boss; Aldgate restaurateur-*cum*-dope
pusher Sempel survives to "assist the police with their inquiries"
(p.27, 79, 125, 136). An unintended highlight of *Death of a
Socialite* is Brandon's wide-eyed treatise on the dire effects of
marijuana use; warning that smoking the drug results in "blood-
lust, in the most horrible forms," a police medical officer suggests, in all seriousness, that its popularity amongst Mexicans
probably accounts for "half the stabbings and killings and the
rest of it to which that people are so prone . . ." (p.27).

Other less-than-pleasant Jewish characters in post-war
detective stories include the abrasive and grasping Madame
Alfrege in Agatha Christie's *The Hollow* (admittedly Christie's
last significant "lapse" in this regard. See Chapter 3). Joe
Coburn is the "short, fat, red-faced" manager of the seedy "Hide
and Seek" nightclub in the northern English town of Manville.
When a desperate young woman employee begs Coburn for a
salary advance, he brutally offers her "the sack" instead
(Richard Goyne, *The Man in the Trilby Hat*, 1946, p.14, 17, 19).
The Machiavellian John Coleby is believed to be Jewish in J.
Jefferson Farjeon's *The Oval Table* (1946). Coleby is a fund-
raiser for the "Society for the Promotion of Jewish Literature,"
and in that capacity he attracts the attention of a rural vicar and
his wife. (The vicar has an active interest in converting Jews.)
The amoral Coleby proceeds to blackmail the clergyman (p.127,
131). In *Death in Dark Glasses* (1952), George Bellairs seems to
be implying that a "smart alec" lawyer is Jewish: Mr Meager is
"swarthy with a look of the Middle East about his face and hair."
Overdressed ("just as if he attended weddings every day"),
Meager hisses "like a cobra" when he speaks (p.201-03). The
otherwise highly entertaining *Murder Pluperfect* (1970), by
Kenneth Giles, contains a slightly jarring throwback to a less
language-sensitive era. In the course of investigating a century-
old West country murder, a Scotland Yard detective encounters
an American folklorist, and muses on the propensity of "Brook-
lyn Jews" to take culture too seriously, "wringing the last drop
out of it before presenting the dessicated remains to some
museum and the rest to a publisher." (The reference is mild
enough, but surely the implicit linking of Jews with academic

acquisitiveness and scholastic predatoriness is unnecessary.)

Brook distinguishes two distinct attitudes towards Jews which he believes have persisted throughout the past two generations: the "Snobbish" and the "Yobbish." According to the first, the Jew is frankly lacking in "class" and "not one of us."[8] This is, of course, merely a continuation of the well-entrenched dislike of the Jew-parvenu, a dislike arguably aggravated by the general *embourgeoisement* of Anglo-Jewry since the war. The "snobbish" attitude is encapsulated in Joanna Cannan's toned-down variant on the nouveau-riche stereotype in *Murder Included* (1950). The upwardly mobile Mr and Mrs Rose (formerly Rosenbaum) are paying guests at a genteel country property, Aston Park. Cannan's portrayal of them is incisive but not unsympathetic; Sidney Rose "has a fancy to be a country gentleman" and zealously rides to hounds. (" 'There's a lot more in huntin' than killin' a fox, you know . . . Hackin' home after a good day, you're a band of brothers.' He thought of his dropped 'gs,' at last they're beginning to come naturally" [p.88].) That he dresses "to the nines" is an understatement:

Sidney Rose, dark-haired and high-coloured, was wearing riding-breeches and a hacking coat of chestnut brown Harris tweed; his yellow tie was adorned with foxes' masks and hunting whips, a handkerchief to match was in his breast pocket and he wore a yellow waistcoat. His cable-stitch stockings matched his coat. His suede shoes looked and were hand-made. (p.28)

Both Roses dote on the local gentry—in turn, they are sneered at universally as "rather common." Even the servants refer to Mrs Rose as "a lady left on the wrong doorstep" (p.8). Yet, complacent and a bit pretentious though they are, the ultimately harmless couple's hunger for social acceptance is understandable; for all their minor faults, they are generally conceded to be "nice enough."

At a whole other level on the social scale is "Yobbish" Jew-hatred which, says Brook, "stems from the same mentality that has given us in the 1970s and 1980s [and beyond] Paki-bashing and queer-bashing and other exuberances of working class thuggery."[9] Guy Cullingford highlights the persistence of conditioned antisemitism amongst peripheral, and inarticulate, sectors of the British public in *The Whipping Boys* (1958); a stupid London thug, accused of sexually harrassing a young girl, refers to his victim as "some bitch . . . who works for some Sheenies down the road" (p.164).

In the main, post-war writers have preferred to discard outdated generalisations about Jewish financial sleight-of-hand, criminality, unscrupulousness, cunning or vulgarity. In some cases, they have clearly outgrown them. Laurence Meynell would seem to be a case in point. In 1941, Meynell's description of the seedier aspects of Soho and London's theatre district, in *The Creaking Chair,* includes flippant references to cafes run by negroes ("never very far from police surveillance"), brothels, less-than-salubrious businessmen "of Hebraic extraction" who converse "with eloquently expressive hands," a Jewish boxing entrepreneur, and "a vast number of cheap dress shops each with a luscious dark Jewish beauty standing in the doorway" (p.13, 68, 80). It is a much more reflective (dare I say, enlightened?) Meynell who justifies thus his hero's decision not to bring to justice the slayer of a notorious con-man in the post-war *Give Me the Knife* (1954):

I made up my mind to do nothing. It had nothing to do with me. In the last, what is it, ten years? Some eight million people have been murdered in Europe and we none of us sleep any the worse for it. I couldn't see that the death of one more man, and a worthless one at that, mattered all that much. (p.187)

In *Die by the Book* (1966), Meynell touches quite astutely on the compatibility or otherwise of "Jewishness" and "Englishness," and ponders on acculturation. The book details the machinations of a criminous group of international bibliophiles, bent on obtaining and selling a thirteenth-century illuminated manuscript known as the "Mexe Book of Hours." Sidney Umberton, an unsophisticated suburban accountant who happens to be the nephew of one of the world's great book-collectors, becomes an unsuspecting pawn in the complex scheme. Easily hoodwinked, his good-natured co-operation with the conspirators brings about his death.

Meynell portrays Sidney as an enthusiastic assimilationist; he arrives home to wife and three children (in middle class Chesham Terrace) promptly each night, bearing the *Evening Standard,* and treats himself to a quiet half-hour at the local pub before dining late. ("[I]t was an English thing to do . . . nothing could be more traditional or in character.") He does, however, fail to share his wife's love of the "idiot box," subscribing quietly to the view that television was "the greatest self-inflicted wound civilisation had suffered since the invention of gunpowder . . . Inbred in his bones there was the racial consciousness of too much real horror and tragedy for the slick, brittle, potted parody to make much appeal." While unlikely "to suffer, as some of his immediate ancestors had done, in a bloody pogrom," the hapless Sidney (we are told) is yet "vulnerable to the minor hurts of life" (p.28-29). Gretton, one of the conspirators, describes him thus:

Judy's going to tell you he's rather sweet, really . . . Of course he's sweet. He's a sweet little, clever Jew boy. As sharp as you could find 'em in any commercial matter and a dewy-eyed innocent in most other ways. I know the type well. You wouldn't stand a chance of selling him a gold brick in a hundred years. Even if it was a genuine one. He would always know a friend round the corner who would let him have the same article at seven and a half off. But you can sell him friendship. The Jew trying to forget that he's a Jew, struggling to swim in the Gentile sea, is always a lonely creature.

He wants to talk to you, to anybody. He wants to be able to tell you about the Public school he was never at, and how keen he is on cricket (which he has never played), and how much he loves beer (which makes him sick). He wants you to clasp him to your English bosom. Hail fellow, well met, jolly good chums together. Away from his office and the so-much per cent business he's a monumental sucker. And thank God for it. (p.57, 58)

When depicted at all after 1945, Jews are most likely to appear as victims or survivors. Cyril Hare portrays a gifted refugee who applies his talents to the investigation and solution of a country-house slaying in the delightful *An English Murder* (1951). As a Christmas guest at isolated Warbeck Hall, "Dr

Wenceslaus Bottwink, sometime Professor of Modern History at the University of Prague," finds himself pitted against the highly unpleasant son of the house, Robert Warbeck, President of the neo-Fascist League of Liberty and Justice. "He sounds like a Jew," Warbeck sneers, and subsequently proceeds to denigrate Bottwink as a "Jew boy" intent on luring a woman guest back to Palestine. (In the course of the action, we discover that Bottwink is both a Concentration Camp and Ghetto survivor.) Once Warbeck has become a scarcely lamented corpse, Bottwink applies his "foreign" lens to the puzzle—and uncovers the truth, thanks to his perceptions of what constitutes typical English behaviour (p.7, 12, 30, 38, 48).

Robert Warbeck has an equally unpleasant counterpart in the third of Raymond Postgate's crime novels, *The Ledger Is Kept* (1953). Following the murder of a civil servant at a British atomic plant, suspicion falls on one of the dead man's colleagues, John Blunt. Blunt turns out not to be the culprit, but he is ultimately exposed as Hans Bormann, former Fascist ("one of Mosley's crowd, or indeed, even more violent") and Soviet spy (p.182-84). When an obnoxious former disciple of Mosley disappears while on a sea voyage, one of the ship stewards ("a displaced person from Central Europe") inevitably comes under suspicion, in Leo Bruce's excellent *Dead Man's Shoes* (1958).

More poignant than the murky ends of former Fascists are explorations of the continued suffering of refugees and displaced persons who either remain captives of their pasts, or are victims of British bureaucratic insensitivity. In *Murder Maestro Please* (1952) by Delano Ames, investigations into the shooting of a ne'er-do-well playboy uncover connections to the tragic wartime saga of a family of Jewish musicians; two gifted young women succeed in escaping Poland only to find themselves doubly isolated in a less-than-hospitable Camden Town. Anthony Gilbert, who rendered a murder victim named Sammy Rubinstein distinctly unsympathetic in *Murder by Experts* (1936),[10] makes amends with the portrayal of the unhappy Else Mount in *Death Against the Clock* (1958). Mrs Mount, "a refugee from Hitler's policy of Aryanism," had lost her mother and two young brothers when their hiding place was betrayed, and had seen her first husband shot. Remarried and settled in a provincial English town, she is described as "a tall dark woman, with the remains of a haggard beauty, who would never completely recover from her experiences under the Nazis and the horror and fear of her escape." In the course of the novel, in which Mrs Mount's grim experiences provide a link to the killing of an elderly spinster, the author makes the important point that a frequent by-product of publicising a police investigation must be the unjust revelation of innocent people's personal tragedies or disturbing pasts (p.29, 33-34, 128-29, 177).

Ngaio Marsh, who examined the position of the German-speaking refugee with delicacy, in *Death and the Dancing Footman*, revisits the theme in *Off with His Head* (1956). Although not Jewish, Mrs Bunz, an earnest albeit comic folklorist, fled to England as an anti-Fascist in the 1930s. Questioned by Alleyn about a murder which takes place in the midst of a traditional rural festival, she declares: "I do not care for policemen. My dear husband and I were anti-Nazis. It is better to avoid such encounters" (p.129). Marsh tells us:

She remembered all the things that had happened to her husband and herself in Germany before the war and the formalities that had attended their arrival in England. She remembered the anxieties and discomforts of the first months of the war when they had continually to satisfy the police of their innocuous attitude, and she remembered their temporary incarcerations while this was going on. (p.226)

Two death-camp survivors ponder on Jewish vulnerability and resilience in Len Deighton's thriller *Funeral in Berlin* (1964) while in another Deighton book, *Yesterday's Spy* (1974), an idealistic ex-communist, who had accepted Soviet expansionism without question, ultimately acknowledges, in the face of Stalinist and post-Stalinist antisemitism, that he is a Jew, first and foremost.[11] A Holocaust survivor is an apparent suicide in George Sims' *The Last Best Friend* (1967), and the plot of V.C. Clinton-Baddeley's *Death's Bright Dart* (1967) revolves around the exposure of a former Nazi war criminal. A similar motif appears in two P.D. James novels. A nurse who once worked in a German death-camp is among the characters in *Shroud for a Nightingale* (1971); a series of murders in the more recent *Origi-*

nal Sin (1994) prove to be linked to the wartime slaying of a Jewish family. The solution to *Original Sin* is ultimately provided by Daniel Aaron, a young detective assisting James' series sleuth Commander Adam Dalgliesh.

James' Detective Aaron is an oddity in British crime fiction. James Yaffe, who has compiled a survey of the "Jewish detective story" in America—i.e. novels featuring consciously Jewish sleuths (like Kemelman's Rabbi Small, Telushkin's Rabbi Winter, Richard Fliegel's Shelley Lowenkopf or Andrew Bergman's Jake LeVine)—contends that the phenomenon has been made possible by growing Jewish self-confidence in the wake of the creation of the state of Israel and the growth of ecumenicism. However, Yaffe has discovered only one practitioner of the overtly "Jewish detective story" in England. (Europe, of course, has a much smaller population, but he believes that Jews still feel less secure there than in America, major post-war changes notwithstanding.) S.T. Haymon's books feature a Norwich policeman, Benjamin Jurnet, in love with a Jewish woman who insists he convert to Judaism. In the course of the series, Inspector Jurnet studies for conversion and, simultaneously, undergoes a spiritual crisis which brings his personal relationship with "Jewishness" into relief. The Haymon novels include *Death and the Pregnant Virgin* (1980), *Stately Homicide* (1984), *Ritual Murder* (1982, in which mediaeval accusations that Jews killed William of Norwich reverberate in the killing of a choirboy), *Death of a God* (1987), and *A Very Particular Murder* (1989).[12]

One of the most likeable (and ultimately tragic) characters in any of the gifted Ruth Rendell's novels is Vivien, far and away the most "normal" member of the bizarre commune featured in *A Fatal Inversion* (1987; published under Rendell's *nom-de-plume,* Barbara Vine). A devotee of alternative therapies and meditation and strongly opposed to formal education, Vivien has worked as a children's nanny and spent time on a kibbutz, and seeks to discover in her own way "what she was doing in the world, what the meaning of life was, and to learn how to be good." Believing it wrong to live on social security benefits, Vivien contributes practically to her fellow residents' well-being by baking bread, cleaning and doing their laundry. As the action of the book spins out of control, she becomes more and more the sole voice of sanity and reason. Also filling the role of rational "touchstone," to whom her amateur investigator lover can turn for common sense advice, is the highly intelligent and liberated Rachel in Ruth Dudley Edwards' *The School of English Murder* (1990). One of the book's more enjoyable passages is a dialogue between Rachel and her gentile lover, Robert, in which she gleefully accuses him "of having a capacity for guilt that is positively Jewish" (p.89). The recent vogue for mystery novels set in mediaeval England has seen occasional, atmosphere-evoking references to Jews. P.C. Doherty, for instance, highlights contemporary perceptions of Jewish sagacity in *An Ancient Evil* (1994); Royal clerk Alexander McBain chooses to eat only white bread, having been advised by a Jew physician from Salerno that "rye bread gives you strange dreams" (p.63). American writer Faye Kellerman, similarly, cleverly studies the situation of Jewish "conversos" in Elizabethan England in *The Quality of Mercy* (1989).[13] Almost invariably, such references are positive and, as a general rule, any Jew in a modern British detective/crime novel is likely to have been treated with insight or sympathy. Traditional derogatory stereotyping is a relict of an increasingly remote past, rendered obsolete by fashion and heightened reader sensibility.

Conclusion

At the outset of *Victims or Villains,* I indicated that my aim was to examine in some detail the incidence and extent of anti-semitic characterisations, remarks or references in English detective fiction, specifically, although not exclusively, during the Golden Age. My survey proceeded from the assumption that the treatment of Jews in crime and detective fiction might provide us with accurate insights into the real-life perceptions and attitudes of the reading public of two or three generations ago. Interpreting the evidence has been complicated by the fact that historians are in disagreement as to the true significance and profundity of British antisemitism during the first half of this century. One school of thought has argued that organised Jew-hatred was confined to the "lunatic fringe," generally marginal to British society as a whole, and usually temporal in nature (i.e. linked to specific factors such as refugee immigration in the 1930s, and relatively transient). Another school suggests that twentieth-century *Judeophobia* was and is far more widespread, part of a long-standing and deep-seated English tradition. By logical extension, deductions about the significance/profundity of antisemitic generalisations in the detective story must take into account whether such statements are superficial, the echo (more often than not) of ignorance or insensitivity, or the literary manifestation of a much more malignant and pathological world view.

Utilising multiple examples culled from the literature, my study has examined the treatment of Jews in British crime and detective writing, from the form's beginnings (with Conan Doyle) to the post-1945 period, paying particular attention to the work of the 1920s and 1930s. In what I have referred to as the "Prelude" to the Classic era (bounded by the advent of Sherlock Holmes and the end of the Great War), the founding fathers and mothers of the genre formulated the fundamental features of the standard whodunit, such requisites as the omniscient investigator and his/her less able offsider, the closed circle of suspects, the "least likely" culprit, the "red herring," the "genteel" slaying of an (often) unlamented victim, a predictable (usually comfortable) social *milieu* inhabited by standardised and readily recognisable supporting characters. Spotted regularly, if often fleetingly, among the last were Jews, usually depicted according to entrenched literary convention, and as we have seen, in tune with popular contemporary prejudices. Important pioneers like Hornung, Orczy, Le Queux, Oppenheim, Fletcher and Freeman articulated deliberately or otherwise widespread perceptions of Jews. Generally defined and disdained as they were by the British public as either excessively influential wealthholders or cunning immigrant paupers (in both cases, essentially "alien" and therefore untrustworthy), it is hardly surprising that the stock characterisations of Jews, enshrined in fiction during this period, were predicated on their relation to money.

The dominant image of the Jew throughout the early period (and, indeed, throughout the entire time-frame surveyed) was the Jew-financier, whether as banker, investor, moneylender, pawnbroker or "lowly" dealer. This image clearly derived from outdated and invalid perceptions that Jews dominated financial markets both at home and abroad. Related recurring images included the Jew-megalomaniac bent on affecting the fate of nations, the Jew-criminal (be it petty pickpocket, embezzling "individualist," gangster or underworld czar), and the Jew-*parvenu*. Frequently these stereotypes overlapped, the usurious moneylender, for instance, often functioning on the periphery of the underworld, as "fence" or confidence trickster. The Jew-plutocrat, outwardly a pillar of the English establishment, occasionally even boasting a knighthood, sometimes dabbled on the quiet in espionage or crime. (Orczy's Sir Leopold Messinger is a case in point; later manifestations include Greene's Sir Marcus or Horler's Wilfred Abrahams and Isidore Sava.)

These images recurred frequently enough for them to have become established stereotypes within the genre by 1920, and they proliferated and multiplied during the interwar years as the market for detective stories expanded, and as Jewish visibility became more pronounced and problematic. John Buchan is credited with furnishing popular literature with the Jew-revolutionary prototype and, in the wake of October 1917, the Jew-as-Bolshevik made regular appearances hand-in-glove with the older stereotypes. In response to renewed fears that Jewish capitalists might be engaged in dastardly plots to take over the world (fears fuelled by dissemination of *The Protocols of the Elders of Zion* and the propaganda of emergent Fascist groups), a number of writers reactivated Jewish "conspiracy theory," some even indulging irrational fantasies about collusion between Jew-plutocrats and Jew-socialists to further undermine a social fabric severely frayed by the Great War. In the 1920s, residual anti-Germanism and resentment at apparent familial financial links between Anglo and German Jewry, ensured reappearances of the Jew as German spy or as war-profiteer (Oppenheim's Mrs Abrahams or Yates' Dunkelsbaum, for instance). Dislike of Jews encompassed derogatory descriptions of them as sexually promiscuous and physically repellent, even deformed or racially inferior. Occasionally, the simple depiction of a character who had unattractive physical attributes and a foreign-sounding name was enough to make the reader presume "Jewishness." (The yellow-faced lawyer Maurice Meister, in Edgar Wallace's *The Ringer* [1927], is a cogent example.) Discontent at influxes of refugees into England after 1933 manifested itself in updated profiteering myths (the Jew as black-marketeer), claims that Jews were fomenting war to avenge themselves on the Third Reich, charges of fifth-column activity, even quite surreal accusations of Jew-Nazi collaboration (as in Sydney Horler at his most outrageous)!

While the employment of such stereotypes and descriptions was the norm in the Golden Age (persisting into the World War II years), it would be inaccurate, and unjust to more "sensitive" craftspersons, to deny that less negative references surfaced in the literature from time to time, even prior to the rise of Nazism. I have noted A.E.W. Mason's thoughtful comment on the Dreyfus case and how, a decade or so on, Sayers, Christie and Cox all went "against the grain" in depicting relatively sympathetic Jewish characters (as did Allingham, Maugham, and Hichens on occasion). The course of the 1920s and 1930s saw a subtle and gradual move away from the portrayal of Jewish *group* involvement in crime and conspiracy (by Buchan,

McNeile, Chesterton, *et al*) to a preferred focus on wrong-doing by Jewish *individuals*. 1933 can be seen as something of a watershed; by that date, a number of writers were straining at the restrictions of conforming to the rigid formulae of the whodunit (such as the cliched treatment of sinister Orientals and Jew-saboteurs). Much more importantly, the plight of continental Jewry nudged a number of previously complacent writers into revaluating the standard, unnecessary employment of Jewish stereotype. The incidence of gratuitous references to Jews dropped markedly from that time. While the persistence of the fictional Jew-villain testified to ongoing dislike of Jews amongst the British public, such depictions were offset more and more by increasingly sophisticated examinations of the Jew in pre-war and wartime situations. Ngaio Marsh, Christianna Brand, and Raymond Postgate produced particularly sympa-thetic portraits of Jews under duress. Negative images continued to appear, with sharply diminished frequency, in the decade or so after 1945, but these were more than balanced by characterisa-tions which sought to examine aspects of Jewish identity or the situation of the Jew (sometimes still a first-generation immi-grant) in English society. Striking instances can be found in the work of Laurence Meynell and Anthony Gilbert.

As regards the Golden Age specifically: Jews appear, or are mentioned, with undeniable frequency in the writing of the period. Given the wide range of titles and authors surveyed (and found wanting) by the current study, it would be difficult to argue with Dilys Wynn's disquiet at the pervasiveness of seem-ingly antisemitic sentiment, or with her finding that "most of the better-known authors are guilty of it."[1] Well-embedded though negative stereotypes and literary conventions were in the mind-sets of a number of influential precursors of the Golden Age, it is also indisputable that they were reinvigorated and multiplied alarmingly during the interwar years, parallel with the intensifi-cation of *Judeophobia* abroad—and at home. Similar expres-sions of Jew-dislike manifested themselves elsewhere in British popular culture, notably as racist caricatures in light periodicals such as *London Opinion* and *Punch;* on radio, stage and music-hall; in non-crime fiction, comic books and picture postcards; even occasionally in the movies. Although George Orwell once

contended that "Jew-jokes" disappeared from cards and vaude-
ville routines following the rise of Hitler, Kushner maintains that
humour of this sort continued throughout the war (only slightly
modified by "the realisation that a degree of constraint was necessary.") He also cites a 1944 complaint regarding "increasing
antisemitism" in home-grown films. In mainstream fiction,
enlightened novels such as Phyllis Bottome's *The Mortal Storm*
or Peter Mendelssohn's *Across the Dark River* competed for
sales with such "throwbacks" as Richard Hillary's *The Last
Enemy* (presenting the Jew as cringing coward) or Elizabeth
Kyle's *The White Lady* (the Jew as all-powerful financier).[2]

In terms of art reflecting life, the congruence of character
types portrayed and perpetuated by crime writers (and other pur-
veyors of popular culture) with mainstream perceptions of Jews
(as recorded by historians like Kushner or contemporary
observers like Sidney Salomon) tends to confirm the importance
and reliability of literature as socio-historical evidence. I can
only agree with William O. Ayedelotte's succinct finding: "the
interest of detective stories to the historian is that they shed light
on the people who read them."[3] Put simply, the portrayal of Jews
in light fiction seems to reflect widespread attitudes to them as a
group and individuals in real life; in terms of the historical
debate over British antisemitism, it provides evidence of what
appears to have been an extensive public disdain or, at least,
misconception.

While speculating on the degree to which crime fiction
reflected or reflects public perception, it is worth considering
the obverse: the degree to which sentiments expressed in crime
writing impacted on, and influenced, readers' views and prejudices. By way of a particularly extreme example of the
process, George Mosse has claimed that Adolf Hitler's personal conception of Jews based itself on stereotyped depictions
in a popular German bestseller of the late nineteenth century,
Die Buttnerbauer. Mosse argues that the first impressions
Hitler gained from his reading were reinforced by encountering
traditionally-garbed Jews in the streets of Vienna years later.[4]
More pertinently, Watson has tentatively posited a link
between McNeile's full-on nationalism (including Bulldog
Drummond's black-shirted patriots who mete out summary jus-

tice to Jew-Bolsheviks and other leftists in *The Black Gang*) and the philosophy and regalia of 1930s Fascists. "It is a matter of conjecture whether the rise of Fascism in Europe and the outbreak of the second world war were helped along by the large section of society that found echo in [the writing of Golden Age nationalists]," Watson observes.[5] Whether or not the troubled public profile of the Jew in the interwar years was reinforced by persistent hostile barbs in the preferred recreational reading of the day is likewise open to question, although it is not unlikely that sentiments expressed enjoyed some credibility among readers who had little or no other contact with Jews.

At the same time, I would suggest that it is possible to overemphasise both the abundance of fictional examples of Jew-dislike, or their significance. Wynn is clearly guilty of overstatement when she contends that such references amount to "a virulent, insidious attempt to verbally annihilate a race."[6] Jews appear throughout the literature in time-honoured conspiratorial, flashy, criminous or un-English guises, even very occasionally as unsuspected hero. Rarely, however, is the Jewish character more than a supporting player—on many occasions, he or she is little more than an "extra," the stereotype being employed fleetingly, as a kind of shorthand, either to elicit an immediate response or to provide atmosphere or colour to a scene or description. Recurrently, villainous Jews tend to rank more often among underworld underlings and accomplices, or dubious characters dabbling at the margins of subversive activity, than as truly evil criminal masterminds though, of course, a number of significant exceptions are noted in the text. It is even more rare for the Jew to be the whodunit's culprit notwithstanding that his or her involvement in subsidiary nefarious doings is often exposed as a result of the primary investigation. "The unpleasant Jew was there, then, simply as a cardboard figure of villainy, but not as the villain," writes W.D. Rubinstein of the period under review.[7] The most striking of the few instances where the Jew does turn out to be the murderer occurs in Anthony Berkeley Cox's *The Silk Stocking Murders;* the character Pleydell is a very skillful reworking of the traditional Jew-financier stereotype. Furthermore, it might well be argued that the mere inclusion in a detective story of a criminal character who happens to be Jewish does not, in itself, constitute antisemitism. "Fiction is conflict," writes American crime novelist Richard Martin Stern:

[A]nd almost inevitably there must be less-than-sympathetic characters. If, for reasons of storyline, one of those less-than-sympathetic characters must be black, hispanic, oriental, or any other race, so be it . . . each ethnic group or background has its share of admirable, abominable, foolish, heroic, untrustworthy, and thoroughly dependable persons, and to believe otherwise, in my opinion, is to wear blinders.

(Stern warns, however, that any writer who "goes out of his way" to treat ethnic characters as sordid, foolish or criminal, is guilty of stereotyping.)[8] Jews may have been an object of passing concern or merely a minor irritant for extensive sectors of the English public in the interwar period, but they loomed large on the horizon of very few ordinary Britishers. In the same way, Jews undoubtedly appear frequently in Golden Age fiction, but more often than not they are peripheral to the action.

Neither, of course, should we be led by the recurring presence of caricatured Jews, particularly in the work of those "Golden Agers" who flourished in the 1920s, into the assumption that most detective fiction writers were singlemindedly racist. It should be stressed that Jews were particularly prominent as the only sizeable immigrant group in Britain at the turn of the century and for three or four decades after. As such, they served inevitably as a focus of discontent and publicity, just as subsequent waves of Pakistanis or West Indians have done. Like the Huguenots and Irish before them, refugees from Russia/Poland or Germany/Austria entered "a host society which was ethnically fairly homogeneous and with a strong cultural tradition. Thus . . . significance was attached to the new arrivals out of all proportion to their numbers."[9] Public ambivalence about foreign migrants was reinforced by the fact the newcomers were also Jews, and this ambivalence was reflected in popular reading-matter. While I endorse Wynn's estimate that fictional references to Jews outstrip unflattering descriptions of other ethnic minorities, it would be futile to deny that dagger-wielding Italians, fiery Spaniards, "niggers," drunken Irishmen, grasping Scotsmen, as well as dim-witted country yokels, also make regular appearances. Yet, as Rubinstein suggests, we tend not to draw any inference from their presence regarding writers' personal prejudices against any or all of these groups. Differentiation in the case of Jews obviously grows out of our post-Holocaust awareness of what negative stereotyping could—and did—lead to in Europe.[10]

Agatha Christie, to take the most obvious example, appears to have been, to all intents, a kindly and benign, albeit somewhat complacent, human being who probably had no personal feelings either way towards Jews, but who, unfortunately, lacked either the perceptiveness or wit, or literary flexibility, to transcend the limits of her class and time in this regard. Yet even Christie, it can be conceded, could surprise on occasion (see *Giant's Bread*). Sayers, on the other hand, may well have felt she had an "axe to grind" against Jews, as "alien" beings at odds with her High Church beliefs, yet the majority of the Jewish characters in her novels and stories are insignificant. On the one occasion Sayers looked in detail at Anglo-Jewry (in *Whose Body*), her depiction of the Levy family was not unsympathetic. Elsewhere (and notwithstanding that such popular contributors to the genre as Crofts, Gilbert, Allingham, Rhode, Wade, Adams, MacDonald and Fletcher are all cited in the present study), few if any Golden Age craftspersons seem to have shared the intense personal or ideological dislike of "the Jew" displayed by the xenophobic McNeile, Horler or Freeman, or the paranoid Chesterton.[11] Intrusive, and sometimes distressing, as the characterisations and slurs are, it seems reasonable to ascribe them more to ignorance and insensitivity, even lack of creative flair or a too-scrupulous adherence to tried-and-true literary conventions, than to any real malice or aversion on the part of their creators.[12] Any Jew who appears in the writing of Francis Beeding would seem to be automatically a villain, for example, yet there is no evidence to suggest that Beeding (or, more accurately, the two writers who together operated under that pseudonym) was a Jew-hater in real life. Stereotyped Jewish no-hopers likewise grace the pages of spy-specialist Valentine Williams, yet Stafford notes that Williams "almost worshipped the Reuter family" and was horrified by Nazi treatment of the Jews in the 1930s.[13] Buchan and Oppenheim were both guilty of propagating demeaning antisemitic clichés in their earlier work. Oppenheim compounded the offence by rendering one-dimensional Jewish characters who played more important roles than usual in *The Treasure-house of Martin Hews* and *Aaron Rodd Diviner*. Even so, Buchan and Oppenheim attempted to redress the balance in *A Prince of the Captivity* and *Last Train Out*, respectively. When read today, the disturbing racist fantasies of Sydney Horler are easily eclipsed by the insightful analysis of the Jewish situation in the greatly superior writing of Anthony Berkeley Cox. It should be noted that a number of the more enduring late arrivals to the Golden Age (such as Innes, Blake, Marsh, Crispin, and Hare) discarded or rejected the use of such offending stereotypes well before some of their veteran peers.

Judging by the continued popularity of Hercule Poirot, Miss Marple, Lord Peter Wimsey, and other lesser sleuths, Golden Age detective novels and stories have an appeal and a timelessness which vastly outweigh their consequence as literature. Part of that appeal undoubtedly has to do with nostalgia and an enthusiasm for a more genteel, less complicated past. Yet, as accessible specimens of popular culture, they remain valid and revealing resources for students or social historians intent on exploring and understanding day-to-day Britain in the first half of this century. The England in which the bulk of the books and stories are set is substantially a neverland; nevertheless, there are frequent echoes or hints at the darker and less romantic aspects of its functioning. A rigid class system and unquestioning often unthinking endorsement of King, Country and a dubious status quo, may well have nurtured a superficial external stability, but it also masked a plethora of inequities, intolerances, misconceptions and injustices just below the surface.

The multiple, usually negative, references to Jews in crime and detective fiction prior to World War II are a prime example. They illuminate and contribute to a general picture of widespread dislike or ignorance, or at the very least, insensitivity, towards Jews in interwar Britain. As well, they provide telling, if indirect, comment on the standing of the Jew within British society before the cataclysmic events in Europe (a) alerted Britain and the rest of the world to the devastating consequences of anti-semitism unchecked, and (b) impelled ordinary people to rethink, revise, and reassess their attitudes.

Notes

Introduction

1. For a particularly incisive analysis of Golden Age escapism as a natural reaction to the trauma of the Great War (comparable, in that regard, to Restoration comedy), see Robert Barnard's fine article, "The English Detective Story" in *Whodunit? A Guide to Crime, Suspense and Spy Fiction,* ed. H.R.F. Keating, New York, 1982, p.30-36.

2. Colin Watson, *Snobbery with Violence: English Crime Stories and Their Audience,* London, 1971, p.95. For lighthearted contemporary acknowledgements of the immense popularity of the detective story, see two short stories by enduringly popular non-mystery writers of the period: "Strychnine in the Soup" by P.G. Wodehouse (*Mulliner Nights,* 1933) and "The Mystery of Oaklands" by Richmal Crompton (*William,* 1929).

3. George Grella, "Murder and Manners: The Formal Detective Novel," in *Dimensions of Detective Fiction,* ed. Larry L. Landrum, Pat Browne & Ray B. Browne, Bowling Green, Ohio, 1976, p.37.

Grella dubs the detective novel "one of the last outposts of the comedy of manners in fiction." In tune with the national literary heritage (he believes), it "avoids and condemns the existence of violence, disorder or anti-social action, favouring instead wholeness, harmony and social integration, the stable virtues of an essentially benevolent and correct society." *ibid.,* p.55.

4. See: Watson, p.95; Robin Winks, "Introduction" to *Detective Fiction: A Collection of Critical Essays,* Englewood Cliffs, New Jersey, 1980, p.8; LeRoy Lad Panek, *An Introduction to the Detective Story,* Bowling Green, Ohio, 1987, p.120-43; Julian Symons, *Bloody Murder: From the Detective Story to the Crime Novel. A History,* Harmondsworth, Middlesex, 1974, p.105-40; Ernest Mandel, *Delightful Murder: A Social History of the Crime Story,* London, 1984, p.22-30. Howard Haycraft, *Murder for Pleasure: The Life and Times of the Detective Story,* New York, 1941, limited the Golden Age to 1918-1930 (although, of course, he was writing only a decade on). Robert Barnard extends the period to include the First World War years

(Robert Barnard, "The Golden Age," in *Hatchards Crime Companion: 100 Top Crime Novels Selected by the Crime Writers' Association,* ed. Susan Moody, London, 1990, p.63-68).

5. For a useful overview of the Golden Age, see Earl F. Bargainnier, *The Gentle Art of Murder: The Detective Fiction of Agatha Christie,* Bowling Green, Ohio, 1980, p.4-20.

6. Colin Watson, "Mayhem Parva and Wicked Belgravia," in *Crime Writers: Reflections on Crime Fiction,* ed. H.R.F. Keating, London, 1978, p.55.

7. See Robert E. Briney, "Sinister Orientals," in Steinbrunner, Chris & Penzler, Otto, *Encyclopaedia of Mystery and Detection,* New York, 1976, p.302-04; Robin W. Winks, "Sinister Orientals: Everybody's Favourite Villains," in *Murder Ink: The Mystery Reader's Companion,* ed. Dilys Wynn, New York, 1977, p.491-93; Watson, *Snobbery with Violence,* p.109-36.

8. See Chapter 2, "Days of Empire: British Imperialism," in Frankie Y. Bailey's *Out of the Woodpile: Black Characters in Crime and Detective Fiction,* New York, 1991, p.11-28. The short stories appear respectively in Conan Doyle's *The Casebook of Sherlock Holmes* (1927) and Chesterton's *The Wisdom of Father Brown* (1914).

9. Dilys Wynn, "Antisemitism and the Mystery," in *Murder Ink: Revived, Revised, Still Unrepentant,* New York, 1984, p.133.

10. Colin Holmes, *Antisemitism in British Society 1876—1939,* London, 1979, p.214.

11. Watson, *Snobbery with Violence,* p.123, 135.

12. W.D. Rubinstein, *A History of the Jews in the English-speaking World: Great Britain,* London, 1996, p. 292-93.

13. Wynn, p.133.

14. Tony Kushner, *The Persistence of Prejudice: Antisemitism in British Society during the Second World War,* Manchester, 1989, p.107-33.

15. Holmes, p.219.

16. Watson, "Mayhem Parva and Wicked Belgravia," p.48.

17. Claude Cockburn, *Bestseller: The Books That Everyone Read 1900—1939,* London, 1972, p.2-3.

Cockburn goes on to note—tellingly: "A person may truthfully claim that he is not bothered by . . . this or that tendency expressed in a book . . . But the fact that, for example, antisemitism in the book does not bother him is already proof that he is so uncivilised as to be incapable of realising that antisemitism is disgusting, dangerous and anti-social." *ibid.*, p.10.

18. Gina M. Mitchell & Colin Holmes, "In his Image: a Study of Jews in the Literature of Guy Thorne," *Patterns of Prejudice* 9(1), 1975, p.18.

19. Watson, *Snobbery with Violence*, p.135.

20. Symons, p.8-10.

21. Chris Steinbrunner & Otto Penzler, *Encyclopaedia of Mystery and Detection*, New York, 1976; John M. Reilly, ed., *Twentieth Century Crime and Mystery Writers*, 2nd ed., New York, 1985; Jacques Barzun & Wendell Hertig Taylor, *A Catalogue of Crime*, New York, 1971; *Dictionary of Literary Biography: Vol 77. British Mystery Writers 1920—1939*, Detroit, 1989.

22. See Julian Symons, *Criminal Practices: Symons on Crime Writing '60s to '90s*, London, 1994, p.156. Symons identifies a dislike of Jews as part of Chandler's "general illiberality" and notes that the creator of Philip Marlowe once informed publisher Hamish Hamilton that it was only a question of time before gentiles would have to wear armbands on the streets of Los Angeles. Along with the assortment of dagoes, wops, broads, niggers and fags who populate Chandler/Marlowe's California in *The High Window* (1942) are: "a Jew called Morris" who supplies another character with a Colt 32 (p.73); a cynical old pawnbroker "in a tall black skull-cap," with business premises on Santa Monica Boulevard (p.89-90, 192); the unlucky numismatist Elisha Morningstar (who, Marlowe tells us, has "a sort of dry musty smell like a fairly clean Chinaman" [p.52-58]); a no-questions-asked medico, Dr Carl Moss, "a big burly Jew with a Hitler moustache, pop eyes and the calmness of a glacier" (p.172, 214); and "a fat greasy sensual Jew" who frequents a downtown nightclub in the company of a "tall stately bored showgirl" (p.125). Less offensively, *The Big Sleep* (1939) includes a "tall, handsome white-haired Jew in lean dark clothes, with about nine carats of diamonds on his right hand" (p.27); and a small, dark woman (with "the fine drawn face of an intelligent Jewess") who provides Marlowe with details of the rare book trade (p.32).

23. Gina M. Mitchell, "Caricature of the Bulldog Spirit: When Peace seems Dull," *Patterns of Prejudice* 8(5), 1974; Gina M. Mitchell, "John Buchan's Popular Fiction: A Hierarchy of Race," *Patterns of Prejudice* 7(6), 1973; Bryan Cheyette, *Constructions of "the*

Jew" in English Literature and Society: Racial Representations 1875—1945, Cambridge, 1993.

24. David Stafford, *The Silent Game: The Real World of Imaginary Spies,* Revised edition, Athens, Georgia, 1991; James Yaffe, "Is This Any Job for a Nice Jewish Boy? (Jews in Detective Fiction)," in *Synod of Sleuths: Essays on Judeo-Christian Detective Fiction*, Metuchen, New Jersey, 1990.

25. For instance, Gina M. Mitchell, "British Novels Present a New Image of the Jew," *Patterns of Prejudice* 10(5), 1976; Charlotte Lea Klein, "The Changing Image of the Jew in Modern English Literature," *Patterns of Prejudice* 5(2), 1971; Charlotte Lea Klein, "English Antisemitism in the 1920s," *Patterns of Prejudice* 6(2), 1972; John A. Morris, "Fascist Ideas in English Literature," *Patterns of Prejudice* 13(4), 1979; Bryan Cheyette, "Jewish Stereotyping and English Literature 1875—1920: Towards a Political Analysis," in *Traditions of Intolerance: Historical Perspectives on Fascism and Race Discourse in Britain,* ed. T. Kushner & K. Lunn, Manchester, 1989; Edgar Rosenberg, *From Shylock to Svengali: Jewish Stereotypes in English Fiction,* London, 1961; Montagu Frank Modder, *The Jew in the Literature of England: To the End of the 19th Century,* Philadelphia, 1944; Harold Fisch, *The Dual Image: The Figure of the Jew in English and American Literature,* London, 1971.

26. W. D. Rubinstein, Letter to the author, 23 Nov. 1997.

27. Klein, "The Changing Image of the Jew in Modern English Literature," p.27.

28. Mitchell, "British Novels Present a New Image of the Jew," p.26.

29. Cecil Roth, *A History of the Jews in England,* 3rd edition, Oxford, 1964, p.270.

30. W. D. Rubinstein, "Recent Anglo-Jewish Historiography and the Myth of Jix's Antisemitism (Part 1)," *Australian Journal of Jewish Studies* 7(1), 1993, p.41.

31. Tony Kushner, "The Impact of British Antisemitism 1918—1945," in *The Making of Modern Anglo-Jewry,* ed. David Cesarani, Oxford, 1990, p.192; Gisela C. Lebzelter, *Political Antisemitism in England 1918—1939,* New York, 1978, p.27-28; Todd M. Endelman, *Radical Assimilation in English Jewish History 1656—1945*, Bloomington & Indianapolis, 1990, p.191.

32. Rubinstein, Letter to the author.

33. Frank Felsenstein, *Antisemitic Stereotypes: A Paradigm of Otherness in English Popular Culture 1660—1830*, Baltimore & London, 1995, p.1.

Felsenstein refers here to the expulsion of the Jews from England in 1290 (until 1656), the first of several such mass deportations throughout Europe in the Middle Ages. Jews were evicted from most of France in the forteenth century, from Spain and Portugal in 1492-97, and prohibited from living in Russia from the fifteenth to mid-eighteenth centuries. In the case of England, expulsion was in response to royal indebtedness to Jewish moneylenders and to acccusations of Ritual murder. The first known charge of ritual murder against mediaeval Jewry occurred at Norwich with the killing just prior to Easter 1144 of William, a Christian child. Subsequently, the "blood libel" (specifically, the allegation that Jews murdered non-Jews, particularly Christians, in order to obtain blood for Passover or other rituals) spread throughout Europe leading to widespread persecution and multiple massacres. (Another famous English instance, the murder of little Sir Hugh of Lincoln, was "immortalised" in folksong form and by Chaucer.) The most notorious modern recurrence of the Blood libel was the Mendel Beilis Case in Russia in 1911; the myth was also revived in the 1930s by Nazi propagandist Julius Streicher in *Der Sturmer* and by British Fascist Arnold Leese.

Allied to mediaeval claims of ritual murder were allegations that Jews poisoned wells (thus facilitating the spread of the Black Death). The "Wandering Jew" (a mystical figure, cursed because he rebuffed Christ on the way to crucifixion, and doomed to roam the earth until Judgement Day) is a ubiquitous legend which has been traced to the New Testament; the myth flourished during the Middle Ages and still surfaces in modern times. The English connection pointed out by Felsenstein was the first written account of the legend, communicated by an Armenian Archbishop to the monks of St Albans in 1228. For more detail, see Louis Golding, *The Jewish Problem,* Harmondsworth, Middlesex, 1938, p.58-70, 121; Joseph Gaer, *The Legend of the Wandering Jew,* New York, 1961, p.vii-18 *passim.*

34. Leon Poliakov, *The Aryan Myth: A History of Racial and Nationalist Ideas in Europe,* New York, 1974, p.255. Quoted by Geoffrey Field, "Antisemitism with the Boots Off: Recent Research on England," *Wiener Library Bulletin,* 1982, p.26.

35. Rubinstein, "Recent Anglo-Jewish Historiography . . . ," p.45; Geoffrey Alderman, *Modern British Jewry*, Oxford, 1992, p.209-320 & *passim*; Geoffrey Alderman, "Antisemitism in Britain" (Review article), *Jewish Journal of Sociology* 31(2), 1989, p.125.

36. Kushner, "The Impact of British Antisemitism," p.192.

37. Holmes, p.117, 227; Rubinstein, Letter to the author; Endelman, p.206.

38. Elaine R. Smith, "Jewish Responses to Political Antisemitism and Fascism in the East End of London, 1920—1939," in *Traditions of Intolerance: Historical Perspectives on Fascism and Race Discourse in Britain*, ed. Tony Kushner & Kenneth Lunn, Manchester, 1989, p.53.

39. Field, p.43.

40. Lebzelter, p.177; W.F. Mandle, *Antisemitism and the British Union of Fascists,* London, 1968, p.65; Rubinstein, *A History of the Jews in the English-speaking World,* p.28-35 & *passim*.

Chapter 1

1. Rosenberg, p.21-22.

2. Fisch, p.11.

3. Felsenstein, p.2.

4. Fisch, p.13; Olivier Cohen Steiner, "Jews and Jewesses in Victorian Fiction: From Religious Stereotype to Ethnic Hazard," *Patterns of Prejudice* 21(2), 1987, p.25.

5. Rosenberg, p.4.

6. Fisch, p.60-63.

7. Modder, p.350-60, 362.

8. Rosenberg, p.14.

9. Rosenberg, p.14.

10. Field, p.28-29; Elie Halevy, *A History of the English People in 1815*, Book 3, Harmondsworth, Middlesex, 1938, p.83.

By 1850, one-third of the London Jewish community belonged to "the servant-keeping strata of society," and by 1882 (and the beginning of mass immigration from Russia), 15% of London Jewry could be described as upper or upper-middle class, and 42% as middle-class. Endelman, p.73-74.

11. Klein, "The Changing Image of the Jew in English Literature," p.27.

12. Cockburn, p.22-23.

13. Bryan Cheyette, "Neither Black nor White: The Figure of 'the Jew' in Imperial British Literature," in *The Jew in the Text: Modernity and the Construction of Identity,* ed. L. Nochlin & T. Garb, London, 1995, p.35-37; Cheyette, "Jewish Stereotyping and English Literature," p.22-26.

14. H.R.F. Keating, "The Founding Fathers" in *Hatchards Crime Companion,* p.60.

15. Rubinstein, *A History of the Jews in the English-speaking World,* p.460-61; W.D. Rubinstein, Letter to the author, 23 Nov. 1997.

16. Derrick Murdoch, *The Agatha Christie Mystery,* Toronto 1976, p.109-15; H.R.F. Keating, "The Founding Fathers" in *Hatchards Crime Companion: 100 Top Crime Novels Selected by the Crime Writers' Association,* ed. Susan Moody, London, 1990, p.57-62; Symons, *Bloody Murder,* p.81-104.

17. Quoted by Alan K. Russell in "Introduction" to *The Rivals of Sherlock Holmes,* Vol. 2, ed. A.K. Russell, Seacaucus, New Jersey, 1979, p.xiii.

18. Marcia Leveson, "The Mineral Revolution, Fiction and the Jewish Image in South Africa," in *Patterns of Migration 1850—1914: Proceedings of the International Academic Conference of the Jewish Historical Society of England & the Institute of Jewish Studies, University College, London,* ed. A. Newman & S.W. Massil, London, 1996, p.187-96.

19. Rubinstein, *A History of the Jews in the English-speaking World,* p.113.

20. *ibid.,* p.148-49; Holmes, p.113, 117; Field, p.28-29; Alderman, *Modern British Jewry,* p.193.

21. Rubinstein, p.148-52; see also W.D. Rubinstein, "The Anti-Jewish Riots of 1911 in South Wales: a Re-examination," *Welsh History Review,* Dec. 1997.

22. LeRoy Lad Panek, *The Special Branch: The British Spy Novel, 1890—1980,* Bowling Green, Ohio, 1981, p.7.

23. Field, p.28-29.

24. Solomon Grayzel, *A History of the Jews: From the Babylonian Exile to the Present,* Revised edition, New York, 1968, p.554.

25. Rubinstein provides evidence to suggest that White, usually cited as an antisemite, was more ambivalent in his attitudes than generally supposed. At one point, for instance, he was hired by Baron de Hirsch to investigate Jewish conditions in Czarist Russia. Rubinstein,

A History of the Jews in the English-speaking World, p.138-39.

26. Steinbrunner & Penzler, p.23; Barzun & Taylor, p.50.

27. John Atkins, *The British Spy Novel: Styles in Treachery,* New York, 1984, p.49.

28. Vivian D. Lipman, *The Jews in Britain Since 1858,* Leicester, 1990, p.139.

29. Symons, *Bloody Murder,* p.236; Stafford, p.23-29.

30. Steinbrunner & Penzler, p.387.

31. Stafford, p.50; Julian Symons, *Criminal Practices,* p.92.

32. Rubinstein, Letter to the author; Information from Colin Thornton-Smith, 25 Apr. 1998.

33. Symons, *Bloody Murder,* p.100.

34. By Steinbrunner & Penzler, p.188, and Murdoch, p.111, respectively.

35. Steinbrunner & Penzler, *ibid.,* p.48.

36. Cheyette, *Constructions of "the Jew" in English Literature and Society,* p.187-88.

37. *ibid.,* p.193.

38. H.R.F. Keating, *Crime and Mystery: The 100 Best Books,* London, 1987, p.27.

39. Steinbrunner & Penzler, p.83; Owen Edwards, "Chesterton and Tribalism," *Chesterton Review* 6(1), 1979, p.57. Quoted by Cheyette, *Constructions of "the Jew" in English Literature and Society,* p.190.

40. Quoted by Cheyette, *ibid.,* pp.182, 186.

41. Steinbrunner & Penzler, p.49.

42. Cheyette, *Constructions of "the Jew" in English Literature and Society,* p.187-88.

43. Panek, *The Special Branch,* p.17; Standish, p.56.

44. Keating, "The Founding Fathers," p.57; "Haycraft-Queen Definitive Library of Detective-Crime-Mystery Fiction: Two Centuries of Cornerstones 1748-1948," in *Murder Ink: The Mystery Reader's Companion,* ed. D. Wynn, New York, 1977, p.18-22.

45. Quoted by Cheyette, *Constructions of "the Jew" in English Literature and Society,* p.68.

46. Mitchell, "John Buchan's Popular Fiction," p.24, 26; Quoted by Cheyette, *ibid.,* p.62.

47. Stafford, p.63-64.

48. Mitchell, "John Buchan's Popular Fiction," p.27.

Chapter 2

1. Wynn, p.133.

2. Robert Graves & Alan Hodge, *The Long Weekend: A Social History of Great Britain 1918—1939*, London, 1985 [1940], p.300-01; see also Panek, *An Introduction to the Detective Story,* p.120.

3. Endelman, p.194; Malcolm Muggeridge, *The Thirties: 1930-1940 in Great Britain,* London, 1967, p.263-64. Quoted by Field, p.39.

4. Quoted by Sidney Salomon, *The Jews of Britain*, Revised edition, London, 1938, p.224.

5. Salomon, p.220, *passim.*

6. Kushner, *The Persistence of Prejudice,* p.107-14, 117-23, 189, 192, 193.

7. Thurlow, p.27; Shmuel Almog, "Antisemitism as a Dynamic Phenomenon: The 'Jewish Question' in England at the end of the First World War," *Patterns of Prejudice* 21(4), 1987, p.12; Holmes, p.113-26; Field, p.27-29, 32; Alderman, "Antisemitism in Britain," p.126.

8. Sharman Kadish, *Bolsheviks and British Jews: The Anglo- Jewish Community, Britain and the Russian Revolution,* London, 1992, p.244; Holmes, p.143.

9. Holmes, *ibid.*, p.113-26; Field, p.27-29; Thurlow, p.28; Richard Thurlow, "The 'Jew Wise': Dimensions of British Political Antisemitism, 1918-39," *Immigrants and Minorities* 6(1), 1987, p.44-47.

10. Field, *ibid.*, p.28; Thurlow, "Racial Populism in England," p.28-30.

11. Endelman, p.192; Rubinstein, Letter to the author.

12. Cheyette, *Constructions of "the Jew" in English Literature and Society*, p.200.

13. The journals *New Witness* and *G.K.'s Weekly* abound with references by Chesterton (and others) to Jewish plutocrats.

14. Watson, *Snobbery with Violence*, p.131; Holmes, p.217; Michael Finch, *G.K. Chesterton,* London, 1986. Cited by Dean Rapp, "The Jewish Response to G.K. Chesterton's Antisemitism 1911-33," *Patterns of Prejudice* 24(2-4), 1990, p.75.

15. Rubinstein, *A History of the Jews in the English-speaking World,* p.114-16; Maisie Ward, *Gilbert Keith Chesterton*, Harmondsworth, Middlesex, 1958 [1944], p.185-86, 267; Michael Coren, *Gilbert: The Man Who Was G.K. Chesterton*, London, 1989. Cited by Rapp, *ibid.*

16. Margaret Canovan, *G.K. Chesterton: Radical Populist*, New York, 1977, p.136. Quoted by Rubinstein, *ibid.*, p.114-16.

17. Quoted by Cheyette, *Constructions of "the Jew" in English Literature and Society*, p.201.

18. *ibid.*, p.202.

19. Mitchell, "John Buchan's Popular Fiction," p.26.

20. *ibid.*, p.27-30; Cheyette, *Constructions of "the Jew" in English Literature and Society*, p.69.

21. Mitchell, *ibid.*, p.24, 26.

22. Mitchell, "Caricature of the Bulldog Spirit," p.27-28; Richard Usborne, *Clubland Heroes: A Nostalgic Study of Some Recurrent Characters in the Romantic Fiction of Dornford Yates, John Buchan and Sapper,* Revised edition, London, 1974, p.142; Barrie Hayne, "Sapper," in *Twentieth Century Crime & Mystery Writers,* ed. John M. Reilly, New York, 1985, p.788.

23. Gertrude Himmelfarb, "John Buchan: An Untimely Appreciation," *Encounter* 15, 1960, p.49; Alastair Buchan, Letter to *Encounter* 15, 1960, p.83. Both quoted in Mitchell, "John Buchan's Popular Fiction," p.26-28.

24. Usborne, p.98.

25. Mitchell, "John Buchan's Popular Fiction," p.30.

26. Atkins, p.60.

27. Usborne, p.148; Stafford, p.112.

28. Stafford, p.111-12.

29. Mitchell, "Caricature of the Bulldog Spirit," p.29.

30. Quoted *ibid.*

31. *ibid.*, p.30.

32. Mitchell, "Caricature of the Bulldog Spirit," p.27-28.

33. Stafford, p.108; Watson, *Snobbery with Violence,* p.71; Atkins, p.61; Panek, *The Special Branch*, p.79-80.

34. The parity of Greene's "entertainments" to the classic Crime or Detective novel could well be the subject of debate. Barzun & Taylor include *A Gun for Sale* in *A Catalogue of Crime*, p.216. Symons includes remarks on Greene's work in his survey of spy stories in *Bloody Murder,* p.243-44.

35. Fisch, p.88. For more on Beeding and Greene, see Panek, *The Special Branch,* p.84-97, 112-37.

36. Cited by Stafford, p.99.

37. Rubinstein, *A History of the Jews in the English-speaking World*, p.488.

38. Elsewhere in *Stamboul Express,* Greene alludes to the alleged superiority of Jewish business strategies in a confrontation between the Jew Myatt and the English agent Moult:

Moult was not a Jew; he had no subtlety, no science of evasion; if he wished to lie, he would lie, but the lie would be confined to the words; he had no knowledge how the untrained hand gives the lie to the mouth. In dealing with an Englishman Moult found one trick enough; as he introduced the important theme or asked the leading question, he would offer a cigar; if the man was lying, however prompt the answer, the hand would hesitate for the quarter of a second. Myatt knew what the Gentiles said of him: "I don't like that Jew. He never looks you in the face." You fools, he would triumph secretly, I know a trick worth two of that. He knew now, for example, that young Moult was not lying (p.14-15).

39. Salomon, p.137.

40. Fisch, p.88; Rosenberg, p.300.

41. Cited by Stafford, p.98-99.

42. Bill Pronzini, *Gun in Cheek: A Study of "Alternative" Crime Fiction,* New York, 1982, p.121-22; Stafford, p.113-15; Watson, *Snobbery with Violence,* p.85-93.

43. Watson, *ibid.*, p.86, 135.

44. Sydney Horler, *Strictly Personal,* quoted by Watson, *ibid.,* p.135.

45. Stafford, p.115; Panek, *The Special Branch,* p.98. See also Bill Pronzini, *Son of Gun in Cheek,* New York, 1987, p.200.

46. Kushner, *The Persistence of Prejudice,* p.114-15.

47. John Morris, "The Fiction of Dornford Yates: Best-selling Prejudice," *Patterns of Prejudice* 11(4), 1977, p.27-28. Another enormously popular writer in his day, Yates fits marginally into the Crime and Mystery genre. (Barzun & Taylor judge his books—insofar as they are "mysteries"—as belonging "to the perfunctory type in which critical attention cannot linger without unfairness to itself and the author"). In comparing Yates to Buchan and McNeile, Morris detects a similar "sense of a desperate need for enterprise, courage, danger and the preservation of established order." Like his mentors, Yates unashamedly targets foreigners as "the enemy." The Jewish servant of a French nobleman misappropriates his dead master's fortune and

identity in *She Fell Among Thieves* (1935). *ibid.*; Barzun & Taylor, p.447.

48. Evelyn Waugh, *The Diaries of Evelyn Waugh,* ed. Michael Davie, London, 1976, p.423; Harold Nicolson, quoted by Kushner, *The Persistence of Prejudice*, p.109.

49. Kushner, *ibid.*, p.109-10.

50. Cited in Watson, *Snobbery with Violence*, p.135-36.

51. For detail, see Morris, "Fascist Ideas in English Literature," p.23-28.

52. Waugh, p.66, 293; Rosenberg, p.300.

53. Mary Cadogan, *Richmal Crompton: The Woman behind William*, London, 1986, p.117-18; Kay Williams, *Just—Richmal: The Life and Work of Richmal Crompton Lamburn,* Guildford, 1986, p.143-44.

54. Kristin Thompson, *Wooster Proposes, Jeeves Disposes or Le Mot Juste,* New York, 1992, p.34-37.

55. Ted Morgan, *Maugham: A Biography,* New York, 1980, p.140-42.

56. Rubinstein, *A History of the Jews in the English-speaking World,* p.304.

57. A case could be put, as well, that Allingham intended the character Wardie Samson to be recognised according to Jewish stereotype in *Flowers for the Judge* (1936). A former associate of the now-reformed Lugg, Campion's valet, Samson is the rascally but not unlikeable patriarch of a family firm in Camden Town which specialises in manufacturing illegal duplicate keys. Allingham also includes a (presumably) Jewish moneylender in the 1958 book *Hide My Eyes* (see Chapter 5).

Chapter 3

1. H.R.F. Keating, ed., *Agatha Christie: First Lady of Crime,* London, 1977, p.7.

2. Symons, *Bloody Murder,* p.110, isolates Christie, Sayers, Cox and the American S.S. Van Dine (creator of Philo Vance) as the outstanding contributors to crime-writing in the 1920s. In *Watteau's Shepherds: The Detective Novel in Britain 1914-1940,* Bowling Green, Ohio, 1979, p.111, LeRoy Lad Panek calls Cox, arguably, the most important of all contributors to the Golden Age.

3. Gillian Gill, *Agatha Christie: The Woman and Her Mysteries*, New York, 1990, p.89-95; Janet Morgan, *Agatha Christie: A Biography*, London, 1984, p.264-66; Charles Osborne, *The Life and Crimes of Agatha Christie*, London, 1982, p.17, 33, 37, 45, 57, 61, 66, 70-71, 84, 87, 118, 125, 141-42, 165, 193; Robert Barnard, *A Talent to Deceive: An Appreciation of Agatha Christie*, London, 1980, p.23-24.

4. James Brabazon, *Dorothy L. Sayers: a Biography*, London, 1981, p.216-19; Janet Hitchman, *Such a Strange Lady: A Biography of Dorothy L. Sayers*, New York, 1975, p.99-101; Nancy-Lou Patterson, "Images of Judaism and Antisemitism in the Novels of Dorothy L. Sayers," *Sayers Review* 2(2), 1978, p.17-24; Philip L. Scowcroft, "Was Dorothy L. Sayers Racist?" *Sidelights on Sayers*, VII, 1984; Jessica Mann, *Deadlier Than the Male: An Investigation into Feminine Crime Writing*, London, 1981, p.169; Catherine Kenney, *The Remarkable Case of Dorothy L. Sayers*, Kent, Ohio, 1990, p.292-93.

5. Rubinstein, *A History of the Jews in the English-speaking World*, p.303-04.

6. Malcolm J. Turnbull, *Elusion Aforethought: The Life and Writing of Anthony Berkeley Cox*, Bowling Green, Ohio, 1996, p.28, 40, 94, 132.

7. Gill, p.89; Barnard, *A Talent to Deceive*, p.23-24.

8. Osborne, p.17.

9. Barnard cites *Chimneys* as a "first-class romp," by far the best of Christie's "thrillers" (as opposed to her more traditional murder-puzzles), but he decries her "xenophobic remarks" as likely to "make the flesh creep." Barnard, *A Talent to Deceive*, 23-24, 195.

10. Gill, p.89.

11. It is worth noting that in her memoirs (*An Autobiography*, 1977), Christie recalls how, following his demobilisation, her first husband went to work in the City for a financier she calls "Mr Goldstein." She remembers that Archie Christie referred quite casually to his boss as "Old Yellowface" (p.254, 272-73).

12. See Gill, p.91-95, for her analysis of *Giant's Bread*.

13. Christie's husband, Max Mallowan, recalled that Jordan was a Nazi agent who actively undermined British authority in Iraq: "it seemed extraordinary that this artistic and cultured man could succumb to the new Hitlerian regime." Max Mallowan, *Mallowan's Memoirs*, London, 1977, p.87.

14. Osborne, p.70; Rubinstein, *A History of the Jews in the English-speaking World*, p.303; Gill, p.90-91; Barnard, *A Talent to Deceive*, p.24.

15. Barnard, *A Talent to Deceive, ibid.*, p.24.

16. Rubinstein, *A History of the Jews in the English-speaking World*, p.303.

17. Morgan, p.265. Barnard notes that offending remarks in early Christie novels (and in the Sayers canon as well) have never been removed in English reprints, but that they have been silently edited out in later U.S. editions—"which may conceivably be good for race relations but is bad for the social historian." Barnard, *A Talent to Deceive*, p.23.

18. Other "possibly Jewish" characters in latter-day Christie are Professor Eckstein, Britain's most eminent scientist (*Passenger to Frankfurt*, 1970), Ella Zielinsky, secretary to movie star Marina Gregg (*The Mirror Crack'd from Side to Side*, 1962); Colonel Ephraim Pikeaway, head of the Special Branch (*Cat Among the Pigeons,* 1959; *Passenger to Frankfurt; Postern of Fate*, 1973); and business magnate Otto Morgenthal (*They Came to Baghdad*). "Possible Jews" in early (to middle) Christie include the defrauding banker in "The Disappearance of Mr Davenheim" (*Poirot Investigates*, 1924), the wealthy Mr and Mrs Opalsen ("The Jewel Robbery at the Grand Metropolitan," *Poirot Investigates*), the literary agent Rosenkraun (*The Sittaford Mystery*, 1931), sisters Esther and Rachel Lawes in the short story "The Gipsy" (*The Hound of Death and Other Stories*, 1933) and Dr Rosen ("The Four Suspects," *The Thirteen Problems*, 1932). Isaac Pointz and Leo Stein, Hatton Garden diamond merchants, are duped out of a priceless gem in the short story "The Regatta Mystery" (*The Regatta Mystery*, 1939). A detective story writer falls victim to a scam involving Anna Rosenberg, a fictitious "German Jewess" who made a spurious fortune in the second-hand clothes trade, in "Mr Eastwood's Adventure" (*The Listerdale Mystery*, 1934). Another Rosenberg, described as "a disgusting Central European," causes a rift between the flamboyant Basil Blake and his current platinum blonde girlfriend (*The Body in the Library*, 1942, p.29-30). A curio-dealer is described as "a small Jew with cunning eyes" in the early short story "Within a Wall" (*Royal Magazine*, Oct. 1925; reprinted in *While the Light Lasts*, 1997). Hercule Poirot deduces that the great tragic actress Linda Arden, nee Goldenburg, may have had "central European blood in her veins—a strain of Jewish, perhaps" (*Murder on the Orient Express*, 1934, p.184).

19. Gill, p.89-91; Morgan, p.264-65.

20. *ibid.*

21. Gill, *ibid.*, p.89-91; Barnard, *A Talent to Deceive*, p.24.

22. The exceptions are *The Unpleasantness at the Bellona Club* and *The Documents in the Case*. Hitchman (p.100) also exempts *The Nine Tailors*; clearly she has overlooked a passing remark made by Superintendent Blundell in Chapter 2 (Part 3) of that book.

23. Barnard, "The English Detective Story," p.34.

24. Hitchman, p.100.

25. Scowcroft, p.17.

26. It is worth noting that in *Thrones Dominations*, the five chapter fragment of a projected fifth Wimsey-Vane novel by Sayers, recently completed by Jill Paton Walsh, Wimsey is credited with having enjoyed a pre-marital affair with a Jewish opera-star in Vienna. In the course of *Thrones Dominations,* he sponsors the woman's escape to England. For this reader, the liaison seems a little contrived. Swedish academic Marianne Thormahlen, who contributed a recent review of the novel to the *Dorothy L. Sayers Society Bulletin* (136, Apr. 1998), argues: "The trick of reintroducing Peter's former mistress, the Viennese singer, as the persecuted Jewess—the obligatory 1990s Holocaust touch—is beneath the dignity of both authors. . . ."

27. Hitchman, p.100-01.

28. Scowcroft, p.16-17; Patterson, p.23.

29. Rubinstein, *A History of the Jews in the English-speaking World,* p.304, 491; Barbara Reynolds, *Dorothy L. Sayers: Her Life and Soul,* London, 1993, p.378; Letter to the author from Christopher Dean, Chairman of the Dorothy L. Sayers Society, Jan 1997.

30. Letter from Sayers to Sir Wyndham Deedes, quoted in Brabazon, p.216-17.

31. Brabazon, p.219. Contributors to *The Future of the Jews: a Symposium,* ed. J.J. Lynx, London, 1945, included Louis Golding, Sir Norman Angell, and Elizabeth A. Allen. Galley-proofs of Sayers' essay, "The Future of the Jews in Britain," are held at the Marion E. Wade Centre, Wheaton College, Illinois.

32. Brabazon, p.216-18; Patterson, p.21-22; Mann, p.169; Kenney, p.292-93; Rubinstein, *A History of the Jews in the English-speaking World,* p.345-46.

33. Dorothy L. Sayers, *The Man Born to Be King,* London, 1942, p.113.

34. Brabazon, p.217.

35. *Time and Tide,* 6 May 1933.

Chapter 4

1. Ronald A. Knox, "A Detective Story Decalogue," in Introduction to *Best Detective Stories of 1928,* ed. R.A. Knox, London, 1929. Reprinted in *The Art of the Detective Story: A Collection of Critical Essays,* ed. Howard Haycraft, New York 1946, p.195; "The Detection Club Oath," in Haycraft, *ibid.,* p.198.

2. In this regard, it is worth highlighting again the hysterical Eliza Tebbutt's claim that a conspiracy is afoot "to murder all persons of British birth and establish the supremacy of the Jews in England" in Dorothy L. Sayers' *Murder Must Advertise* (1933, p.272). Miss Tebbutt's claim is cited as evidence of her general instability.

3. Rubinstein, *A History of the Jews in the English-speaking World,* p.304; Rubinstein, "Charles Dickens, R. Austin Freeman and the Spirit of London," p.325; W.D. Rubinstein, Communication to the author, 9 Apr. 1998. Similarly, Rubinstein cites the unlikely marriage of Freddie Arbuthnot and Rachel Levy (in Sayers' *Strong Poison*) as "a propos of nothing else in the story," and suggests that Sayers may well have been making "a deliberate point" in the face of escalating European antisemitism. Rubinstein, *A History of the Jews in the English-speaking World, ibid.*

4. Quoted by Cheyette, *Constructions of "the Jew" in English Literature and Society,* p.69-70.

5. Cheyette, *ibid.*; see also Mitchell, "John Buchan's Popular Fiction," p.30.

6. Lebzelter, p.67, 85, 86; Rubinstein, *A History of the Jews in the English-speaking World,* p.204, 212.

7. Thurlow, "Racial Populism in England," p.30.

8. *Daily Telegraph,* 8 Nov. 1935.

9. Golding, p.141, 151.

10. Oliver Sacks, *The Jewish Question,* London. 1937, p.17.

11. Rubinstein, *A History of the Jews in the English-speaking World,* p.313; Endelman, p.194.

12. Kushner, "The Impact of British Antisemitism, 1918-1945," p.194-95.

13. Haycraft, *Murder for Pleasure,* p.198.

14. Margaret Lewis, *Ngaio Marsh: A Life*, London, 1991, p.77.

15. Also conceivably Jewish (although there is no real evidence other than his name) is Alfred Meyer, an unloved theatrical impressario whose head is smashed by a malevolently propelled magnum of champagne in Marsh's *Vintage Murder* (1937).

16. John Dickson Carr was, of course, American. However, he is frequently included in rosters of English Golden Age writers because he lived in Britain during the period in question, and because he specialised in mysteries with English settings. See Panek, *Watteau's Shepherds*, p.145-84.

17. George Orwell, "Antisemitism in Britain," *Contemporary Jewish Record* 8(2), 1945, p.166.

18. Rubinstein, Letter to the author.

19. Kushner, *The Persistence of Prejudice*, p.107-23 *passim*, 131.

20. Orwell, p.170.

21. Colin Holmes, *John Bull's Island: Immigration and British Society 1871-1971,* London, 1988, p.145.

22. Howard M. Sachar, *Diaspora: An Inquiry into the Contemporary Jewish World,* New York, 1985, p.144.

23. Kushner, *The Persistence of Prejudice,* p.118.

24. Bill Pronzini, *Gun in Cheek: A Study of "Alternative" Crime Fiction,* New York, 1982, p.120-22.

25. Kushner, *The Persistence of Prejudice,* p.123.

26. Elizabeth F. Duke, "Manning Coles," in *Twentieth Century Crime and Mystery Writers,* p.184.

27. Rubinstein, Letter to the author.

28. Kushner, *The Persistence of Prejudice,* p.192.

29. *ibid.*, p.112.

30. *ibid.*, p.119.

31. *ibid.*, p.120-22.

32. I am grateful to Bill Rubinstein for alerting me to Witting's novel, and for making a copy available.

33. Kushner, *The Persistence of Prejudice,* p.223.

34. *ibid.,* p.131.

35. Kushner, *ibid.,* p.109-10, cites Brandon's portrait of Isaac Levant as a literary perpetuation of one aspect of the "Jew-devil" image, i.e. the sexual predator with a "strange power" over women.

Chapter 5

1. Quoted in Kushner, *The Persistence of Prejudice,* p.131. For detail on Orwell's complex attitudes towards Jews and anti-Jewish prejudice, see David Walton, "George Orwell and Antisemitism," *Patterns of Prejudice* 16(1), 1982, p.19-34.

2. Kushner, *ibid.*

3. Mitchell, "British Novels Present a New Image of the Jew," p.26.

4. *ibid.,* p.27; Rubinstein, *A History of the Jews in the English-speaking World,* p.304. Rubinstein notes that James Bond makes a point of identifying the wealth-crazed Goldfinger (in Fleming's 1959 novel of that name) as not Jewish. ("Thirty years before, an equivalent character in a British 'thriller' would in all likelihood have been a Jew.") Rubinstein, *ibid.*

5. Stephen Brook, *The Club: The Jews of Modern Britain,* London 1989, p.382-90; Rubinstein, *A History of the Jews in the English-speaking World,* p.367-87.

6. Brook, *ibid.,* p.397; Rubinstein, *ibid.,* p.387-89.

7. Brook, *ibid.,* p.395.

8. *ibid.,* p.382.

9. *ibid.*

10. W.D. Rubinstein, Communication to the author, May 1997.

11. Mitchell, "British Novels present a New Image of the Jew," p.27; Atkins, p.215.

12. Yaffe, p.23, 50-55. S.T. Haymon's books and P.D. James' *Original Sin* aside, I have "unearthed" only one discernibly Jewish sleuth in my survey of English crime-writing terrain. Peter Cheyney included a marginally relevant comic sketch titled "Abie the Sleuth" in his 1944 miscellany *Making Crime Pay.* Cheyney emulates the jargon and style of the American "hardboiled" school in this mildly diverting (but ultimately inconsequential) skit about a small-time New York gangster, Abie Hymie Finkelstein, who attempts unsuccessfully to become a private detective a la Marlowe or Spade.

13. *ibid.,* p.55.

Conclusion

1. Wynn, p.133.

2. Orwell, "Antisemitism in Britain," p.166; Kushner, *The Persistence of Prejudice*, p.111, 115-16, 125, 131-33.

3. William O. Ayedelotte, "The Detective Story as a Historical Source," in *Dimensions of Detective Fiction*, ed. Larry L. Landrum, Pat Browne & Ray B. Browne, Bowling Green, Ohio, 1976, p.69.

4. George L. Mosse, *Germans and Jews: The Right, the Left and the Search for a "Third Force" in Pre-Nazi Germany,* London, 1971, p.62.

5. Watson, *Snobbery with Violence*, p.71, 136.

6. Wynn, p.133.

7. Rubinstein, *A History of the Jews in the English-speaking World,* p.293.

8. Richard Martin Stern, Contribution to "Symposium: Writers' Views on Creating Black Characters," in Bailey, p.125.

9. Kadish, p.46.

10. Rubinstein, Letter to the author.

11. As it is, I noted earlier Freeman's "about face" on Jews in *Mr Polton Explains.* See Chapter 5.

12. An insensitivity which obviously extended from author to reader. As Colin Watson has observed: "The fact of a public generally unaware of the ugliness of ethnic intolerance has to be accepted if one is to understand how so much popular fiction of racialist flavour came to be written without qualm and read without protest in the years before the second World War." Watson, *Snobbery with Violence,* p.123.

13. Stafford, p.98, 123-24.

Bibliography

Primary Sources
Editions of short stories, novels cited in the text.

Adams, Herbert. *The Old Jew Mystery.* London: Collins, 1936.

——. *The Sloane Square Mystery.* London: Methuen, 1925.

Allingham, Margery. *Coroner's Pidgin.* Harmondsworth, Middlesex: Penguin, 1950 [1945].

——. *The Crime at Black Dudley.* Harmondsworth, Middlesex: Penguin, 1950 [1929].

——. *Flowers for the Judge.* Harmondsworth, Middlesex: Penguin, 1944 [1936].

——. *Hide My Eyes.* Harmondsworth, Middlesex: Penguin, 1960 [1958].

——. *Look to the Lady.* Harmondsworth, Middlesex: Penguin, 1950 [1961].

——. *Mystery Mile.* Harmondsworth, Middlesex: Penguin, 1950 [1930].

Ames, Delano. *Murder Maestro Please.* Harmondsworth, Middlesex: Penguin, 1963 [1952].

——. *No Traveller Returns.* London: Nicholson, 1934.

Ashdown, Clifford. "The Assyrian Rejuvenator" [1902]. Reprinted in *The Rivals of Sherlock Holmes: Early Detective Stories.* Ed. Hugh Greene. Harmondsworth, Middlesex: Penguin, 1971.

Bailey, H.C. *Mr Fortune's Practice.* London: Methuen, 1923.

Barr, Robert. *The Triumphs of Eugene Valmont.* New York: Dover, 1985 [1906].

Beeding, Francis. *The Five Flamboys.* London: Hodder & Stoughton, 1929.

Bell, Josephine. *Death on the Borough Council.* Harmondsworth, Middlesex: Penguin, 1944 [1937].

Bellairs, George. *Death in Dark Glasses.* London: Gifford, 1952.

Bennett, Arnold. *The Grand Babylon Hotel.* London: Collins, c1915 [1902].

Bentley, E.C. *Trent Intervenes.* London: Dent, 1986 [1938].

——. *Trent's Last Case.* New York: Harper & Row, 1978 [1913].

Bentley, John. *Pattern for Perfidy.* London: Hutchinson, 1946.

Bentley, Nicholas. *The Tongue-tied Canary.* Harmondsworth, Middlesex: Penguin, 1954 [1948].

Berkeley, Anthony [A.B. Cox]. *The Layton Court Mystery.* London: Herbert Jenkins, 1925.

——. *Not to Be Taken.* Harmondsworth, Middlesex: Penguin, 1946 [1938].

——. *The Silk Stocking Murders.* New York: Doubleday, 1928.

——. *Trial and Error.* London: Hodder & Stoughton, 1937.

Blake, Nicholas. *The Case of the Abominable Snowman.* London: Collins/Fontana, 1961 [1941].

——. *The Smiler with the Knife.* London: Collins/Fontana, 1965 [1939].

Brand, Christianna. *Heads You Lose.* Harmondsworth, Middlesex: Penguin, 1950 [1941].

Brandon, John G. *Death in Duplicate.* London: Wright & Brown, 1945.

——. *Death of a Socialite.* London: Wright & Brown, 1957.

——. *Mr Pennington Goes Nap.* London: Wright & Brown, 1940.

Bruce, Leo. *Dead Man's Shoes.* Chicago: Academy Chicago, 1987 [1958].

Buchan, John. *Greenmantle.* London: Hodder & Stoughton, 1916.

——. "The Grove of Ashtaroth." *The Moon Endureth.* London: Hodder & Stoughton, 1963 [1912].

——. *Huntingtower.* Harmonsworth, Middlesex: Penguin, 1956 [1922].

——. *Mr Standfast.* London: Hodder & Stoughton, 1919.

——. *A Prince of the Captivity.* London: Hodder & Stoughton, 1933.

——. *The Thirty-nine Steps.* London: Pan, 1959 [1915].

——. *The Three Hostages.* Harmondsworth, Middlesex: Penguin, 1953 [1924].

Cannan, Joanna. *Murder Included.* Harmondsworth, Middlesex: Penguin, 1958 [1950].

Cassells, John. *Meet the Picaroon.* London: John Long, 1957.

Charteris, Leslie. *Enter the Saint.* London: Hodder & Stoughton, 1930.

Chesterton, G.K. *Autobiography.* London: Hutchinson, 1936.

——. *Four Faultless Felons.* London: Cassell, 1953 [1930].

——. *The Incredulity of Father Brown.* London: Cassell, 1926. Reprinted in *The Father Brown Stories.* London: Cassell, 1953.

——. *The Innocence of Father Brown.* London: Cassell, 1911. Reprinted in *The Father Brown Stories.*

——. *Man Alive*. London: Nelson, 1912.

——. *The Man Who Knew Too Much and Other Stories*. London: Cassell, 1922.

——. *The Man Who Was Thursday: A Nightmare*. Harmondsworth, Middlesex: Penguin, 1938 [1906].

——. *The Paradoxes of Mr Pond*. London: Cassell, 1936.

——. *The Wisdom of Father Brown*. London: Cassell, 1914. Reprinted in *The Father Brown Stories*.

Cheyney, Peter. "Abie the Sleuth." *Making Crime Pay*. London: Faber, 1944.

Christie, Agatha. *An Autobiography*. New York: Dodd Mead, 1977.

——. *At Bertram's Hotel*. London: Collins, 1965.

——. *The Big Four*. London: Collins, 1979 [1927].

——. *The Body in the Library*. Harmondsworth, Middlesex: Penguin, 1953 [1942].

——. *Cards on the Table*. London: Collins, 1956 [1936].

——. *The Clocks*. London: Collins, 1963.

——. *Death in the Clouds*. London: Collins/Fontana, 1957 [1935].

——. *Hallowe'en Party*. London: Collins, 1969.

——. *The Hollow*. London: Collins, 1946.

——. *The Hound of Death and Other Stories*. London: Collins/Fontana, 1964 [1977].

——. *The Labours of Hercules*. London: Collins, 1948.

——. *The Listerdale Mystery*. London: Collins/Fontana, 1961 [1934].

——. *Lord Edgware Dies*. London: Collins, 1955 [1933].

——. *The Murder of Roger Ackroyd*. London: Collins, 1926.

——. *Murder on the Links*. Harmondsworth, Middlesex: Penguin, 1936 [1923].

——. *Murder on the Orient Express*. Harmondsworth, Middlesex: Penguin, 1948 [1934].

——. *The Mysterious Affair at Styles*. Harmondsworth, Middlesex: Penguin, 1935 [1920].

——. *The Mysterious Mr Quin*. Harmondsworth, Middlesex: Penguin, 1953 [1930].

——. *The Mystery of the Blue Train*. London: Collins, 1953 [1928].

——. *One Two Buckle My Shoe*. London: Collins/Fontana, 1959 [1940].

——. *Parker Pyne Investigates*. Harmondsworth, Middlesex: Penguin, 1953 [1934].

——. *Partners in Crime*. London: Collins/Fontana, 1958 [1929].

——. *Passenger to Frankfurt: An Extravaganza.* London: Collins, 1970.

——. *Peril at End House.* London: Collins, 1966 [1932].

——. *Poirot Investigates.* London: Pan, 1955 [1924].

——. *Poirot's Early Cases.* London: Collins, 1974.

——. *The Regatta Mystery.* New York: Dell, 1959 [1939].

——. *Sad Cypress.* London: Collins, 1951 [1940].

——. *The Secret Adversary.* London: Triad/Panther, 1976 [1922].

——. *The Secret of Chimneys.* London: Bodley Head, 1958 [1925].

——. *The Seven Dials Mystery.* London: Collins/Fontana, 1954 [1929].

——. *The Sittaford Mystery.* London: Collins, 1966 [1931].

——. *Ten Little Niggers [And Then There Were None].* London: Collins/Fontana, 1963 [1939].

——. *They Came to Baghdad.* London: Collins, 1951.

——. *Three Act Tragedy.* London: Collins, 1971 [1935].

——. *While the Light Lasts.* London: Harper/Collins, 1997.

Clinton-Baddeley, V.C. *Death's Bright Dart.* New York: Dell, 1982 [1967].

Cole, G.D.H., & Margaret Cole. "A Lesson in Crime" [1932]. Reprinted in *Ten Modern Mystery Stories.* Ed. L. Derwent & J.R. Crossland. London: Collins, 1965.

Coles, Manning. *Drink to Yesterday.* London: Hodder & Stoughton, 1951 [1940].

——. *Pray Silence.* London: Hodder & Stoughton, 1940.

Cox, A.B. *O England!* London: Hamish Hamilton, 1934.

Crispin, Edmund. *The Case of the Gilded Fly.* Harmondsworth, Middlesex: Penguin, 1954 [1944].

Crofts, Freeman Wills. "The Case of the Avaricious Moneylender." *Murderers Make Mistakes.* London: Pan, 1953 [1947].

——. *The Crime at Guildford.* London: Collins, 1935. Reprinted as *The Crime at Nornes.* New York: Dodd Mead, 1935.

——. *The Groote Park Murder.* Harmondsworth, Middlesex: Penguin, 1946 [1923].

Crompton, Richmal. "The Mystery of Oaklands." *William.* Sydney: Dymock's, 1947 [1929].

——. "William and the Nasties." *William the Detective.* London: George Newnes, 1935.

Cullingford, Guy. *The Whipping Boys.* Harmondsworth, Middlesex: Penguin, 1964 [1958].

Dane, Clemence, & Helen Simpson. *Enter Sir John*. New York: Cosmopolitan, 1928.

Deighton, Len. *Funeral in Berlin*. London: Jonathan Cape, 1964.

Detection Club. *The Floating Admiral*. London: MacMillan, 1981 [1931].

Dickson, Carter [John Dickson Carr]. *And So to Murder*. Harmondsworth, Middlesex: Penguin, 1951 [1941].

Doherty, P.C. *An Ancient Evil*. London: Headline, 1994.

Doyle, Sir Arthur Conan. *The Adventures of Sherlock Holmes*. Harmondsworth, Middlesex: Penguin, c1938 [1892].

——. *The Casebook of Sherlock Holmes*. Harmondsworth, Middlesex: Penguin, 1951 [1927].

——. *The Memoirs of Sherlock Holmes*. Harmondsworth, Middlesex: Penguin, c1938 [1894].

——. "The Story of the Jew's Breastplate" [1899]. Reprinted in *The Rivals of Sherlock Holmes*. Vol 2. Ed. Alan K. Russell. Secaucus, New Jersey: Castle Books, 1979.

——. *A Study in Scarlet*. London: Lippincott, 1890 [1887]. Reprinted in *The Complete Sherlock Holmes Long Stories*. London: John Murray & Jonathon Cape, 1929.

Du Maurier, Daphne. *Early Stories*. London: Todd, 1955.

——. *I'll Never Be Young Again*. London: Heinemann, 1949 [1932].

——. *The Progress of Julius*. London: Heinemann, 1952 [1933].

Edwards, Ruth Dudley. *The School of English Murder*. London: Victor Gollancz, 1990.

Farjeon, J. Jefferson. *The Oval Table*. London: Collins, 1946.

Fletcher, J.S. *The Mysterious Chinaman*. London: Herbert Jenkins, 1923.

——. *The Perilous Crossways*. London: Ward, Lock & Co, 1914.

Freeman, R. Austin. *Best Dr Thorndyke Detective Stories*. Ed. E.F. Bleiler. New York: Dover, 1973.

——. "The Brazen Serpent." *The Exploits of Danby Croker*. London: Duckworths, 1916. Reprinted in *My Funniest Story*. London: Faber, 1932.

——. *The Famous Cases of Dr Thorndyke (aka The Dr Thorndyke Omnibus)*. London: Hodder & Stoughton, 1929.

——. *Mr Polton Explains*. London: Hodder & Stoughton, 1940.

Frome, David. *The Man from Scotland Yard*. London: Readers' Library, c1933 [1932].

Galsworthy, John. *"Loyalties" with Two Other Plays.* London: Pan, 1953.

Gilbert, Anthony. *Death Against the Clock.* London: Collins, 1958.

——. *Murder by Experts.* London: Collins, 1936.

Giles, Kenneth. *Murder Pluperfect.* London: Gollancz, 1970.

Goyne, Richard. *The Man in the Trilby Hat.* London: Stanley Paul, 1946.

Graeme, Bruce. *Impeached.* London: Hutchinson, 1933.

Greene, Graham. *Brighton Rock.* Harmondsworth, Middlesex: Penguin, 1943 [1938].

——. *A Gun for Sale.* Harmondsworth, Middlesex: Penguin, 1974 [1936].

——. *Stamboul Train.* London: Heinemann & Bodley Head, 1974 [1932].

Gribble, Leonard. "The Case of Jacob Heylyn" [1937]. Reprinted in *My Best Mystery Story.* London: Faber, 1939.

Grierson, Francis. *The Yellow Rat.* London: Collins, 1929. Reprinted as *Murder at the Wedding.* London: Collins, 1932.

Griffith, George. "I.D.B.: Being Tales of the Diamond Fields." *Pearson's Magazine*, Nov. & Dec. 1897. Reprinted in *The Rivals of Sherlock Holmes, Vol 2*. Ed. Alan K. Russell. Secaucus, New Jersey: Castle Books, 1979.

Hare, Cyril. *An English Murder.* Harmondsworth, Middlesex: Penguin, 1956 [1951].

——. *Suicide Excepted.* Harmondsworth, Middlesex: Penguin, 1956 [1939]; London: Hogarth Press, 1986.

Heyer, Georgette. *A Blunt Instrument.* London: Panther, 1961 [1938].

Hichens, Robert. *Bella Donna.* Philadelphia: Lippincott, 1909.

——. *The Paradine Case.* New York: Doubleday, 1947 [1933].

Holt, Henry. *The Mystery of the Smiling Doll.* London: Collins, 1939.

Horler, Sydney. *The Man Who Walked with Death.* London: Hodder & Stoughton, 1941.

——. *Miss Mystery.* London: Hodder & Stoughton, 1928.

——. *Nighthawk Mops Up.* London: Hodder & Stoughton, 1944.

——. *The Return of Nighthawk.* London: Hodder & Stoughton, 1940.

——. *Wolves of the Night.* London: Readers' Library, 1932.

Hornung, E.M. *Raffles [The Amateur Cracksman].* Harmondsworth, Middlesex: Penguin, 1936 [1899].

Iles, Francis [A.B. Cox]. "It Takes Two to Make a Hero." *Saturday Book 3.* London: Hutchinson, 1943. Reprinted as "The Coward." *Ellery Queen's Mystery Magazine* Jan. 1953.

James, P.D. *Original Sin.* London: Faber, 1994.

——. *Shroud for a Nightingale.* London: Sphere, 1973 [1971].

Jenkins, Herbert. *Malcolm Sage, Detective.* London: Herbert Jenkins, 1921.

Keverne, Richard. *The Black Cripple.* London: Collins, 1941.

——. *Carteret's Cure.* Harmondsworth, Middlesex: Penguin, 1950 [1926].

——. *The Shadow Syndicate.* Harmondsworth, Middlesex: Penguin, 1946 [1930].

Le Queux, William. "A Run with Rosalie." *Cassell's Magazine* 1906. Reprinted in *The Rivals of Sherlock Holmes, Vol 2.* Ed. Alan K. Russell. Secaucus, New Jersey: Castle Books, 1979.

Lorac, E.C.R. *Rope's End, Rogue's End.* London: Collins, 1942.

Lowndes, Marie Belloc. *A Chink in the Armour.* New York: Longmans, Green & Co., 1937 [1912].

MacDonald, Philip. *The Mystery at Kensington Gore.* London: Collins, 1975 [1932].

——. *X versus Rex.* Harmondsworth, Middlesex: Penguin, 1955 [1933].

McNeile, H.C. ("Sapper"). *The Black Gang.* London: Hodder & Stoughton, 1922. Reprinted in *Bulldog Drummond: His Four Rounds with Carl Peterson.* London: Hodder & Stoughton, 1967.

——. *The Final Count.* London: Hodder & Stoughton, 1926. Reprinted in *Bulldog Drummond: His Four Rounds with Carl Peterson.* London: Hodder & Stoughton, 1967.

——. *The Island of Terror.* London: Hodder & Stoughton, 1931.

——. *Jim Maitland.* London: Hodder & Stoughton, 1923.

——. *The Saving Clause: Stories by "Sapper."* London: Hodder & Stoughton, 1927.

Marsh, Ngaio. *Death and the Dancing Footman.* London: Collins/Fontana, 1958 [1942].

——. *Death at the Dolphin.* London: Collins, 1967.

——. *Death in a White Tie.* Geneva: Heron Books, 1981 [1938].

——. *Died in the Wool.* London: Collins, 1946.

——. *Light Thickens.* London: Collins/Fontana, 1984 [1982].

——. *Off with His Head.* London: Collins, 1956.

——. *Photo-Finish.* London: Collins/Fontana, 1982 [1980].

——. *Vintage Murder.* Harmondsworth, Middlesex: Penguin, 1940 [1937].

Mason, A.E.W. *At the Villa Rose.* Harmondsworth, Middlesex: Penguin, 1962 [1910].

Maugham, W. Somerset. *Ashenden.* London: Heinemann, 1928.

Meynell, Laurence. *The Creaking Chair.* London: Collins, 1941.

——. *Die by the Book.* London: Collins, 1966.

——. *Give Me the Knife.* London: Collins, 1954.

Oppenheim, E. Phillips. *Aaron Rodd Diviner.* London: Hodder & Stoughton, 1920.

——. *Ambrose Lavendale Diplomat.* London: Hodder & Stoughton, 1920.

——. *Last Train Out.* London: Hodder & Stoughton, 1952 [1941].

——. *The Mysterious Mr Sabin.* London: Brown Watson, 1963 [1898].

——. "The Secret of the *Magnifique*" [1913]. Reprinted in *More Rivals of Sherlock Holmes: Early Detective Stories.* Ed. Hugh Greene. Harmondworth, Middlesex: Penguin, 1971.

——. *The Treasure House of Martin Hews.* London: Hodder & Stoughton, 1929.

Orczy, Baroness Emmuska. "The Inverted Five." *Skin'o'My Tooth: His Memoirs by His Confidential Clerk.* London: Hodder & Stoughton, 1928.

——. *Lady Molly of Scotland Yard.* New York: International Polygonics, 1981 [1910].

——. "The Regent's Park Murder." *The Man in the Corner.* New York: Dodd Mead, 1909.

Pirkis, C.L. "A Princess's Vengeance." *Ludgate Magazine*, May 1893. Reprinted. *The Rivals of Sherlock Holmes, Vol 2.* Ed. Alan K. Russell. Secaucus, New Jersey: Castle Books, 1979.

Postgate, Raymond. *The Ledger Is Kept.* Harmondsworth, Middlesex: Penguin, 1958 [1953].

——. *Somebody at the Door.* London: Ian Henry, 1976 [1943].

——. *Verdict of Twelve.* New York: Alfred Knopf, 1940.

Punshon, E.R. *The Crossword Mystery.* Harmondsworth, Middlesex: Penguin, 1948 [1934].

Rhode, John. *The Double Florin.* London: Geoffrey Bles, 1924.

Rohmer, Sax. *The Dream Detective.* New York: Dover, 1977 [1920].

"Sapper." *See* McNeile, H.C.

Sayers, Dorothy L. *Busman's Honeymoon.* London: New English Library, 1977 [1937].

——. *Clouds of Witness.* London: Victor Gollancz, 1978 [1926].

——. *Five Red Herrings.* London: Victor Gollancz, 1978 [1931].

——. *Gaudy Night.* London: Victor Gollancz, 1935.

——. *Have His Carcase.* London: Victor Gollancz, 1978 [1932].

——. *Lord Peter Views the Body.* London: New English Library, 1977 [1928].

——. *The Man Born to Be King.* London: Victor Gollancz, 1942.

——. *Murder Must Advertise.* London: Victor Gollancz, 1978 [1933].

——. *The Nine Tailors.* London: New English Library, 1977 [1934].

——. *Striding Folly.* London: New English Library, 1973.

——. *Strong Poison.* London: Victor Gollancz, 1978 [1930].

——. *Unnatural Death.* London: Victor Gollancz, 1978 [1927].

——. *Whose Body?* London: New English Library, 1977 [1923].

Sayers, Dorothy L., & Jill Paton Walsh. *Thrones Dominations.* London: Hodder & Stoughton, 1998.

Sayers, Dorothy L., & Muriel St Clare Byrne. "Busman's Honeymoon." *Famous Plays of 1937.* London: Victor Gollancz, 1937.

Sims, George. *The Last Best Friend.* Harmondsworth, Middlesex: Penguin, 1971 [1967].

Sykes, W. Stanley. *The Missing Moneylender.* Harmondsworth, Middlesex: Penguin, 1945 [1931].

Verner, Gerald. *White Wig.* London: Mellifont Press, c1950 [1935].

Vine, Barbara [Ruth Rendell]. *A Fatal Inversion.* Harmondsworth, Middlesex: Penguin, 1987.

Wade, Henry. *The Duke of York's Steps.* New York: Grosset & Dunlap, 1929.

——. *The Dying Alderman.* Harmondsworth, Middlesex: Penguin, 1945 [1930].

——. *Policeman's Lot.* London: Constable, 1933.

Wallace, Edgar. *The Four Just Men.* London: Dent, 1985 [1905].

——. *The Mind of Mr J.G. Reeder.* London: Pan, 1967 [1925].

——. *The Ringer.* London: Hodder & Stoughton, 1927.

Wentworth, Patricia. *Miss Silver Intervenes.* London: Hodder & Stoughton, 1951 [1944].

Westmacott, Mary [Agatha Christie]. *Absent in the Spring.* London: Collins, 1973 [1944].

——. *Giant's Bread.* London: Collins, 1973 [1930].

White, Ethel Lina. *An Elephant Never Forgets.* London: Collins, 1937.

Witting, Clifford. *Measure for Murder.* London: Hodder & Stoughton, 1945.

Wodehouse, P.G. *The Code of the Woosters.* Harmondsworth, Middlesex: Penguin, 1953 [1938].

——. "The Ordeal of Osbert Mulliner." *Mr Mulliner Speaking.* London: Herbert Jenkins, 1929.

——. "Strychnine in the Soup." *Mulliner Nights.* London: Herbert Jenkins, 1933.

Yates, Dornford. *Berry and Co.* London: Ward, Lock & Co, 1920.

——. *She Fell among Thieves.* London: Dent, 1985 [1935].

Secondary Sources

Alderman, Geoffrey. "Antisemitism in Britain" (Review article). *Jewish Journal of Sociology* 31(2), 1989.

——. *Modern British Jewry.* Oxford: Clarendon Press, 1992.

Almog, Shmuel. "Antisemitism as a Dynamic Phenomenon: The 'Jewish Question' in England at the End of the First World War." *Patterns of Prejudice* 21(4), 1987.

Atkins, John. *The British Spy Novel: Styles in Treachery.* New York: Riverrun, 1984.

Aydelotte, William O. "The Detective Story as a Historical Source." *Dimensions of Detection Fiction.* Ed. Larry L. Landrum, Pat Browne & Ray B. Browne. Bowling Green, Ohio: Bowling Green State University Popular Press, 1976.

Bargainnier, Earl F. *The Gentle Art of Murder: the Detective Fiction of Agatha Christie.* Bowling Green, Ohio: Bowling Green State University Popular Press, 1980.

Bailey, Frankie Y. *Out of the Woodpile: Black Characters in Crime and Detective Fiction.* New York: Greenwood, 1991.

Barnard, Robert. "The Golden Age." *Hatchards Crime Companion: 100 Top Crime Novels.* Ed. Susan Moody. London: Hatchards, 1990.

——. "The English Detective Story." *Whodunit? A Guide to Crime, Suspense and Spy Fiction.* Ed. H.R.F. Keating. New York: Van Nostrand Reinhold, 1982.

——. *A Talent to Deceive: An Appreciation of Agatha Christie.* London: Collins, 1980.

Barzun, Jacques, & Wendell Hartig Taylor. *A Catalogue of Crime.* New York, Harper & Row, 1971.

Brabazon, James. *Dorothy L. Sayers: A Biography.* London: Victor Gollancz, 1981.

Briney, Robert E., C. Steinbrunner & O. Penzler, eds. "Sinister Orientals." *Encyclopaedia of Mystery and Detection.* New York: McGraw-Hill, 1976.

Brook, Stephen. *The Club: The Jews of Modern Britain.* London: Pan, 1990 [1989].

Cadogan, Mary. *Richmal Crompton: The Woman behind William.* London: Allen & Unwin, 1986.

Cheyette, Bryan. *Constructions of "The Jew" in English Literature and Society: Racial Representations 1875 1945.* Cambridge: The University Press, 1993.

——. "H.G. Wells and the Jews: Antisemitism, Socialism and English Culture." *Patterns of Prejudice* 22(3), 1988.

——. "Jewish Stereotyping and English Literature 1875 1920: Towards a Political Analysis." *Traditions of Intolerance: Historical Perspectives on Fascism and Race Discourse in England.* Ed. T. Kushner & K. Lunn. Manchester: The University Press, 1989.

——. "Neither Black nor White: The Figure of 'The Jew' in Imperial British Literature." *The Jew in the Text: Modernity and the Construction of Identity.* Ed. L. Nochlin & T. Garb. London: Thames & Hudson, 1995.

Cockburn, Claude. *Bestseller: The Books That Everyone Read 1900-1939.* London: Sidgwick & Jackson, 1972.

Duke, Elizabeth. "Manning Coles." *Twentieth Century Crime and Mystery Writers.* Ed. John M. Reilly. 2nd edition. New York: St. Martin's Press, 1985.

Endelman, Todd M. *Radical Assimilation in English Jewish History 1656-1945.* Bloomington & Indianapolis: Indiana University Press, 1990.

Felsenstein, Frank. *Antisemitic Stereotypes: A Paradigm of Otherness in English Popular Culture 1660-1830.* Baltimore & London: Johns Hopkins University Press, 1995.

Field, Geoffrey G. "Antisemitism with the Boots Off: Recent Research on England." London: *Wiener Library Bulletin,* 1982.

Fisch, Harold. *The Dual Image: The Figure of the Jew in English and American Literature.* London: World Jewish Library, 1971.

Frankenstein, Ernst. *Justice for My People: The Jewish Case.* London: Nicholson & Watson, 1943.

Gaer, Joseph. *The Legend of the Wandering Jew.* New York: New American Library, 1961.

Gill, Gillian. *Agatha Christie: The Woman and Her Mysteries.* New York: Free Press, 1990.

Golding, Louis. *The Jewish Problem.* Harmondsworth, Middlesex: Penguin, 1938.

Graves, Robert, & Alan Hodge. *The Long Weekend: A Social History of Great Britain 1918-1939.* London: Cardinal, 1985 [1940].

Grayzel, Solomon. *A History of the Jews: From the Babylonian Exile to the Present.* Revised edition. New York: New American Library, 1968.

Grella, George. "Murder and Manners: The Formal Detective Novel." *Dimensions of Detective Fiction.* Ed. Larry L. Landrum, Pat Browne & Ray B. Browne. Bowling Green, Ohio: Bowling Green State University Popular Press, 1976.

Halevy, Elie. *A History of the English People in 1815.* Book 3. Harmondsworth, Middlesex: Penguin, 1938.

Haycraft, Howard, ed. *The Art of the Mystery Story: A Collection of Critical Essays.* New York: Grosset & Dunlap, 1946.

——. *Murder for Pleasure: The Life and Times of the Detective Story.* New York: Grosset & Dunlap, 1941.

"Haycraft-Queen Definitive Library of Detective-Crime-Mystery Fiction." *Murder Ink: The Mystery Reader's Companion.* Ed. D. Wynn. New York: Workman Publishing, 1977.

Hayne, Barrie. "Sapper." *Twentieth Century Crime and Mystery Writers.* Ed. John M. Reilly. 2nd edition. New York: St Martin's Press, 1985.

Hitchman, Janet. *Such a Strange Lady: A Biography of Dorothy L. Sayers.* New York: Harper & Row, 1975.

Holmes, Colin. *Anti-Semitism in British Society 1876-1939.* London: Edward Arnold, 1979.

——. *John Bull's Island: Immigration and British Society 1871-1971.* London: MacMillan, 1988.

Kadish, Sharman. *Bolsheviks and British Jews: The Anglo-Jewish Community, Britain and the Russian Revolution.* London: Frank Cass, 1992.

Keating, H.R.F., ed. *Agatha Christie: First Lady of Crime.* London: Weidenfeld & Nicolson,1977.

——. *Crime and Mystery: The 100 Best Books.* London: Xanadu, 1987.

——. "The Founding Fathers." *Hatchards Crime Companion: 100 Top Crime Novels Selected by the Crime Writers Association.* Ed. Susan Moody. London: Hatchards, 1990.

——. *Murder Must Appetize.* New York: Mysterious Press, 1975.

Kenney, Catherine. *The Remarkable Case of Dorothy L. Sayers.* Kent, Ohio: Kent State University Press, 1990.

Klein, Charlotte Lea. "The Changing Image of the Jew in Modern English Literature." *Patterns of Prejudice* 5(2), 1971.

——. "English Antisemitism in the 1920s." *Patterns of Prejudice* 6(2), 1972.

Kushner, Tony. "The Impact of British Antisemitism, 1918-1945." *The Making of Modern Anglo-Jewry.* Ed. David Cesarani. Oxford: Basil Blackwell, 1990.

——. "The Paradox of Prejudice: The Impact of Organised Antisemitism in Britain during an Anti-Nazi War." *Traditions of Intolerance: Historical Perspectives on Fascism and Race Discourse in Britain.* Ed. T. Kushner & K. Lunn. London: Frank Cass, 1992.

——. *The Persistence of Prejudice: Antisemitism in British Society during the Second World War.* Manchester: The University Press, 1989.

Kushner, Tony, & Kenneth Lunn, eds. *Traditions of Intolerance: Historical Perspectives on Fascism and Race Discourse in Britain.* London: Frank Cass, 1989.

Lambert, Gavin. *The Dangerous Edge.* New York: Grossman, 1976.

Lebzelter, Gisela C. *Political Antisemitism in England 1918-1939.* New York: Holmes & Meier, 1978.

Leveson, Marcia. "The Mineral Revolution, Fiction and the Jewish Image in South Africa." *Patterns of Migration, 1850-1914: Proceedings of the International Academic Conference of the Jewish Historical Society of England and the Institute of Jewish Studies, University College, London.* London: J.H.S.E. & Institute of Jewish Studies, 1996.

Lewis, Margaret. *Ngaio Marsh: A Life.* London: Chatto & Windus, 1991.

Lipman, Vivian D. *The Jews in Britain Since 1858.* Leicester: The University, 1990.

Lunn, Kenneth. "The Ideology and Impact of the British Fascists in the 1920s." *Traditions of Intolerance: Historical Perspectives on Fascism and Race Discourse in Britain.* Ed. T. Kushner & K. Lunn. London: Frank Cass, 1992.

Lynx, J.J., ed. *The Future of the Jews: A Symposium.* London: Lindsay Drummond, 1945.

Mallowan, Max. *Mallowan's Memoirs.* London: Collins, 1977.

Mandel, Ernest. *Delightful Murder: A Social History of the Crime Story.* London: Pluto Press, 1984.

Mandle, W.F. *Antisemitism and the British Union of Fascists.* London: Longmans, 1968.

Mann, Jessica. *Deadlier Than the Male: An Investigation into Feminine Crime Writing.* London: David & Charles, 1981.

Mitchell, Gina M. "British Novels Present a New Image of the Jew." *Patterns of Prejudice* 10(5), 1976.

——. "Caricature of the Bulldog Spirit: When Peace Seems Dull." *Patterns of Prejudice* 8(5), 1974.

——. "In His Image: A Study of Jews in the Literature of Guy Thorne." *Patterns of Prejudice* 9(1), 1975.

——. "John Buchan's Popular Fiction: A Hierarchy of Race." *Patterns of Prejudice* 7(6), 1973.

Modder, Montagu Frank. *The Jew in the Literature of England: To the End of the 19th Century.* Philadelphia: Jewish Publication Society, 1944.

Morgan, Janet. *Agatha Christie: A Biography.* London: Collins, 1984.

Morgan, Ted. *Maugham: A Biography.* New York: Simon & Schuster, 1980.

Morris, John A. "Fascist Ideas in English Literature." *Patterns of Prejudice* 13(4), 1979.

——. "The Fiction of Dornford Yates: Best-selling Prejudice." *Patterns of Prejudice* 11(4), 1977.

Mosse, George L. *Germans and Jews: The Right, the Left and the Search for a "Third Force" in Pre-Nazi Germany.* London: Orbach & Chambers, 1971.

Murdoch, Derrick. *The Agatha Christie Mystery.* Toronto: Pagurian Press, 1976.

Orwell, George. "Antisemitism in Britain." *Contemporary Jewish Record* 8(2), 1945.

Osborne, Robert. *The Life and Crimes of Agatha Christie*. London: Collins, 1982.

Panek, LeRoy Lad. *An Introduction to the Detective Story*. Bowling Green, Ohio: Bowling Green State University Popular Press, 1987.

——. *The Special Branch: The British Spy Novel 1890-1980*. Bowling Green, Ohio: Bowling Green State University Popular Press, 1981.

——. *Watteau's Shepherds: The Detective Novel in Britain 1914-1940*. Bowling Green, Ohio: Bowling Green State University Popular Press, 1979.

Patterson, Nancy-Lou. "Images of Judaism and Antisemitism in the Novels of Dorothy L. Sayers." *Sayers Review* 2(2), 1978.

Pike, B.A. *Campion's Career: A Study of the Novels of Margery Allingham*. Bowling Green, Ohio: Bowling Green State University Popular Press, 1987.

Pronzini, Bill. *Gun in Cheek*. New York: Coward, McCann & Geoghegan, 1982.

——. *Son of Gun in Cheek*. New York: Mysterious Press, 1987.

Rapp, Dean. "The Jewish Response to G.K. Chesterton's Antisemitism 1911-33." *Patterns of Prejudice* 24(2-4), 1990.

Reynolds, Barbara. *Dorothy L. Sayers: Her Life and Soul*. London: Hodder & Stoughton, 1993.

Rosenberg, Edgar. *From Shylock to Svengali: Jewish Stereotypes in English Fiction*. London: Peter Owen, 1961.

Roth, Cecil. *A History of the Jews in England*. 3rd edition. Oxford: The University Press, 1964.

Rubinstein, W.D. "The Anti-Jewish Riots of 1911 in South Wales: A Re-examination." *Welsh History Review* Dec. 1997.

——. "Charles Dickens, R. Austin Freeman and the Spirit of London." *Elites and the Wealthy in the Modern World*. Brighton: Harvester Press, 1987.

——. *A History of the Jews in the English-speaking World: Great Britain*. London: MacMillan, 1996.

——. "Recent Anglo-Jewish Historiography and the Myth of Jix's Antisemitism (Part 1)." *Australian Journal of Jewish Studies* 7(1), 1993.

Russell, Alan K., ed. *The Rivals of Sherlock Holmes, Vol 2.* Secaucus, New Jersey: Castle Books, 1979.

Sachar, Howard M. *Diaspora: An Inquiry into the Contemporary Jewish World.* New York: Harper & Row, 1985.

Sacks, George. *The Jewish Question.* London: Gollancz, 1937.

Salomon, Sidney. *The Jews of Britain.* London: Hutchinson, 1938.

Samuel, Maurice. *The Great Hatred.* London: Gollancz, 1943.

Scowcroft, Philip L. "Was Dorothy L. Sayers Racist?" *Sidelights on Sayers* VII, 1984.

Smith, Elaine R. "Jewish Responses to Political Antisemitism and Fascism in the East End of London, 1920-1939." *Traditions of Intolerance: Historical Perspectives on Fascism and Race Discourse in Britain.* Ed. T. Kushner & K. Lunn. London: Frank Cass, 1992.

Stafford, David. *The Silent Game: The Real World of Imaginary Spies.* Revised edition. Athens, Georgia: University of Georgia Press, 1991.

Standish, Robert. *The Prince of Storytellers: The Life of E. Phillips Oppenheim.* London: Peter Davies, 1957.

Steinbrunner, Chris, & Otto Penzler. *Encyclopaedia of Mystery and Detection.* New York: McGraw-Hill, 1976.

Steiner, Olivier Cohen. "Jews and Jewesses in Victorian Fiction: From Religious Stereotype to Ethnic Hazard." *Patterns of Prejudice* 21(2), 1987.

Symons, Julian. *Bloody Murder. From the Detective Story to the Crime Novel: A History.* Harmondsworth, Middlesex: Penguin, 1974.

——. *Criminal Practices: Symons on Crime Writing 60s to 90s.* London: MacMillan, 1994.

Thompson, Kristin. *Wooster Proposes, Jeeves Disposes or Le Mot Juste.* New York: James H. Heineman, 1992.

Thormahlen, Marianne. "Review of *Thrones Dominations.*" *Dorothy L. Sayers Society Bulletin* 136, Apr. 1998.

Thurlow, Richard C. "The 'Jew Wise': Dimensions of British Political Antisemitism, 1918-39." *Immigrants and Minorities* 6(1), 1987.

——. "Racial Populism in England." *Patterns of Prejudice* 10(4), 1976.

Turnbull, Malcolm J. *Elusion Aforethought: The Life and Writing of Anthony Berkeley Cox.* Bowling Green, Ohio: Bowling Green State University Popular Press, 1996.

Usborne, Richard. *Clubland Heroes: A Nostalgic Study of Some Recurrent Characters in the Romantic Fiction of Dornford Yates, John Buchan and Sapper.* London: Barrie & Jenkins, 1971.

Walton, David. "George Orwell and Antisemitism." *Patterns of Prejudice* 16(1), 1982.

Ward, Maisie. *Gilbert Keith Chesterton.* Harmondsworth, Middlesex: Penguin, 1958 [1944].

Watson, Colin. "Mayhem Parva and Wicked Belgravia." *Crime Writers.* Ed. H.R.F. Keating. London: BBC, 1978.

——. *Snobbery with Violence: English Crime Stories and Their Audience.* London: Eyre Methuen,1971.

Waugh, Evelyn. *The Diaries of Evelyn Waugh.* Ed. Michael Davie. London: Weidenfeld & Nicolson, 1976.

Williams, Kay. *Just Richmal: The Life and Work of Richmal Crompton Lamburn.* Guildford: Genesis, 1986.

Winks, Robin, ed. *Detective Fiction: A Collection of Critical Essays.* Englewood Cliffs, New Jersey: Prentice-Hall, 1980.

——. "Sinister Orientals: Everybody's Favourite Villains." *Murder Ink: The Mystery Reader's Companion.* Ed. D. Wynn. New York: Workman Publishing, 1977.

Wynn, Dilys. "Antisemitism and the Mystery." *Murder Ink: Revived, Revised, Still Unrepentant.* Ed. D. Wynn. New York: Workman Publishing, 1984.

Yaffe, James. "Is This Any Job for a Nice Jewish Boy? (Jews in Detective Fiction)." *Synod of Sleuths: Essays on Judeo-Christian Detective Fiction.* Ed. Jon L. Breen & Martin H. Greenberg. Metuchen, New Jersey: Scarecrow Press, 1990.

Index